Rewarding Excellence

Rewarding Excellence

Pay Strategies for the New Economy

Edward E. Lawler III

Jossey-Bass Publishers • San Francisco

Jossey-Bass books and products are available through most bookstores. To contact Jossey-Bass directly, call (888) 378–2537, fax to (800) 605–2665, or visit our website at www.josseybass.com.

Substantial discounts on bulk quantities of Jossey-Bass books are available to corporations, professional associations, and other organizations. For details and discount information, contact the special sales department at Jossey-Bass.

 Manufactured in the United States of America on Lyons Falls Turin Book. This paper is acid-free and 100 percent totally chlorine-free.

Library of Congress Cataloging-in-Publication Data

Lawler, Edward E.
    Rewarding excellence : pay strategies for the new economy / Edward E. Lawler III.
      p. cm. — (The Jossey-Bass business & management series)
    Includes bibliographical references and index.
    ISBN 0-7879-5074-2
    1. Compensation management. 2. Pay-for-knowledge systems. I. Series.
HF5549.5.C67 L382 1999
658.3'225—dc21

                                    99-047329

FIRST EDITION
HB Printing 10 9 8 7 6 5 4 3 2 1

The Jossey-Bass
Business & Management Series

Contents

Preface

Forty years ago, I began doing research on reward systems. To say the least, the years since then have been eventful. The world of management, for example, has changed considerably. Today, organizations face a new global economy, a level of competition never anticipated in 1960, and a vast array of technologies that enable them to operate in new and more effective ways. Reward system practices have also changed, though perhaps not as dramatically as technology and the competitive landscape. It is much clearer today how to design reward systems that are powerful drivers of individual and organizational behavior.

This book is based on the premise that to capture the full power of a reward system in today's competitive environment, organizations need to focus on rewarding excellence in all areas. Outstanding individuals need to be highly rewarded because they are worth more and because rewards for performance are motivating. Teams need to be rewarded for their performance as well, and in many cases stock and bonuses for company performance should be given to all employees.

Part One of the book argues that organizations should adopt a new logic of organizing that recognizes the new competitive realities and that today's key sources of competitive advantage are human capital, core competencies, and organizational capabilities. Parts Two and Three show why the old reward systems, which focus on jobs and merit pay, don't do an adequate job of developing and motivating either individuals or organizations. As a result, they fail to contribute to the competitive advantages that organizations need in order to be successful in today's environment. What is needed is a shift to reward systems that attract and retain the right mix of individuals and that motivate excellent performance.

The impact of reward systems, especially pay systems, on motivation and performance is well understood. There are few mysteries here. Reward systems should reward individuals for developing their skills and abilities as well as for their performance. When this is done correctly, reward systems can make a significant and important contribution to organizational effectiveness.

What is new and different—and the main focus of this book—is a new approach to designing reward systems that can more effectively attract, retain, and motivate individuals. As I point out in Part Two, organizations must carefully craft a set of reward system practices in order to attract, retain, and develop the right mix of talent. In almost every situation, this means paying individuals rather than jobs and focusing on the individuals' market value. When organizations focus on rewarding people for what they can do, organizations develop not only valuable human capital but also new organizational capabilities and core competencies that provide a competitive advantage.

Part Three focuses on rewarding performance. Effective reward systems are key to motivating outstanding performance and to implementing organizations' strategic plans. The challenges here involve deciding how to measure and reward performance and how much of an individual's pay to base on performance. In order for rewards to be effective motivators, they must represent a significant portion of a total reward package. In traditional pay systems that rely on merit pay, this simply cannot happen. Thus, I argue strongly for using bonuses, stock, and other forms of variable pay to reward performance.

Part Four provides an integrated view of the pay practices that reward excellence and points out how an organization's total reward system needs to be designed to optimally contribute to organizational effectiveness. It specifically focuses on reward system practices that support and fit with the high-performance organization model (explained in Chapter One) that has become so popular over the last decade. There I strongly argue that the old reward system practices simply don't do the job.

Rewarding Excellence is not just about how to pay individuals; it is about how to design and manage complex organizations. The book focuses on pay systems and therefore should be particularly interesting to those who are designing and managing organizational pay systems. It should also be of interest to anyone who is involved in designing and managing complex organizations that can compete effectively in today's business environment.

Rewarding Excellence draws on the extensive research literature on reward systems but focuses on the application of research findings, as well as on specific pay and reward system practices. I discuss the types of practices that should be used by different kinds of organizations. I also provide useful advice on how managers should conduct performance appraisals, decide what to pay people who work for them, and perhaps most important, how to structure a pay system for their organization. I give guidelines about the appropriateness of practices such as team-based pay, 360-degree performance appraisals, and skill-based pay. These discussions provide a meaningful blueprint for managers who must make decisions about the design and operation of pay systems.

Acknowledgments

For the last twenty years, I have been a member of the Center for Effective Organizations at the University of Southern California in Los Angeles. The research of the center has focused heavily on reward systems, and I have drawn extensively on this research in writing this book. I have particularly profited from the work of Jay Galbraith, Gerry Ledford, Allan Mohrman, and Susan Mohrman. Their work has shaped my thinking about reward systems and organizational design.

The Center for Effective Organizations is truly a unique entity that has enabled me to do research that is relevant to both theory and practice. It is supported by a group of over fifty corporations and by the Marshall School of Business at the University of Southern California. Because of this support I have had the opportunity to study the reward practices of innumerable organizations and to develop and test many of the ideas I present in this book. Several members of the center have helped me with the preparation of this manuscript; I would especially like to thank Kristan Venegas and Dustin Pendill for their support.

My wife, Patty, has supported me continuously throughout the writing of this book. She has encouraged me when I have been discouraged and motivated me when I have been negligent, but more than anything she has provided her love and a supportive relationship. For this I am very grateful and truly fortunate.

October 1999   EDWARD E. LAWLER III
Los Angeles, California

The Author

EDWARD E. LAWLER III is professor of management and organization in the Marshall School of Business at the University of Southern California. He is also director of the school's Center for Effective Organizations.

After receiving his Ph.D. degree from the University of California-Berkeley in 1964, Lawler joined the faculty of Yale University as assistant professor of industrial administration and psychology; three years later he was promoted to associate professor.

Lawler moved to the University of Michigan in 1972 to become a professor of psychology and a program director in the Survey Research Center at the Institute for Social Research. In 1978, he became a professor in the Marshall School of Business at the University of Southern California. The following year, he founded and became the director of the University's Center for Effective Organizations.

Business Week has recognized Lawler as one of the worlds' leading management experts. The American Compensation Association and the Society for Human Resource Management have given him their career achievement awards for his many contributions to HR management. He has consulted with many corporations and governments on pay and organizational effectiveness.

Lawler is the author and coauthor of more than two hundred and fifty articles and thirty books. Recent books include *The Ultimate Advantage* (1992), *Organizing for the Future* (1993), *From the Ground Up: Six Principles for Creating the New Logic Corporation* (1996), *Tomorrow's Organization* (1998), *Strategies for High Performance Organizations: The CEO Report* (1998), and *The Leadership Change Handbook* (1999), all published by Jossey-Bass.

Rewarding Excellence

Introduction

I believe that a major revolution is occurring in the way organizations are managed. The revolution is being driven by new technologies and by the major social and political changes that have led to the globalization of business and to the increasing numbers of democratic, capitalist countries. Billions of people have recently entered, or are about to enter, the capitalist world. A smaller but very significant number have entered the world of electronic connectedness as a result of the growing popularity of the Internet, satellite TV, cellular phones, and videoconferencing.

The combined effects of technological and political change on organizations are enormous and multifaceted. Increasingly, organizations are finding that in order to be competitive in the new global economy they have to reinvent themselves in important ways. This is true of their basic organizational structure, their global reach, and their use of information technology. It is also true of their reward systems.[1]

Performance Demands

The shift toward capitalism and global capital markets, and along with it the lowering of trade barriers, is perhaps the most important new source of pressure on organizations to raise their performance levels. These changes have created many opportunities for growth but have also created many new competitors and more demanding investors. The growing power of institutional shareholders has enabled them to put more pressure on management to produce exceptional returns to shareholders. Retirement funds and mutual funds now hold large ownership shares in many corporations and have become active critics of their performance. This has led to the resignation of some CEOs and the restructuring of many corporate boards.

The 1990s saw a number of major companies—AT&T, Sears, IBM, General Motors, and Compaq Computers—oust their CEOs because of poor corporate financial performance. In the compensation arena, the pressure on boards and senior management to produce high returns for shareholders has had a number of effects, including the growing tendency for board members and senior executives to be required to own stock in their companies. It has also contributed to the proliferation of stock option plans. The reality is that in today's global economy, companies are competing for financial capital, not just with other companies in their country and continent but with companies all over the world. Today, financial capital can and does move quickly to wherever it can earn the best return.

The performance pressure on corporations is heightened by the increased power of buyers. A recent survey of CEOs identified rising customer expectation as the most important challenge they face.[2] Virtually every product and service in the world is in surplus. There is an oversupply of cars, television sets, and restaurants. The result is a subtle but important shift of power from sellers to buyers—a shift that has been accelerated by the tremendous amount of information buyers now have that helps them make more intelligent purchases. The Internet, television, and a host of other communication devices allow consumers to compare products and services and to make increasingly well-informed buying decisions. The Internet has also created a new distribution channel that is changing the way many products are bought. It is forcing both retailers and business-to-business suppliers to redesign their business models. Never before have organizations been subject to as much performance and change pressure as they are today, and there is every reason to believe that the pressure will continue to increase.

Knowledge Growth

It is an understatement to say that the last half of the twentieth century was marked by a knowledge explosion. The technological advances of that era were truly incredible. New knowledge led to the creation of new industries and to our ability to send people to the moon, as well as to communicate with each other on earth in new and much cheaper and more effective ways. The future promises the continued development of technology and scientific knowledge. Corporations' spending on research and development continues to grow, as does the number of scientific discoveries.

The rapid and continuing growth of knowledge and information technology has had two important effects on organizations. First, it has made the traditional bureaucratic form obsolete—a form based on an information-distribution model that assumes a scarcity of information and a high cost of transmitting it. With the growth of computers and information technology, these assumptions are no longer valid. Because information can be easily and cheaply transmitted, important new organizational forms have developed that are based on a new logic of organizing, which I will discuss in Chapter One. It is almost certain that most organizations will use these forms as they adapt to the new technical and competitive realities.

Second, the rapid growth of technology has made knowledge management and development increasingly critical issues in organizations.[3] It has changed the very structure of jobs and what individuals are expected to know and do. More and more jobs have become knowledge work. This is true for individuals writing software programs for Microsoft, as well as for many production workers. The production worker of the past typically was responsible for performing a simple, repetitive task. In many cases today, production workers may be, for example, running a programmable machine tool, doing statistical process control, or working on scheduling and dealing with suppliers. In short, much of the old work is gone, having been replaced by new work that requires employees to be knowledgeable decision makers and capable of understanding their organization's business strategy, work, and customers.

New Deal

The performance demands that organizations face, combined with the rapid growth in technology and changes in the nature of work, have led to an important change in the relationship between employers and employees. One part of this change is the much-discussed shift from a relatively permanent employment relationship to one that is much more transitory.[4] Another part— the most significant part—is the transfer of power from employers to employees. Yes, corporations are engaging in and will continue to engage in large and frequent layoffs. Yes, workers have less job security. Yes, individuals have to worry much more about their careers and skills. But the fact is that an increasing number of employees have the upper hand when it comes to their relationships with corporations. Of course not every employee has the upper hand. Who has it and who doesn't depends on who has the skills and knowledge organizations need and on how scarce and important those skills and that knowledge are.

Organizations are increasingly desperate for employees who can provide knowledge and skills that give them a competitive advantage in today's business environment. Human capital is increasingly critical to organizational effectiveness. Thus, obtaining, developing, and managing human capital can be an important source of competitive advantage if it is managed and organized in a way that leads to high performance.

Historically, employers were in charge of the work relationship. People applied for jobs, were granted an interview, and were selected by the organization. But this relationship is changing in sports, entertainment, information technology, consulting, finance, education, and a host of other industries. Increasingly, organizations must recruit and compete for talent. They have to focus on capturing the right human capital, that is, being able to hire the most talented people. Sometimes by hiring the right people they can capture not just key human capital but some of the competencies and capabilities of their major competitors.

The power of human capital is most visible in the rewards that are received by CEOs, entertainers, sports figures, and technology experts. The best people in these professions can command incredibly high pay. Those in the greatest demand can negotiate for personalized reward packages that often include a variety of perks such as first-class airfare, luxury hotel suites when travel is required, home loans, and limousine or helicopter transportation between home and office.

In sports and entertainment there is a long tradition of agents negotiating contracts and helping manage careers. Agents have begun to represent senior executives and technology experts as well. Agents help with public relations, as well as with their clients' career development and contract negotiations. A good guess is that as human capital continues to become more valuable and job security becomes less available, an increasing number of employees will recognize that they are now in a market position that makes it worth using agents to get a maximum return on their human capital. It is also likely that more and more employees will seek job security terms in their employment contracts.

In sports the best baseball, football, and basketball players make forty or fifty times more than the less-well-paid performers. This provides an interesting contrast with traditional salary ranges, which rarely allow the best performer to earn even 30 percent more than the least effective performer. The key difference is that in traditional jobs the best performer may not be adding much more value than the least effective performer. In sports and other kinds of highly skilled work, the best performers often add a tremendous amount more value. In sports the stars draw more viewers to TV and bring more fans into the stands. CEOs can potentially make billions of dollars of difference in the total return to shareholders by increasing earnings and their company's stock price.

Professional sports provide many dramatic examples of the difference between the salaries of outstanding performers and those of other team members. In 1998, for example, the top-paid players at virtually every position in the National Football League made more than $3 million. In the case of the highest-paid position—quarterback—Dan Marino of the Miami Dolphins made $7.5 million. On every team there were also many players making the league minimum of $131,000 a year—quite a pay range for individuals on the same team and playing the same position.

The range for American football is probably somewhat narrower than it would be if not for the salary cap that the owners put in place to keep themselves from paying "too much" for human capital. It strictly limits the total amount that any team can spend on employing players. Judging from what has happened in major league baseball in the United States, which does not have a salary cap, most likely the salary cap in football has limited the pay of very top players and served to restrict the range of salaries. In baseball, the top players now make over $15 million a season, whereas the lower-paid players' salaries are similar to those in professional football. In basketball, which has a "soft" cap, Michael Jordan made over $30 million in 1998. An analysis by *Fortune* magazine suggests that the money was well spent: it estimates that he has produced nearly $1 billion in revenue for the NBA during his career.[5]

Human Capital and Organizational Performance

In baseball and other professional sports the highest-paying teams by and large win the most games. In 1997 the Florida Marlins had one of the highest payrolls, and they won the World Series. In 1998 they decided they could not afford to be a high-paying team and traded a number of their higher-paid players; as a result, they dramatically reduced both their payroll and their performance. The New York Yankees, however, increased their payroll to the second highest in baseball and replaced the Marlins as the World Series winners. In 1998 the highest-paying team in baseball—the Baltimore Orioles—had a losing season, demonstrating that it is not just how much you spend that matters. How you spend also matters.

The lesson from all this is clear. If organizations want to attract high performers and be high performers, they have to be willing to reward excellent performers highly. This requires abandoning traditional pay structures and practices in which the best performers are only paid a little more than average and below-average performers. This may be acceptable in a traditional bureaucratic organization but not in an organization in which individuals make the difference between winning and losing or between being a highly profitable company and just an average, run-of-the mill company. In today's new economy companies have to invest money in human capital in order to make money.

The importance of human capital is clearly reflected in the stock price of many knowledge-work companies. For example, Microsoft has little in the way of plant and equipment but a high stock value because of its intellectual capital. In 1999 its market value was the highest of any U.S. corporation, higher than the value of General Electric, General Motors, DuPont, and a host of other firms with many more employees and a great deal more in physical assets.

The idea that employees are a critical part of an organization's worth is not new. In the 1960s and 1970s there was an effort to put the human assets of corporations on their balance sheets.[6] This effort failed to gain significant momentum, in part because it mistakenly argued that people should be thought of as assets. But assets can be bought and sold because they are owned. People cannot be bought and sold because they are not owned. People are better thought of as human capital investors.[7] Capital is owned by investors, not by an organization, and can be invested or not, depending on the return that is offered for it and how it is treated.

Employees invest time, energy, intelligence, and skills; organizations must pay them for that investment. Organization members, in essence, forgo the opportunity to put their human capital into other organizations in order to work for just one. Individuals continuously choose where they will invest their human capital. They also make active choices about improving and developing their capital. Those who do not improve their skills and knowledge often find that they are worth less, whereas those who make wise investments find that they are worth more.

Companies must deal with individuals who have significant and continuously changing market values. Many of these individuals can move easily to other corporations that want their skills and knowledge and are willing to pay a fair market price for them. In today's highly competitive world, every employee is a free agent, just as every company is free to downsize, de-layer, and change its strategy. Thus, the market value of human capital must be accurately reflected in the compensation amounts received by human capital investors; otherwise, they will not remain members of the organization. The bonds of loyalty have been broken as a result of layoffs, downsizing, and the loss of job security. New bonds that are based on rewards need to be created.

Perhaps the most intense war for talent is taking place at the senior executive level. A study by the McKinsey consulting firm found that companies are seeing a shortage of executive talent and feel they have to focus a great deal of their attention on the recruitment, development, and retention of senior executives.[8] Three-quarters of corporate officers surveyed by McKinsey said that their companies had insufficient talent to fill their senior management ranks. Not surprisingly, given this result, the study argues that attracting talent is critical to the long-term effectiveness of every major corporation. Because of the changing nature both of corporations and the business environment, executives are an increasingly important key to the success of major corporations.

Simply stated, being a successful executive requires more talent and motivation than it used to. Today it is not good enough to simply be a good manager. A successful executive has to be an exceptional leader and manager, as well as something of a visionary.

As their ability to offer stock ownership and other financial incentives has increased, mid-sized and small companies are becoming increasingly competitive when it comes to attracting top management talent. They can frequently offer reward packages that include an upside potential that cannot be matched by most large corporations. Thus, large companies that used to be able to dominate the competition for talent are finding themselves increasingly in tough battles with companies that previously were not in their league. Clearly, attracting and retaining talent is more difficult than it used to be and is increasingly centered on financial rewards. As the idea of lifetime careers, secure jobs, and loyalty to a single company has disappeared, highly talented individuals increasingly are looking for the best financial deals.

In today's environment, attracting human capital means not only competing with other corporations but in many cases with self-employment. Many talented people don't have to work for a corporation; they can be self-employed. Thus, corporations must provide a job in which individuals can do what they want to do better than they can do it on their own.

In the case of organizations that make products requiring extensive financial capital, the argument for creating large corporations is obvious. However, in many knowledge-work activities such as consulting, architecture, and film production, corporations have a much harder time proving to individuals that it is worth their time and effort to sign on with them. Being part of a virtual organization may be much more attractive.

A dramatic example of the potential advantage that an individual can have operating alone is provided by the management guru Tom Peters. He started his career working as a consultant for McKinsey but left for a variety of reasons, not the least of which was the opportunity to get a higher return on his human capital by operating as an individual. At McKinsey, the royalties on an author's books go to the corporation rather than the author. By leaving McKinsey, Peters was able to receive the royalties on the multimillion-copy sales of his many books—a clear example of the benefits of operating alone.

The privately owned SAS Institute, a leading software company, has taken a broad-based approach to obtaining and retaining talent. It is frequently cited as one of the best places to work. The company offers a number of attractive benefits to its employees, including a free health clinic, two day-care centers, private offices for everyone, flexible hours, a pianist in the subsidized cafeteria, year-end bonuses and profit sharing, a 35,000-square-foot recreational facility, and a thirty-five-hour workweek in an industry that is known for its long work hours. SAS also ties individuals into the community of Cary, North Carolina, where it is located. SAS offers 10 percent discounts on land in a subdivision the CEO has developed; employees also get discounts on memberships at the country club he owns. Finally, employees get a tuition break if their children are admitted to a private academy in Cary. One of the effects of this generous, reward-rich environment is extremely low turnover. According to one report it hovers at around 4 percent—much lower than the industry average, which is probably closer to 20 percent.[9]

The low turnover rate may also in part be accounted for by benefits the company does *not* offer: tuition reimbursement for M.B.A. degrees and stock options. Both are likely to lead to turnover. Giving stock options can lead to the "Microsoft problem"—individuals cashing out their stock options and ending up so rich they no longer need to work. And giving tuition reimbursement for an M.B.A. means that employees can increase their market value through education and as a result be motivated to move on to a higher-paying position elsewhere. In short, SAS has done a creative job of putting together a benefits package that effectively locks its employees in for the long term.

Some consulting firms, including the largest, Andersen Consulting, have been even more direct than SAS in developing programs that train individuals and at the same time retain them. Before they invest in training, they require individuals to sign a contract requiring them to pay the organization back for the cost of training unless they work for a certain period of time after the training is completed. This is an obvious attempt to be sure that training does not make employees more mobile. In some cases it can be an effective approach, but when a person is in high demand, hiring organizations will offer to "buy the employee out" by simply paying the amount that is owed to the organization that provided the training.

There is no guarantee that employees who have significant human capital will use it in ways that improve an organization's performance. The reward system challenge, therefore, is to attract the right kinds of human capital and to motivate it to develop and perform in ways that increase shareholder value. Unless their reward system accomplishes these two objectives, most organizations simply cannot be effective in a highly competitive business environment. It is of course one thing to say that an organization must attract the right human capital; it is another to do this effectively at a reasonable cost. Simply spending large amounts of money is not enough; the money must be spent in ways that attract and develop the right people.

Rewards and Excellence

The old reward practices and systems that worked well in nationally focused, bureaucratic, capital-intensive, hierarchical, steady-state, near-monopoly corporations such as the old General Motors and AT&T simply don't fit the realities of today's business environment. Dramatic change is needed, and it is not difficult to identify what the key theme of today's reward systems should be: *a focus on rewarding excellence.* Many factors argue for excellence being the number-one focus of any organization's reward system, including the ability to attract and retain the best people and to motivate the kind of performance that an organization needs in order to succeed in the new economy.

Creating reward systems that focus on excellence and treat employees as human capital investors requires a major change in the way most systems operate.[10] Reward systems typically treat employees as job holders who are rewarded according to the size and nature of their jobs and how well they perform their jobs.[11] Viewing them as human capital investors suggests a different approach to rewards in two respects. First, it suggests basing rewards on the value of the human capital that people bring to the organization.

What their job is at a particular moment is much less important than the value of their knowledge and skills. Second, it suggests rewarding people according to how effectively they use their human capital—their knowledge, skills, and competencies—to help the organization improve its business performance.

Creating reward systems that recognize the value of human capital and reward performance excellence is not easy. It requires a careful articulation among an organization's reward system, business strategy, organization design, information systems, and employees. I will begin our discussion of how it can be done by considering how reward systems impact organizational effectiveness.

Part One

Rewards and Organizational Performance

Chapter One

Organizational Effectiveness
The New Logic

Evidence that the business environment is increasingly competitive is everywhere. In virtually every business, organizations have been able to improve their products and services dramatically in four areas: (1) quality, (2) production costs, (3) speed to market, and (4) innovation.

In the past, companies had some slack in one or more of these areas. If an organization could get a product out quickly, customers would pay more for it and would tolerate defects. Or if the price were low enough, customers would accept poor quality, some slowness in service, or both. Today there is little tolerance for substandard performance in any area. Customers want and get value, and that means speed, cost, quality, and innovation. Even more significantly, they do not have to tolerate sub-par performance; they can readily turn to alternative sources that offer faster, cheaper, better, and more innovative products and services.

Changes in the Business Environment

Why is business competition so different today? Why does it take ever-higher performance levels to be successful? The explanation rests in the four major changes in the business environment I mentioned in the Introduction: (1) a global economy, (2) worldwide labor markets, (3) instantly linked communications, and (4) global capital markets.

A Global Economy

The globalization of business has occurred primarily because of the fall of communism, the growth of capitalism, the reduction of trade barriers, and the decline of government-managed economies. Communism, monopolies, and government ownership of business are out; free markets and capitalism are in. This has brought new competitors with new and different management styles and powerful competitive advantages (for example, relatively cheap skilled labor) into many markets.

Worldwide Labor Markets

Because the workforces in different countries have different skills and wages, organizations can now draw on a wider variety of workers and working conditions. This has led to the creation of organizational structures and business strategies that are global in their reach. Because of the increasing ease of moving information and, in some cases, production around the world, work is moving to wherever needed skills exist at the best price. For example, a significant amount of electrical engineering work has moved to Israel, and software development is increasingly being done in India, Russia, and a number of East Asian countries. Low-skilled jobs have moved to less developed countries where individuals work for low wages. Ultimately, this is likely to mean that the only work that will remain in more developed countries will be highly skilled work or the kind of face-to-face delivery work that is required in many service businesses.

Instantly Linked Information and Communication

Information technology is enabling organizations to be designed and managed in dramatically different ways. Personal computers, company networks, the Internet, expert systems, and a host of voice and video communication devices make it possible for everyone in even the largest and most complex organizations to have their organizations' business model and information on their desks. As Bill Gates has pointed out, the Web changes everything.[1]

Individuals and teams can easily and quickly gain access to large databases concerning particular products, processes, and customers. Networks can help employees from around the world form a consensus for action, produce innovative decision-making models that make it easier for individuals to work together on products and services, and reduce the response time to customer requests. This is in sharp contrast to the conditions that shaped traditional organizations: information was expensive to obtain and difficult to move. Thus, organizations sought ways to create efficient chains of command to move information up the line for centralized decision making, and they created specialized units that could operate independently to perform single steps in production and service processes.

Global Capital Markets

The development of information technology, in combination with the reductions of trade barriers and the globalization of the economy, has led to global financial markets. Investors can quickly and easily move their financial capital around the world in search of the highest possible returns. Increasingly, large amounts of capital are being held by institutional investors whose sole focus is on investing people's money in order to get a high rate of return. Because of the open trading of currencies and information technology, investors can easily move money not just from one company to another but from one country to another in their search for the best return.

The development of global capital markets has dramatically increased the pressure on companies to pay attention to the return they produce for their shareholders; this has led to changes at the top of many corporations. Boards of directors are not simply rubber stamps for management; increasingly, they are active, independent groups who hold senior management accountable for the returns their shareholders get. In the United States, boards are becoming more willing to intervene when the performance of a company is sub-par.

The pressure on boards and senior management to produce high returns for shareholders has had a number of effects, including the growing tendency for board members and senior executives to look for new sources of competitive advantage. It also has led to the increased adoption of new management practices. The reality is that in today's global economy, companies are competing for capital with business opportunities around the globe and must find a source of competitive advantage.

The New Competitive Advantage

The nature of today's business environment suggests an important conclusion about where competitive advantage can be found in the future. It is not likely to be found simply in the quality of an organization's financing, its access to natural resources, or its country of operation. These conditions are available to many companies and thus are not likely to provide an advantage. But an organization's ability to match its human resources, organization design, and management approach to its business strategy can create a difficult-to-match advantage—an effective organization.

Organizational effectiveness increasingly depends on organizations being able to develop their own approach to organizing and managing and to continuously improve it. This is not easy to do but is increasingly the key source of competitive advantage in today's global businesses. Not only is it a powerful source of competitive advantage, it has the potential to be a sustainable source of competitive advantage.

Until the 1980s the importance of management and organization in building a competitive advantage was not fully appreciated by many executives because companies in the United States and western Europe all used the same management style and competed only with each other. The success of a number of Japanese companies, with their focus on total quality management, called attention to just how important management and organization are. Today, with global competition, organizations that simply follow the traditional approaches to organizing and managing appear to be destined to perform at a mediocre level or worse.[2] The competitive world has simply left behind many of the practices that in the past were regarded as leading to effectiveness. This, more than anything else, is why many traditionally successful companies have become corporate dinosaurs in today's environment.

They are still concentrating on doing the old things better instead of concentrating on how to redesign themselves and create new management systems that fit today's social, economic, and business realities.

Going into the 1980s, AT&T had all the traditional competitive advantages: the highest possible financial rating and, as a result, access to the lowest-cost capital; world-class core competencies in key telecommunications and computing technologies; a research laboratory (Bell Labs) that was respected for its ability to innovate and make technological breakthroughs; a great, global brand name; and a monopoly on many phone services in the United States.

Despite its many strengths, AT&T did not fair well during the last two decades of the twentieth century. The opening of the long-distance market to competition caused AT&T to lose a significant portion of its market share to start-up companies. The company also proved unsuccessful at managing a computer company, NCR, it acquired and ultimately sold it at a multibillion-dollar loss. AT&T then put its equipment business into a new company, Lucent Technologies, which has shown some of the entrepreneurial spirit and innovation that AT&T has had trouble building into its own operations. In 1999 Lucent had a market value that equaled that of AT&T, even though it had only half the revenue.

Few doubt that AT&T would have continued to be successful if the rules of the game had stayed the same. Unfortunately for AT&T, the rules changed dramatically, and the company has had to struggle to change itself into a lean, competitively oriented organization that can earn the kind of returns on capital that will satisfy its shareholders. In order to do this, it is having to reinvent itself. The traditional bureaucratic approaches it had used so successfully in a monopoly environment simply don't work now. The very same things that led to its being widely praised as a well-managed company are significant handicaps today.

AT&T's lifetime employment contract and its development of managers based on a careful analysis of what has succeeded in the past are two major practices that don't fit today's competitive business environment. Similarly, its pay system, which focused on job size and seniority with little pay at risk and little pay for performance, hardly fits an environment in which shareholders are demanding high returns on their money and customers are demanding low rates, quick responses, and a strong focus on service. In its defense, AT&T now recognizes this and has begun to change. For the first time, it has brought in an outsider to be CEO, and the company has changed some of its organization and management practices.

In one respect, focusing on organization and management in order to gain competitive advantage is not new. Organizations have always tried to do a better job of organizing and managing themselves. However, they have operated with traditional thinking about what works and what doesn't. They have accepted the wisdom of using established management methods such as job descriptions, performance appraisal systems, budgets, and hierarchies and have believed that the way to gain competitive advantage is to use those methods more skillfully. What is needed today is a new logic of organization and management, not better execution of traditional management practices.[3]

Convincing evidence that new management practices can provide competitive advantages is beginning to accumulate. For example, a study I conducted showed that in 1996, Fortune 1000 companies that were high users of employee involvement and total quality management had higher returns on equity and returns to shareholders than did low users.[4] This replicated my earlier study on the 1993 financial performance of Fortune 1000 companies and fits with other studies relating financial performance to management practices.[5]

Organizational Capabilities

The message is clear. In order to be successful, organizations must have capabilities that allow them to coordinate and motivate behavior in ways that are tuned to the marketplace and produce levels of performance that differentiate them from their competitors. Every organization must understand what capabilities it needs in order to compete in its market and then develop them by creating the appropriate organizational designs and management systems.

What are some key organizational capabilities? They include the ability to focus on quality, understand customers, operate on a global basis, be a low-cost operator, learn, respond quickly to the business environment, speed products to market, and a host of other capabilities that I will discuss throughout this book. Today, organizational success frequently requires not just a single, world-class organizational capability but the right combination of many; it may take two or three that are exceptional and a number of others that are world-class.

Organizational capabilities don't exist in one place—in the heads of a few technology gurus or in a set of patents, for example. They rest in a combination of the skills and knowledge of the workforce and the reward system, culture, processes, and overall design of an organization. They typically require the coordinated behavior of many individuals and systems.[6]

The performance improvement that General Electric has made over the last decades can in part be attributed to the development of a number of key organizational capabilities. When Jack Welch became the CEO of GE in early 1981, he immediately recognized that it needed a significant downsizing and cost-reduction effort. He proceeded to make a number of changes in the organization that substantially reduced its costs and gave GE the capability to be a relatively low-cost producer. By reducing the corporate staff and putting the business units on their own to be either financial successes or failures, he moved GE toward becoming a customer-focused organization. He increased motivation by threatening to sell the businesses that didn't become number one or number two in their markets. The combination of these and other moves created a group of businesses that are focused on the market rather than on the corporate hierarchy and that are relatively low-cost, market-responsive operations.

Welch has also taken steps to improve the quality capability within GE. He mandated adoption of the Six Sigma program, which was developed by Motorola, and gave each business unit within GE the funds to support its implementation. He changed the bonus plan in each of the GE business units to include measures of quality. The results are positive: GE has improved the quality of its products and added to its organizational capabilities.

It is not enough to change one element of an organization in order to add a capability. It takes changes in the reward system, and it takes training, organization design, and process changes to develop world-class capabilities.

Core Competencies

Organizational capabilities are not the same as core competencies. Core competencies, also a possible source of competitive advantage, are technical areas of expertise such as Boeing's expertise in the aerodynamics of flight, Microsoft's expertise in computer science, Honda's competency in making gasoline engines, and Sony's ability to miniaturize products.[7] The longevity of the competitive advantage an organization gains from its core competencies depends on how easy they are to copy. There is always the risk that others can duplicate or capture them because they often reside in the minds and skills of a small number of employees. The easiest way to acquire competencies in these cases is to hire key employees away from an organization that has them. Apple did just this when it started. It sought out and hired people from Xerox's Palo Alto, California, research facility who developed the software operating system for Xerox's innovative personal computer, the Star. They went on to develop the Apple operating system, which provided Apple with a significant competitive advantage.

Employees may also leave on their own and take core competencies with them to create new, competing organizations. One of the most dramatic examples occurred during the 1970s. Fairchild, which pioneered the development and production of semiconductors, combined a high level of technological competency with a well-deserved, bad reputation for the way it managed and treated employees. This combination made it difficult for Fairchild to maintain a technological advantage, despite the pioneering development work it did on semiconductors. Departing employee after employee simply took knowledge of Fairchild's core competency in semiconductors with them and used it to start competing companies that were better managed. Whereas some of these new companies—Intel, AMD, and others—are among the most successful semiconductor firms in the world today, Fairchild is out of business.

Finding Competitive Advantage

Although it is important to acquire, develop, and protect core technological competencies, it is clear that they are neither enough by themselves for success nor necessarily the best source of a sustainable competitive advantage. Organizational capabilities, particularly those oriented toward understanding customers and speeding technology to market with the best possible quality and at a reasonable cost, are often more important.

The Xerox personal computer experience I mentioned earlier provides a good example of this point. Xerox had a significant technological lead in the personal computer business. It developed the first PC for office use, as well as the software that proved so important to Apple's early success. However, it lacked the organizational capabilities to capitalize on its technological core competencies and, as a result, is not in the computer business today.

It is up to an organization's executives to manage the development of a strategy that identifies the kind of performance that is needed, to communicate the need for that performance through mission and values statements, and to develop the needed competencies and capabilities. They can only do this well if they have a good understanding of the environment the organization faces and how business strategies and performance are related to competencies and capabilities. This relationship is shown in the Diamond Model (see Figure 1.1), which shows that organizational effectiveness results when there is a fit among four points: (1) strategy, (2) competencies, (3) capabilities, and (4) the environment.

Figure 1.1. The Diamond Model.

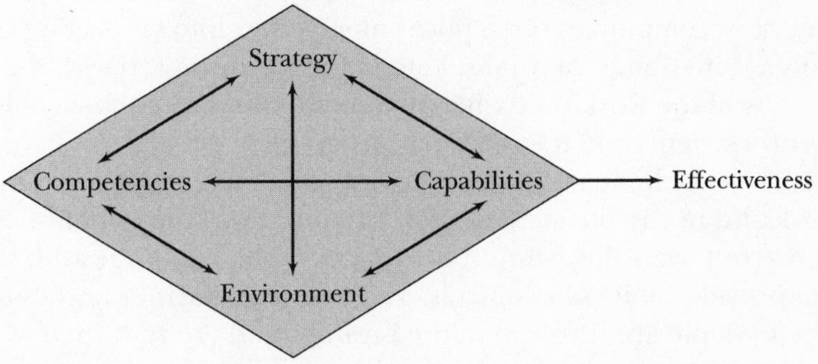

The New Logic of Organizing

It is one thing to say that organizations can gain a competitive advantage by creating the right competencies and capabilities. It is quite another to specify what the major design features of an organization need to be in order to create them. Fortunately, a considerable amount of research and practical experience suggests a new logic of organizing. If followed, it can lead to the creation of high-performance organizations that can develop the right competencies and capabilities. It is slowly but surely replacing the bureaucratic logic that was dominant during the twentieth century.[8] The elements of this new logic include business involvement, the effective use of human capital, lateral processes, and product- and customer-focused designs. I will discuss each element in order to provide a general sense of the new logic of organizing.

Business Involvement

In every organization, there must be a way to influence and coordinate the performance of individuals; otherwise, they cannot accomplish the organization's goals. The debate in organizational theory about coordination and control is not about whether control is necessary but about how it is best achieved. The traditional approach argues that control can best be obtained through incentive pay, close supervision, hierarchy, and the careful delineation of responsibilities. There are many problems with this approach; the most serious involve how people react to it. Sometimes workers will be obedient, but even when they are the result is rarely excellence because they do just enough to satisfy the minimum requirements. Still worse, employees often put as much effort into sabotaging controls as into doing their jobs. I am regularly impressed with the ingenuity of the workforce when it comes to defeating management control systems and incentive-pay programs.

The new logic argues that if individuals are involved in their work and in the business of their organization, they will not only figure out what they should be doing and how to do it well, they will provide their own controls. The new logic further argues that when people are involved in the business and are rewarded when the business succeeds, their energy and creativity will be focused on positive results such as improving production processes and creating better products and services instead of on beating the system. As a result, many of the costly bureaucratic control structures in traditional, hierarchical organizations are unnecessary.

Perhaps the simplest way of expressing how involvement works is to say that it is better to have a customer and the external market controlling an individual's performance than to use a set of bureaucratic rules, procedures, and a supervisor for control. In order to move control into the hands of the market and customer, the entire organization has to be structured so that employees can get feedback from customers about their performance and their responses to customer needs. This can guide performance in ways that a supervisor or system cannot duplicate because the customer, not some person or system that is acting as a proxy for the customer, is the ultimate arbiter of success. Thus, the customer is in a position to point employees in the right direction and to prompt change as the competitive environment changes.

Admittedly, hierarchy properly designed and rewarded can allow lower-level employees to act quickly with a high degree of precision and conformity through programmed decisions. But the downside of programmed actions is that strict guidelines and controls may prevent employees from acting on their own to meet a demand or to solve a unique or particularly difficult problem. The result, when it is not business as usual, all too often is slow decision making and poor-quality decisions.

Programmed decisions that are dictated by hierarchy and rule books are particularly problematic when it is difficult to anticipate what decisions need to be made. With the business environment changing rapidly and with more complex customers, products, and services, fewer and fewer of an organization's actions lend themselves to carefully planned, programmed decisions. So unless organizations abandon the bureaucratic approach, they end up with more and more hierarchical "approvals" needed for decisions. As a result, decision makers are overloaded, decision making is slow, and even simple transactions turn into complicated ones.

Decision quality also can become a problem under a hierarchical approach. Decisions made at higher levels in an organization often miss the critical subtleties that the people who are close to the problem and the customers are very well aware of. Besides, in service situations, telling an irate customer that you have to get approval or you are just following the rules does not help to quell anger and dissatisfaction. The opposite often occurs. Customers want immediate action on their requests and problems. They want the first person they encounter to satisfy them. Nordstrom, the department store chain, recognizes this and has given its customer service associates only one rule with respect to refunds and exchanges: satisfy the customer. Ritz-Carlton Hotels has done the same and gives each employee the power to spend thousands of dollars to do it.

Effective involvement depends on developing an organizational structure in which individuals feel accountable for their own and their organization's performance because they have customers who provide them with feedback.[9] An organization cannot meet this challenge just by grafting customer satisfaction measures onto a hierarchical structure that relies on bureaucratic and supervisory control, as well as extrinsic rewards (pay, bonuses) and punishments (firing), in order to coordinate behavior and ensure that customers are satisfied.

The new logic calls for replacing bureaucratic controls with the following components of effective employee involvement:

- Information about business strategy, processes, quality, customer feedback, events, plans, and business results
- Knowledge of the work, the business, and the total work system
- Power to act and make decisions about the work
- Rewards tied to business results, individual growth, capability, and contribution

When these four elements are appropriately positioned in an organization, they can create business involvement and be an effective source of motivation and performance.

Involvement requires that the amounts of information, knowledge, power, and rewards that individuals have be balanced and that all employees have significant amounts of each. This does not mean that those at the top of the organization have any less knowledge, information, power, and rewards than they do in traditional organizations; it does mean that organizations become flatter (that is, have fewer levels) and that the information, power, knowledge, and rewards that were in the middle are pushed down so that they are spread throughout the organization. This is what makes effective decision making and involvement possible at lower levels. Figure 1.2 presents this approach in graphic form.

The figure illustrates how involvement-oriented and hierarchical organizations position these four key elements differently. In well-designed hierarchical organizations, people at the lowest levels have little information, power, knowledge, and rewards, whereas those at the top have large amounts of all four. In the involvement-oriented, high-performance approach, people at the lowest levels have much more of these elements.

Balance among information, power, knowledge, and rewards is critical to effective involvement. In general, this is accomplished when people are rewarded based on how effectively they exercise the power associated with their position and when they have the information and knowledge to exercise power effectively. Individuals should not have more power than they can exercise effectively, given the amount of information and knowledge they have, nor do

Figure 1.2. Organizational Forms.

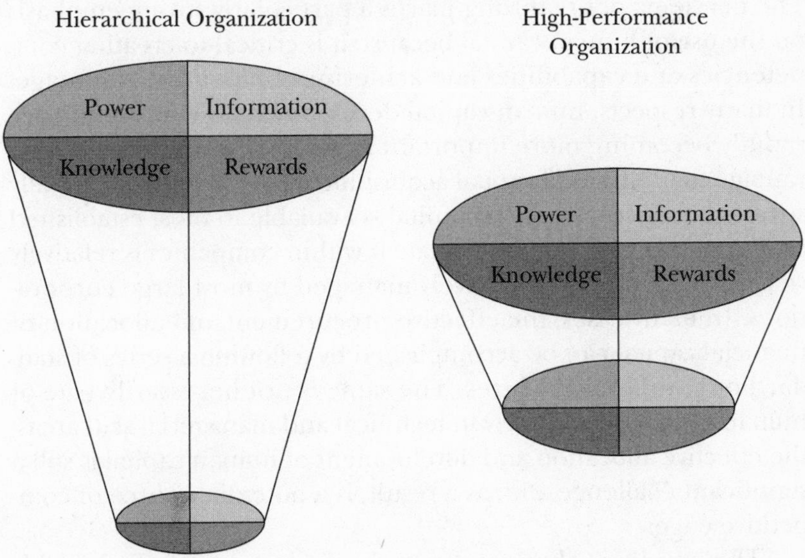

they need significantly more knowledge than they can use, given their power and information. Having more power than knowledge or information is particularly dangerous because it can lead to poor decision making. Finally, as will be considered in the rest of this book, rewards must fit the kind of power individuals exercise, the type of knowledge they have, and the information they receive. Otherwise, individuals will be incorrectly motivated, and there will be a lack of accountability for performance because no consequences are attached to it. Overall, in a well-designed, high-performance organization, individuals

- Understand the business, know its strategy, know how it is doing, and know who their customers and competitors are
- Are rewarded according to the success of the business and, as owners, share in its performance so that what is good for the business is good for them
- Are able to influence important organizational decisions, decide on work methods, participate in business strategy decisions, and work together to coordinate their work

Use of Human Capital

The new logic of organizing places a particularly strong emphasis on the use of human capital because it is critical to creating competencies and capabilities and achieving competitive advantage. In many respects, human capital development and allocation are rapidly becoming more important as a source of competitive advantage than financial capital acquisition and allocation. Generally speaking, low-cost financial capital is available to most established organizations, and how to allocate it within companies is relatively well understood and effectively managed by most large corporations. In many cases, the effective procurement and allocation of financial capital can be accomplished by following a series of standard operating procedures. The same is not necessarily true of human capital. Particularly in technical and managerial skill areas, the effective allocation and development of human capital is still a significant challenge and, as a result, is a potential source of competitive edge.

The new logic changes the traditional equation of who adds value to the organization's products and services significantly. It constantly pushes for individuals throughout the organization to develop their human capital and add value by

- Doing more complicated tasks
- Managing and controlling themselves
- Coordinating their work with the work of other employees
- Suggesting ideas about better ways to do the work
- Developing new products and ways to serve customers

This is in sharp contrast to the traditional, hierarchical organization in which individuals at the lower levels of the organization carry out prescribed, routine, low-value-added tasks in a controlled manner. Senior management adds major value through their work on organizational strategy, corporate finance, and coordinating the work of different groups and functions.

There is little chance for employees to add value to simple, repetitive work. Many relatively untrained low-wage workers in companies and countries around the world can do this work, making the people who do it low-value human capital. This accounts for the current movement of many manufacturing jobs out of developed countries. Employees who are doing simple, repetitive work in the United States, Europe, Japan, and other developed countries are often simply overpaid relative to the global value of their human capital and the value they add to products. Sometimes the only solution to this problem is to move work to low-wage companies and countries. But this is not always the right or the best answer. This kind of "overpayment" of employees may be the result of organizations following the old logic and as a result not allowing their employees to add all the value they can. All too often, when individuals try to add value through making suggestions or managing themselves, the work systems will not let them. Thus, even though employees earn wages that suggest that they add significant value, the organizational designs and structures that support top-down decision making and control do not allow them to add it.

The relationship between compensation levels and knowledge is relatively straightforward. Knowledge has a value that is determined by its scarcity and by the demand for it. Less straightforward and perhaps less well established is the relationship between affordable wage levels and management practices. Simply stated, if work is designed so that employees take on management duties that are typically done by supervisors and staff specialists, then they warrant higher pay. They are in essence adding the value that a highly paid manager or someone in a technical staff role might otherwise contribute.

Information technology, as well as advanced automation processes in the manufacturing world, can help transform work. Information technology is particularly important because it can move business information, and therefore decisions, to virtually anywhere in an organization. Automation in manufacturing, such as the use of robots, can create work that involves high levels of problem solving, technical complexity, and coordination and can thus make it possible for employees to add considerable value and add to their human capital. Employees end up doing programming, skilled maintenance, and machine setup instead of simple, routine, manual tasks. Fewer individuals are needed, but those who remain can be paid good wages because they contribute more to organizational effectiveness.

Today, given the realities of the new global economy, it is critical to structure organizations so that in high-wage countries, employees at all levels add significant value. Organizations can no longer afford the combination of high pay and low-value-added work and workers. By making the assumption that individuals at all levels of the organization can add significant value through the new-logic approach to organizing and through the use of information technology, new-logic organizations often can be cost-effective when traditional ones are not. The key is that individuals must know more and do more. When an organization's work can be designed to help create high-value-added jobs, it can be a win-win situation for organizations and for individuals. Organizations can end up with a competitive advantage, and individuals can end up with higher-paid, more rewarding work.

One immediate, direct effect of creating organizations that have business involvement and include high-value-added work concerns the importance of human capital. Simply stated, organization alone cannot be a source of competitive advantage; excellent employees are needed. Their skills and knowledge are critical to all core competencies and organizational capabilities. Despite this it is probably not correct to think of quality employees as a primary source of sustainable competitive advantage. However, it is correct to think that in combination with the right organization design and management approach they can be a powerful source of competitive advantage.

In order for people to contribute to organization and management as sources of competitive advantage, they must be developed, motivated, and retained. Organizational systems must be designed that attract, retain, and develop individuals with the skills and knowledge that are needed in order for the organization to have the right competencies and capabilities. Doing this effectively is critical to using organization as a source of competitive advantage. Without excellent employees, organizational excellence is impossible. Indeed, without an excellent organization, excellent employees cannot be retained and developed. Therefore, in many ways excellent employees and excellent organization designs are inseparable; they form the foundation on which a high-performance organization can be built.

Lateral Processes

The new logic puts much less emphasis on hierarchical reporting relationships and much more on lateral relationships. It stresses that effective lateral relationships are the key to creating organizations that can perform well with respect to speed, cost, quality, and innovation.[10] Both reengineering and total quality management address this point. They emphasize that when employees at different steps in the work process coordinate their behavior effectively, it can lead to significant gains in organizational performance. The traditional logic of organizing doesn't deny the importance of lateral relationships. Quite the contrary, it views them as so important that they must be closely controlled and monitored through hierarchical management and reward system structures.

There are two major problems with the hierarchical approach. First, individuals tend to compete with each other to move up the hierarchy and please higher-level managers. This occurs for a number of reasons but perhaps the most important is that upward mobility is highly rewarded and available to only a limited number of individuals. All too often employees end up spending their energy and efforts trying to please the boss and the boss's boss rather than concentrating on what is needed to produce a successful product or service, that is, relating to customers, vendors, and other employees at their level with whom they need to work. This is hardly surprising, given that the organization chart shows them reporting to a higher-level manager who controls their financial rewards and career rather than to a peer or customer. Indeed, the only formal connection among peers occurs because they all report to the same level of management.

Second, there is often a lack of focus on important organizational goals. Employees are simply engaging in individual activities rather than trying to accomplish important objectives. Most hierarchical organizations group employees not by customer or product but by common activities such as sales, production, and accounting. They put people together who do the same kind of work (for example, selling or shipping) rather than group those who are trying to accomplish the same organizational goals and are working on the same process. Hierarchical organizations then typically reward them based on how well they do their individual activities, not on how well the organization performs.

When all employees who are working on a product work together and share a common purpose, it increases the chance that the product will be well designed and manufactured. Similarly, when all who serve a particular customer work together, they can go beyond their function or step in the service process because they know and care about how customers are being served. This can lead to a greater ownership of both individual and organizational performance and thus to better service and products.

It can also lead to faster decision making and service because information does not need to be moved to someone higher up to integrate it and make a judgment. It can be done at the point of contact with the customer or product—a particularly crucial advantage in rapidly changing business environments. Further, because a laterally focused organization needs fewer control systems than a hierarchically focused one, it can eliminate levels of management and reduce costs.

Only if all of an organization's systems are designed to support it can an organization truly operate in a lateral manner that produces excellent performance. This means changing the human resource management system, the reward system, the communication system, and the work structures of vertical organizations to ones that are consistent with a lateral approach. Following are some examples of needed changes:

- Employees need the ability to meet in groups and problem solve together.
- Reward systems must be in place that reflect peer input and reward group and team performance.
- Individuals need to be rewarded for lateral learning and career moves.
- Team-based work designs are necessary.
- Communication systems must move information and customer data laterally without going through levels of supervisory control.
- Managers need to facilitate lateral interaction and learning.

Creating the right organization structure is also crucial to creating lateral relationships that reduce costs, improve quality, and speed decision making.

Product- and Customer-Focused Organization Designs

The traditional logic of organizing emphasizes functional excellence and expertise and assumes that good performance grows directly out of these qualities. It further assumes that functional excellence is the result of getting the best possible individuals in each specialty and putting them together. This enables functional specialists to learn from each other as well as to get training and development that is designed for them. The managers, who are usually experts in the specialty, are charged with developing the department's technical competency. In this approach, staff groups in areas such as human resources management, finance, and law typically review the plans and operations of the business units and departments to determine whether they are up to their standards.

The main flaw in this approach is that no single function—not human resources management, not finance, not marketing, not R&D, and not even manufacturing—can, by itself, make a product or serve a customer. Because no single function, even if performed extremely well, can create satisfied customers, most employees do not see a strong relationship between what they do and their organization's success.

The new logic does not discount the need for strong expertise in particularly critical functions. Indeed, this is often key to developing the right core competencies. But the new logic does stress that it's possible to have strong functional expertise in an organization that's not particularly effective. Traditional, functionally structured organizations have trouble developing the teamwork and coordination that lead to successful products and services.

The new logic argues that organizations have to organize around units that are focused on products and customers if they want employees with different specialties to work well together. This ties directly to the idea of control coming from customers and the market, the importance of lateral processes, and the need for individuals at all levels to add significant value. In order for these aspects of the new logic to work, all employees must be part of units in which everyone can see how their behavior affects organizational performance; in other words, they must have a line of sight to the business and its success. Then and only then can individuals feel that they are market-driven, that they are responding to a particular customer or managing a specific product, and that their rewards are tied to the success of a business they can influence.

When an organization is primarily structured into units that are focused on products and customers, it is important to create structures and practices that build technical excellence. As I will discuss in later chapters, the reward system can make a significant contribution to technical excellence if it rewards knowledge development. Various structural features can also be used, including technical councils, overlay teams, and shared learning teams.[11]

The Star Model

What types of practices, structures, and systems does an organization need to put in place in order to follow the new logic? To begin answering this question, a view of the key elements of an organization is needed. For years, researchers, companies, and consultants have studied and debated what the key elements are. The guide that I think provides the most useful way to think about them is the Star Model—so called because, as can be seen in Figure 1.3, it has a pentagonal shape with a five-pointed star inside. The model de-

Figure 1.3. The Star Model.

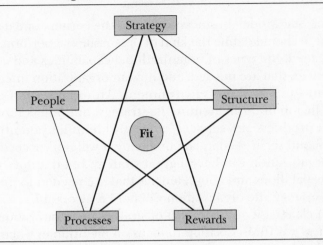

picts the key features of an organization: strategy, structure, rewards, processes, and people.[12]

The five points of the star are connected with lines. These interconnections are important because they indicate that organizational effectiveness requires a good alignment or fit among all five elements. The best test of fit is organizational performance. If it matches the organization's strategy, a good fit has been obtained. A second test of fit involves the positioning of information, power, knowledge, and rewards. When they are present in balanced amounts at all levels in the organization, it means the five points on the star are well balanced with respect to business involvement.

The interconnections in the Star Model have an important implication for organizational change efforts: significant improvements in an organization's performance are likely only if most or all five elements are changed. Doing less runs the risks of putting the organization out of balance, which is more likely to cause problems than to create better performance. The challenge is to develop an approach to organizing that considers all of the elements and how they fit together to create an organization with the right strategy, competencies, and capabilities to succeed. To provide an introduction to the Star Model, I will briefly touch on each of its five points.

Strategy

In the Star Model, business strategy is the cornerstone design element. It should define the kind of organizational performance that is needed, the types of organizational capabilities and core competencies that are needed, and how an organization intends to respond to its business environment. An organization can do a terrific job of implementing its strategy, but unless it offers the right products and services, correctly identifies potential customers, and secures adequate financing it will not succeed. Finally, an organization can have a great strategy, but if it does not have the capabilities and competencies that are needed to implement that strategy, the organization will not be successful.

A clear case of the impact of strategy on organizational effectiveness was IBM's decision to focus on mainframes when the personal computer market and networking were growing. Because of this decision, IBM lost the leadership position in a multibillion-dollar industry. The opposite was true of Compaq Computer, which recognized that computer users were moving to PCs and quickly established a very successful business that focused on providing individuals and companies with PCs and network servers. Dell Computer has successfully challenged Compaq by adopting a slightly different strategy, selling custom computers directly to customers. Dell has done well with this strategy in part because it has the capability to produce customized computers quickly and to deal with end-user customers.

In new organizations, business strategy is usually the first thing to be considered, and it often can be addressed somewhat independently of existing practices and structures. In an existing organization, however, the major organizational practices and systems that are already in place often affect the organization's strategy choices. For example, the reward system often strongly influences the choices organizations make because it has an impact on management decision making (as in the areas of cost cutting and short- versus long-term investing). It is also important to take an organization's current conditions, resources, competencies, and capabilities into account in formulating strategy. In fact, failing to do so runs the risk of generating an entirely unrealistic strategy.

Structure

The second point on the Star Model is the organization's structure, that is, how people are grouped together, who reports to whom, how tasks are assigned, and the nature of the jobs within the organization. Even though there may not be traditional job descriptions and organization charts, critical decisions still need to be made about how individuals are grouped together, how major decisions are made, how many levels of management are created, and a host of other factors. In many respects, because these decisions involve the fundamental building blocks of an organization, they must be closely articulated with the strategy. They are major determinants of how the organization will behave and have significant implications for the kinds of people and reward systems it needs.

Rewards

The third point on the Star Model—reward systems—must closely fit the organization's strategy; the systems must reward the correct behaviors. They also need to be closely articulated with the need for human resources because they are critical in attracting, retaining, and developing employees. Further, they are crucial in making all elements of an organization operate effectively. For example, it does not make sense to combine a structure that calls for teams with a reward system that rewards individual performance excellence. As I will discuss in Chapter Two, a number of design choices must be made correctly if an alignment between the reward system and the other features in the organization is to be achieved.

Processes

Management processes—the fourth point on the Star Model—are the systems that the organization puts into place to help control, manage, inform, and direct its members' behavior, both individually and collectively, so that they focus on the correct strategic actions. Management processes include information and communication systems, budgeting and financial measurement systems, and the behavior of managers, particularly those involved in decision making and setting direction for the organization.

As with the other points on the star, if the measurement and communication processes are out of alignment or are nonexistent, the organization cannot perform effectively. Some key communication processes such as meetings and social events are relatively informal, but most are formal. Budgets, quality controls, and financial information systems are formal means of measuring and communicating performance results. Strategic fit with respect to these systems means correctly measuring and rewarding the behaviors that the strategy says need to be motivated in order for the strategy to be successfully implemented.

People

The final point on the star is people—the organization's human resources. To get the right mix of capabilities and competencies, the organization needs to do an effective job of obtaining, developing, and allocating human capital. Then it must ensure that people who have the right skills and knowledge are motivated to perform effectively. If motivation is to be high, individual needs must fit the rewards offered. As I will discuss further in Chapter Three, reward systems are critical determinants of who is attracted to working for a company, who is motivated to work while there, and who remains as an employee.

Organizational Culture

The five-pointed Star Model does not identify a final determinant of organizational performance: corporate culture. This is omitted because it is not a design parameter in the same way that the features of the Star Model are but develops as a result of the influence of all the major elements. An organization, for example, is seen as having a culture that values innovation not simply because it says it does but because the reward systems, work design, and information processes all support and encourage the behaviors that lead to innovation. Some versions of the Star Model reflect this by placing culture in the center of the star. I prefer to omit it because it cannot be directly controlled the way the major design elements can be.

It is often possible to determine how an organization will perform by looking at its culture because the culture "says" what people in the organization should do and what will be rewarded. For example, in an organization I studied several years ago, the CEO was concerned about creating a more entrepreneurial environment and wondered why there wasn't more innovation and risk taking. He could have answered his own question had he heard what a manager in the company told me: "The culture here is clear: the rewards for successful innovation are uncertain and usually minimal. The punishments for failed risk taking are swift, certain, and usually fatal."

Often the early reward system practices of an organization are particularly important in shaping its culture. They reinforce certain behavior patterns and signal how highly valued different individuals are by the organization. They also attract and retain a certain type of employee and in a host of little ways indicate what the organization stands for and values.

The challenge in changing an organization's culture is to identify what points on the star give the current culture its characteristics and then to figure out how to change them so that the organization can operate with a new and more functional culture. Culture is often difficult to change because the people who have signed up to work for an organization and have continued to work there *like* the existing culture. Unfortunately, all too often those who would welcome change have long since left the organization because they did not like the culture. Thus, proposed changes to structure, process, and rewards are often met by statements like, "We don't do things that way here." This can make reward system changes very difficult to implement when they do not fit the culture of the organization—a culture, ironically, that was most likely shaped by the reward system.

Conclusion

Now that the major features of the new logic have been considered, it is appropriate to turn to the point on the Star Model that is the major focus of this book: the reward system. In order to support the new logic of organizing, it needs to fit the other points on the star in a way that contributes to organizational effectiveness. This is clearly more easily said than done, given the many design choices that need to be made.

Chapter Two

Reward System Design Choices

The number of ways to design and manage reward systems is virtually unlimited; the number of different kinds of rewards that organizations can give is large as well. The key to developing a reward system that creates excellence by supporting an organization's strategy lies in making the right design choices. Although many options exist, effective reward system design involves making a relatively small number of key decisions. I will identify these decisions in this chapter and discuss them in depth throughout the remainder of the book.

Useful in thinking about options for the design and management of reward systems is the process-content dichotomy. The structural or content dimension of a reward system refers to its formal mechanisms, procedures, practices (for example, the salary structure, the profit-sharing formula, the performance appraisal forms)—in short, the nuts and bolts of the system. The process dimension refers to the communication and decision aspects of how the system is designed, managed, and operated. Both process and structure are critical determinants of the effectiveness of reward systems and form an important part of the employment contract between individuals and organizations. I will begin the discussion of design options by focusing on the key structural decisions and then consider process design decisions and different employment contracts.

Structural Decisions

Nine major structural design issues are critical determinants of the impact of a reward system. The first two that will be discussed, job-

or person-based pay and performance-based pay, are the ones that usually get the most attention, but the others are also important and must be aligned with the first two in order for the pay system to be effective.

Job- or Person-Based Pay

The distribution of financial and status rewards in most organizations is based on the types of jobs people do. Indeed, with the exception of bonuses and merit salary increases, the standard policy in most organizations is to evaluate the job rather than the person and then set the reward level.[1] This approach is based on the assumption that job worth can be determined and that the person doing the job is worth only as much to the organization as the job itself is worth. At least part of this assumption is valid in many situations because with the use of techniques such as job evaluation, it is possible to determine what other organizations are paying people to do the same or similar jobs. It is less clear that the worth of people can be equated to the worth of their job. Despite this, it is clear that the approach has one important advantage: it can help an organization ensure that its compensation costs are not out of line with those of its competitors. Further, it gives a somewhat objective basis to the determination of pay.

An alternative to job-based pay that has recently been adopted by a number of organizations is to pay people based on their skills and competencies. This does not necessarily produce pay rates that are dramatically different from those produced by paying for the nature of the job. The skills people have usually match reasonably well with the jobs they are doing. It can, however, result in some employees being paid more than they would have been paid under a job-based system. Or the reverse can happen. Sometimes employees don't have the skills they need to do their job and therefore don't deserve the kind of pay that goes with it; in such instances they are paid less than they would be under a job-based system.

Perhaps the most important changes that are introduced when person-based pay is used occur in the kind of culture and motivation the system produces in an organization. Instead of being rewarded for moving up the hierarchy, people are rewarded for increasing their skills and developing themselves. This can create a culture of concern for personal growth and development and a highly talented workforce.

United Technologies Corporation (UTC) has an interesting approach to paying for knowledge that is targeted at changing the corporate culture. As a corporation it wants to establish a culture of learning and education and has the objective of creating the best-educated workforce in the world. In order to accomplish this objective, UTC has created an employee-scholar program that encourages employees to get a university degree—associate, bachelor's, or advanced. UTC pays for tuition, books, and academic fees and gives employees time off to study. When employees obtain their degree, they are given UTC stock as a graduation reward. One hundred shares of stock are awarded to every employee who achieves a bachelor's, master's, or doctoral degree; fifty shares are awarded to everyone who receives an associate degree.

One unusual feature of the UTC program is that it rewards employees even though the courses they take may not be related to the work they do or the work of the organization. The rationale for this is that UTC wants to create a knowledgeable, learning-oriented workforce, and so its program is designed to do this rather than develop specific job skills. Given that many of the company's businesses are in high-technology fields (such as the manufacture of jet engines) that are changing rapidly, it is easy to see the rationale for this strategy. Legitimate questions can be raised, however, as to whether or not the program would be even more effective if it targeted the specific skills and knowledge that individuals need to do their work.

Skill-based pay has been used frequently in new plant start-ups and in plants that are moving toward high-involvement, team-based management.[2] In factories where skill-based pay has been used, it typically means that many people in the organization can perform multiple tasks; thus, the workforce is knowledgeable and flexible.[3] Flexibility often means that less staff is needed; absenteeism and turnover are reduced as well because people like the opportunity to develop, use, and be paid for a wide range of skills.

Skill-based pay can be challenging to administer, however, because often it is not clear how to assess the pay marketplace and determine how much a skill is worth. There are a number of well-developed systems for evaluating jobs and comparing them to the marketplace, but none do this well with respect to individual skills. Skill assessment also can be difficult to accomplish. Another approach to person-based pay—competency pay—is beginning to be used with knowledge workers and with managers.

In general, person-based pay seems to fit organizations that want to have a flexible, relatively permanent workforce that is oriented toward learning, growth, and development. It also fits situations where organizations need to attract and retain talented individuals who, because of their scarce and valuable skills, need to be paid on the basis of their market value.[4] As I will discuss further in Chapter Six, it has a number of potential advantages and is likely to become the approach of choice for high-performance organizations that want to attract, retain, and develop excellent individuals.

Performance-Based Pay

Perhaps the key strategic decision that needs to be made in the design of any reward system is how much, if any, pay will be based on performance. As I will discuss in the next chapter, this decision is a key determinant of motivation and of who chooses to be a member of an organization. Once the decision about rewarding performance is made, many features of the reward system tend to fall into place.

Most business organizations, as well as many nonprofit and government organizations, say they reward individual performance and call their pay and promotion systems merit systems. Having a true merit-pay or promotion system is often easier said than done, however. Indeed, it has been observed that many organizations would be better off if they didn't try to relate pay and promotion to performance and relied on other systems to motivate performance.[5] The logic for this statement stems from the difficulty of specifying what kind of performance is desired and then determining whether it has been demonstrated. There is ample evidence that a poorly designed and administered merit system can do more harm than good. However, there is considerable evidence that relating rewards effectively to performance can help motivate, attract, and retain outstanding performers.[6]

There are numerous ways to relate pay to performance. The kind of pay reward that is given can vary widely and can include such things as stock, cash, and benefits. In addition, the frequency with which rewards are given can vary tremendously from every few minutes to every few years. Performance can be measured at the individual level so that each person gets a reward based on his or her performance. Rewards can also be based on the performance of groups, business units, and the total organization. Finally, many different kinds of performance can be rewarded. For example, managers can be rewarded for sales increases, productivity volumes, developing subordinates, cost-reduction ideas, and so on.

Many organizations choose to put individuals on multiple performance reward systems. For example, they may use a salary increase system that rewards people for their individual performance. At the same time they may give everybody in a business unit or division a bonus based on the unit's performance. Some plans measure group or company performance and then divide up the bonus pool that is generated among individuals on the basis of their performance, which in effect rewards employees for both individual and group performance.

Rewarding some behaviors and not others has clear implications for performance, so decisions about what is to be rewarded need to be made carefully and with attention to the overall strategic plan of the business. Consideration needs to be given to such issues as short- versus long-term performance, risk taking versus risk aversion, division performance versus total corporate performance, ROI (return on investment) maximization versus sales growth, and so on. Once an organization's strategic plan has been developed to the point that key performance objectives have been defined, the reward system needs to be designed to motivate the appropriate performance. Decisions about such issues as whether to use stock options or cash bonuses, for example, should be made only after careful consideration of whether they support the kind of behavior that is desired.

Future chapters will detail the pros and cons of relating pay to performance and of the many approaches to doing so. A few general points need to be made here, however. Bonus plans are generally better motivators than pay-raise and salary-increase plans. Bonus plans make it possible to substantially vary an individual's pay from time period to time period, which, as I will discuss further in Chapter Three, must happen if pay is to be a motivator of performance. With salary-increase plans, this is very difficult to do because past raises become an annuity.

Approaches using objective measures of performance are better motivators than those using subjective measures because they enjoy higher credibility. As I will discuss in Chapter Eight, considerable evidence exists to show that subjective performance appraisals are often biased and invalid. Instead of contributing to positive motivation and a work climate that improves superior-subordinate relationships, they lead to just the opposite. Employees will often accept the validity of an objective measure, such as sales volume or units produced, when they will not accept a superior's rating. As a result, when pay is tied to objective measures—and made public—it is usually clearer to employees that pay is determined by performance.

Group and organizational bonus plans are generally best at producing integration and teamwork. Under such plans, it is generally to everyone's advantage that individuals work effectively because everyone shares in the financial results of higher performance. If people feel they can benefit from others' good performance, they are likely to encourage and help others perform well. As a result, good performance is likely to be supported and encouraged by everyone when group and organizational plans are used. This is not true under individual plans, which tend to produce competition and little peer support.

A common error in the design of pay-for-performance systems is the tendency to focus on measurable, short-term operating results because they are quantifiable and regularly obtained. Too many organizations reward their top-level managers on the basis of short-term profitability. This can have the obvious dysfunctional consequence of causing managers to be very shortsighted in their behavior and to ignore strategic objectives that are important to the long-term profitability of the organization. Other common errors include giving too-small rewards, failing to clearly explain pay systems, and using poor administrative practices.

In short, the decision as to whether or not to relate pay to performance is a crucial one. The error of automatically assuming that they should be related can lead to serious problems. What is often overlooked is that relating them poorly can have more negative than positive consequences. However, the advantages that come with doing it right are significant.

Market Position

When it comes to the amount of reward given, the absolute amount is not the most significant factor. How much others receive is more critical. The key feature of a reward system is how the amount of reward an organization gives compares to what other organizations give. As I will discuss in Chapter Three, comparative reward levels are a crucial determinant of employee satisfaction. They can strongly influence the kind and number of people an organization attracts and retains, as well as its labor costs.

Organizations frequently have well-developed policies about how their pay compares to that of other companies. For example, some organizations feel it is important to be a leading payer, and they consciously set their pay rates at or above market level. Other organizations are much less concerned about being in a leadership position with respect to pay and as a result are content to target their pay levels at or below the market.

If an organization largely employs knowledge workers who are a key source of its competitive advantage, it may make sense to pay above the market. However, if many of its jobs are low-skilled and people are readily available in the labor market to do them, then a strategy of high pay may not be appropriate. It can increase labor costs and produce a minimum number of benefits.

Organizations do not have to be high payers for all jobs. Indeed, some organizations identify certain key skills they need in order to support their core competency and adopt the stance of being a high payer for them but an average or below-average payer for other skills. This has the obvious advantage of allowing organizations to attract the critical skills they need to support their strategy and to control costs at the same time.

The market position a company adopts with respect to its reward systems can have a noticeable impact on its culture. For example, a policy that calls for above-market pay can contribute to the feeling in an organization that it is elite, that people must be competent to be there, and that they are indeed fortunate to be there. A low-pay-level strategy can lead to just the opposite culture, that is, one in which everyone is looking to leave and employees help one another find better-paying jobs. A policy that puts certain skill groups into a high-pay position but puts the rest of the organization at lower pay levels can contribute to a spirit of elite groups within the organization and cause divisive social tensions.

Finally, it is worth noting that some organizations try to be above average in noncash compensation as a way of competing for the talent they need. They stress factors such as the quality of food in the dining room or child care and concierge services. Other organizations stress interesting and challenging work. This stance can be effective. It gives organizations a competitive edge in attracting people who value these things but raises the question of whether these are the best people to attract.

Internal-External Equity

Organizations differ in the degree to which they stress internal and external equity in their pay and reward systems. Organizations that stress internal equity work very hard to see that individuals doing similar work are paid the same, even though they may be in different locations or businesses. Corporations that focus on internal equity set a corporationwide pay structure for their jobs. They also usually evaluate jobs carefully so that similar jobs can be paid the same, even though they are in different functions or business units.

Organizations that stress external equity typically focus on the labor market as the key determinant of what somebody should be paid. Although a focus on the external market does not necessarily produce different pay for people doing the same job in a company, it may do that. For example, the same job in the auto industry and the electronics industry may be paid quite differently. Thus, focusing on the external market may produce different pay for similar jobs simply because they are in different business units of a company.

A number of advantages and disadvantages are associated with focusing on internal pay comparisons and paying all people in similar jobs the same. This system can make transfers from one location to another easier because pay differences need not be coped with. This is particularly true when the transfer involves a promotion, since it should always lead to a pay increase. In addition, an internal focus can produce an organizational culture of homogeneity and the feeling that everyone working for the company is treated fairly. It also can reduce or eliminate people's tendency to want to move to a higher-paying division or location within the company, as well as the tendency for rivalry and dissatisfaction to develop because of "unfair" internal pay comparisons.

A focus on internal equity can be very expensive, particularly if the organization operates diverse businesses and, as usually happens, pay rates across the corporation are set at the level that the market demands for the corporation's highest-paying business. The disadvantage of this is obvious: the organization pays a lot more than is necessary to attract and retain good people in many of its business units. In some situations, organizations can become noncompetitive in certain businesses and find that they have to limit themselves to businesses in which their pay structure makes them cost-competitive.

The automobile industry provides an interesting example of how organizations can get into cost difficulties by having an internal equity focus with respect to pay. When it comes to pay, the major auto producers in the United States have treated their parts manufacturing operations the same as they have treated their final assembly operations. Both have had very extensive benefit packages and relatively high wages for manufacturing workers. Over time the parts manufacturing operations of these organizations have become increasingly noncompetitive because they have had to compete with organizations that just manufacture parts and pay significantly lower wages. This is not a serious problem for the U.S. operations of DaimlerChrysler because they have always bought most of their parts, but it was and is a serious problem for both Ford and General Motors. They have dealt with it by creating separate companies and putting their auto parts manufacturing into those companies.

The advantages and disadvantages of an external equity focus are generally the reverse of those associated with an internal equity focus. They help ensure that individuals are paid well relative to the market and, as I will discuss further in the next chapter, this can be very important from an attraction and retention point of view. The focus on external equity can also help ensure that an organization's cost structure is in line with the cost structures of its competitors. On the negative side, a focus on external equity may create internal feelings of unfairness and motivate people to seek new jobs simply because they pay more. Career development, in particular the development of senior managers who understand multiple businesses and what is good for the organization, can be overwhelmed by these issues.

In some instances a strong focus on external equity can raise issues of discrimination and the unfair treatment of certain groups. For a considerable number of years, advocates of fair pay for women have argued for a policy called comparable worth. In some state governments within the United States and in parts of Canada, comparable worth is the law. It argues that fairness in compensation requires that work be evaluated in terms of its characteristics and that people be paid according to those evaluations. The fairness argument here is based on the comparatively low wages that are paid for work that has traditionally been done by women (for example, teachers, secretaries, nurses). Advocates of comparable worth argue that the history of discrimination against women has kept the wages associated with women's jobs low by creating an oversupply of job seekers. They go on to argue that this can be corrected by raising the pay for traditional female jobs above their current market price. By paying the job and focusing on internal equity, they maintain, this can be fairly and reasonably accomplished.

Centralized or Decentralized Reward Structure

Closely related to the issue of internal versus external equity is the issue of a centralized versus decentralized reward system structure. Organizations with centralized reward systems typically develop organizationwide, standard pay grades and ranges, standardized job evaluation systems, and perhaps, standardized promotion systems. They also typically assign to a corporate staff group the responsibility for seeing that reward practices are similar throughout the organization. In decentralized organizations, design and administration in the areas of pay, promotion, and other rewards are left to local option. Corporations may have broad guidelines or principles they wish to stand for, but the design and day-to-day administration of the systems is left up to the local entity.

The advantages of a centralized structure rest primarily in the pay administration expertise that can be developed at the central level and the degree of homogeneity that exists across the entire organization. Homogeneity can lead to a clear image of the corporate culture, feelings of internal equity, and the belief that the organization stands for something with respect to rewarding and valuing its human capital. It also eases the job of communicating and understanding what is going on in different parts of the organization. A decentralized strategy allows for local innovation and practices that fit particular businesses. It also reduces the need for administrative overhead at the corporate level.

As is true with the other critical design choices, there is no universally right choice between a centralized and decentralized approach to reward system design. The right choice depends on the strategy and structure of the organization.

A decentralized system tends to make the most sense when an organization is involved in businesses that face different markets and are at different points in their maturity. It allows those unique practices to surface, which can give a competitive advantage to one part of the business but may prove to be a real hindrance or handicap to another. For example, giving such perquisites as cars is often standard operating procedure in one business but not in another. Similarly, bonuses and stock options may be needed to attract one group of people but make little sense for others. Low base pay may make a great deal of sense in a start-up business but not in a traditional "cash cow" business.

The decentralized approach is particularly important to use when disruptive technologies appear. This point has been dramatically made by the growth of the Internet and its impact on organizations. Generally, organizations that have tried simply to add Internet business activities to their existing business units have had great difficulty attracting, retaining, and motivating the kinds of individuals they need. The Internet requires a different business model and, consequently, different pay structures if organizations are going to be successful in e-commerce. The problem is amplified by the fact that individuals with Internet business skills are hot talent and hence able to command unusual pay packages. Such packages are typically outside the allowable structure of the pay systems of most corporations. In most cases, the only way to deal with the pay problems and, indeed, with the entire problem of entering a business that requires a new business model, is to set up an autonomous business unit with its own special reward and people management practices.[7]

As a general rule, centralized reward systems make the most sense when companies are in a single business or a group of businesses that are in the same industry and operate in the same labor markets. In this situation it is hard to argue with the point that local options and local design can lead to unneeded complexity and unfairness when people doing the same kind of work end up being paid differently.

It is particularly important in organizations that are in only one business or several closely related businesses that all the top managers in the business be on the same pay and career system. In this type of company, developing people who understand the entire corporation and can produce synergies across its related businesses is critical to success. Accomplishing this requires corporate practices that ensure that individuals in the business units are motivated to look for multibusiness synergies and to work with other units. It is also important to have people whose career tracks cross over from one business unit to another. This is the best way to develop individuals who understand all of the operations of the different business units. It is only likely to happen if the corporate level takes responsibility for management development and career placement across a variety of business units and puts in place a corporationwide reward system that supports this type of career development.

Degree of Hierarchy

Hierarchical systems pay people larger amounts of money and give them greater perquisites and symbols of office as they move higher up in an organization. In other words altitude is the major factor when it comes to rewards. Typically, no formal decision is ever made to have a hierarchical or an egalitarian approach to rewards in an organization. A hierarchical approach simply happens because it is so consistent with the usual way organizations are run. The effect of a hierarchical approach is to strongly reinforce the traditional hierarchical power relationships in an organization and to create a climate of different status and power levels. In steeply hierarchical reward systems, the reward system often has more levels in it than the formal organization and, as a result, creates additional status differences.

The alternative to a hierarchical system is one in which differences in rewards are not strongly linked to hierarchical level. This may mean that certain rewards are eliminated. For example, in large corporations such as Alcoa and Hewlett-Packard that adopt an egalitarian stance, such things as special offices, reserved parking spaces, executive restrooms, and special building entrances are eliminated. People from all levels in the organization eat together, work together, and travel in elevators together.

As with all reward system strategic choices, there is no right or wrong answer as to how hierarchical a system should be. It depends on the strategy and structure of the organization. In general, a steeply hierarchical system makes the most sense when an organization needs relatively rigid bureaucratic behavior, strong top-down authority, and a strong motivation for people to move up the organizational hierarchy. A more egalitarian approach fits with the new-logic approach to organizing and the desire to retain technical specialists and experts in nonmanagement and lower-level management jobs. A less hierarchical approach tends to encourage decision making by expertise rather than by hierarchical position and creates less focus on upward mobility as a career track. It is not surprising, therefore, that many of the organizations that emphasize perquisites and pay practices that are similar from top to bottom are in high-technology and knowledge-based businesses.

Reward Mix

The reward mix an organization offers is important because it can determine both how many and what type of individuals are attracted to it. For example, highly variable, stock- and bonus-based compensation programs will attract different employees than salary-based programs. The challenge is to design a reward mix that fits the business strategy of the organization. As I will discuss in later chapters, an organization needs to translate its business strategy into an attraction and selection strategy that attracts and retains the "right kind" of people, given its business and organizational models.

The kind of rewards that organizations give can vary widely. Organizations can choose to reward people almost exclusively with cash, downplaying fringe benefits, perks, and status symbols, or they can reward people with a wide variety of fringe benefits and noncash rewards. The money that is given can come in many forms, from stock to retirement pay.

One major advantage of cash is that the value of cash in the eyes of recipients is universally high. When cash is translated into fringe benefits, perks, and other noncash rewards, it may lose part or all of its value for many people; as a result, it may be a poor investment. Life insurance is a good example of a reward that is often valued at less than its cost. Not surprisingly, this is particularly true for young people. However, certain benefits, such as medical insurance, can be obtained at a lower cost through mass purchase, and individuals may value them beyond their actual dollar cost to the organization. Finally, there may be cultural reasons for paying people in the form of perks and status symbols; they send messages about who has authority and power.

Flexible or cafeteria-style fringe benefit programs allow individuals to create a reward package that fits their needs and desires. They have become increasingly popular in part because organizations get the best value for their money by giving people only what they want.[8] These plans also have the advantage of treating individuals as mature adults rather than as dependent people who need their welfare looked after. Finally, they avoid the challenge of trying to determine what employees value and need.

Recently, the movement to flexibility in reward packages has led organizations to move beyond the usual fringe benefits. For example, organizations are now offering people who are in great demand a choice of working conditions. They can choose their working hours and location; they can opt for computers, cellular phones, and a host of other items that allow them to customize their work relationship. In many ways this resembles the manufacturing process called mass customization, which enables organizations to create products or services that are mass-produced and that allow customers to make important choices that shape the product or service to fit their unique situation.

Given the increased number of options that people have with respect to how and where they work, it may be time to implement a "wild" idea that I first advocated in an earlier book.[9] I suggested that organizations compute a total cost that they are willing to spend to have individuals work for them. The cost would include all cash compensation and fringe benefits, as well as the cost of work support systems. For this purpose, work support systems would usually include parking, office space, clerical services, transportation, and electronic equipment. Once organizations have this total cost or expense number in mind, they could then go to prospective employees and ask them to shape an optimally attractive employment package. People would not have to receive things they don't want—a secretary or an office, for example—but could simply "buy" whatever is needed to create an effective and attractive work situation. Once they have done this, the remaining money would be paid to them as cash compensation. Although complicated to manage, this system would ensure that employees only get the support systems, benefits, and perquisites they value.

Job Security

Job security is an important issue to many individuals. It also is a reward that fewer and fewer organizations seem to be willing to offer. Until the 1990s organizations such as AT&T, IBM, and Digital Equipment had either formally stated policies or practices under which no employee was ever laid off or downsized. Other companies had employment stability with respect to their professional or managerial workforces but did have layoffs and plant shutdowns that affected their nonmanagement employees.

Companies are increasingly moving away from guaranteeing employment stability or job security to anyone. In a recent survey of employment contracts that I conducted, most companies responded that to a substantial degree no one has a secure job.[10] Most companies also agreed with statements saying that loyalty to the company is not rewarded and that rewards are not tied to seniority. What is rewarded? The answer in most companies was performance and having the right skills.

The issue of employment stability is a critical one in terms of establishing the nature of the relationship between individuals and organizations. An organization that guarantees stability of employment is in fact making a statement of commitment to its employees that may well lead to loyalty on their part. At the very least, it is offering what may be an attractive reward. The emphasis here is on *may* because not all employees want to be in a highly secure job.

An organization that does not make employment security commitments is likely to have low-loyalty employees who behave like free agents. This is particularly true of employees who are in a contingent work situation (such as that of temporary or contract employees). They are told by the organization that it is not committed to them. The employee response can vary all the way from wanting to join the core or regular employee ranks of the organization to being willing to take any reasonably attractive alternative job opportunity that comes along.

Because of the massive downsizing and restructuring programs that have occurred, it can be argued that most corporations have basically eliminated the possibility of employees being loyal to them.[11] Companies have, in effect, unilaterally chosen a strategy that voids the traditional employment contract and eliminates most employee loyalty. That said, companies may be able to cultivate a committed workforce if they are willing to make some conditional security commitments and develop some substitutes for job security such as the opportunity to learn transferable skills. It is probably true, however, that it is much more difficult to develop a loyal workforce now than it was ten or fifteen years ago when employees had not seen so many companies violate their loyalty policies and move toward new, more temporary relationships with their employees.

Organizations are making much greater use of contingent employees. For example, they are using contract labor, labor provided by temporary agencies, labor provided by their own internal temporary agencies, and outsourced labor. This has led to organizations having multiple types of employees, each with a different employment relationship. Various authors have described this as a "shamrock" approach to employment and as a "rings" approach with a core group in the center.[12] I prefer to think of it as a "sunflower" approach in which there is a center and a number of petals that are attached to the center. There may be many or few petals and a large or small center, depending on the employment strategy of the organization and the business conditions it faces at the time.

The design challenge for an organization is clear. It needs to establish the employment relationships that fit its business strategy and its need for human resources. The emphasis here is on *relationships* (note the plural) because it is unlikely that any single model will fit the business situations that most organizations face. Most probably do need a stable core of employees, but beyond that, different strategies call for different employment stability relationships. In some organizations it may make sense to have a very large core and only a few contingent workers, whereas in other situations just the opposite may be best.

Seniority

Most organizations tie some of the rewards individuals receive at least in part to the length of their service. This is particularly true of retirement benefits, vacation days, and eligibility for fringe benefits. Seniority often affects eligibility for such perquisites as parking spaces and offices. Basing rewards on seniority sends a clear message to employees: their length of service is valued. This often is taken by employees as a sign of loyalty and commitment on the part of an organization. It can encourage employees to stay because all they have to do is remain as an employee to be more highly rewarded. Some companies put a particularly strong focus on length of employment by having celebrations and giving symbols (clocks, citations, rings) to celebrate important anniversary dates.

The alternative to a seniority-based reward system is to essentially ignore seniority, that is, to treat all employees the same regardless of how long they have been with the organization. This approach sends a very different message about what the organization values, particularly with respect to the value that is placed on loyalty.

Whether it is desirable to tie rewards to seniority depends very much on the nature of the relationship an organization wants to develop with its workforce. It clearly makes sense to do so when an organization wants to build a long-term relationship with its employees and needs them to be loyal. The opposite is true, however, if an organization needs to make frequent changes in its employee population and to restructure itself. In this case, rewarding seniority may strike employees as cynical and hypocritical, given that the organization does not seek a long-term relationship with its employees.

Process Issues in Reward Administration

Process issues involve how decisions are made, communicated, and put into practice. They come up frequently with respect to reward systems because organizations constantly have to make reward system design, management, implementation, and communication decisions. The focus here will be on the two critically important process themes—communication policy and decision-making process—that characterize the overall way reward systems are designed and administered.

Communication Policy

Organizations differ widely in how much information they communicate about their reward systems. Some are extremely secretive, particularly in the area of pay. They forbid employees from talking about their pay, give out minimal information about how rewards are decided on and allocated, and have no publicly disseminated information about such things as the market position of pay, the approach to gathering market data, and the budget for pay increases. At the other extreme, some organizations are so open that everyone's pay is a matter of public record, as are the pay administration practices (many new high-involvement plants operate this way). In addition, all promotions are subject to open job postings, and in some instances peer groups discuss people's eligibility for promotion.

The difference between an open and a closed communication policy in the area of rewards is enormous. Like all the other choices that must be made in designing a reward system, however, there is no clear right or wrong approach. Rather, it is a matter of picking a position on the continuum from open to secret that is supportive of the overall culture, organization design, and types of behavior needed for organizational effectiveness. An open system tends to encourage people to ask questions, share data, and ultimately be involved in decisions, whereas a secret system tends to put people in a more dependent position, to keep power concentrated at the top, and to allow an organization to keep its options open with respect to its pay and reward decisions. It can also lead to the creation of a low-trust environment in which people have trouble understanding the relationship between pay and performance. Thus, if strong secrecy policies are in place, a structurally sound pay system may end up being ineffective because it is misperceived.

Open systems put considerable pressure on organizations to do an effective job in administering rewards. If pay administration is done poorly, strong pressures for change usually develop. Ironically, if an organization wants to spend little time administering rewards but still wants to base pay on performance, secrecy may be the best policy, although secrecy may limit the effectiveness of the organization's pay plan.

Decision-Making Process

Reward systems have typically been designed by top management, with staff support, and administered by strict reliance on the chain of command. The assumption is that this provides the proper checks and balances in the system and locates decision making where the expertise rests. In many cases this is a valid assumption and certainly fits well with a management style that emphasizes hierarchy, bureaucracy, and control through the use of extrinsic rewards. It does not fit, however, with an organization that believes in open communication, high levels of involvement, and control through individual commitment to policies. Neither does it fit when expertise is broadly spread throughout the organization.

In discussing the types of decision-making processes that are used with respect to reward systems, it is important to distinguish between decisions about system design and those about ongoing system administration. It is possible to have different styles with respect to these two types of decisions.

There are a number of examples of employees being involved in the design of their pay system. For example, employees have been involved in designing their own bonus systems, and the results have been generally favorable.[13] When employees are involved, it leads them to raise important issues and to provide expertise that is not normally available to the designers of pay systems. Perhaps more important, once the system is designed, the acceptance level and the understanding of the system tends to be very high. This often leads to the rapid start-up of the system and to a commitment to seeing it survive. When systems are designed by line managers rather than by staff support people, greater effectiveness generally results because the managers see the need to support, maintain, and stay committed to their system.

There has also been some experimentation with having peer groups and first-level supervisors handle the day-to-day decision making about who should receive pay increases and how jobs should be evaluated and placed in pay structures. The most visible examples of this are in participative plants that use skill-based pay.[14] In these plants, typically, the work group reviews the performance of individuals and decides whether they have acquired new skills. Interestingly, what evidence there is suggests that this has gone very well. In many respects this is not surprising because peers often have the best information about the performance and skills of their peers and thus are in a good position to make assessments. The problem in traditional organizations is that they lack the motivation to give valid information and to respond responsibly, so their expertise is of no use. In more participative open systems, this motivational problem is less severe and, as a result, involvement in decision making is more effective.

There have been some instances of executives and managers assessing each other. This can work effectively when combined with a history of open and effective communication. Deciding on rewards is clearly not an easy task for groups and should be done only when there is comfort with the confrontation skills of the group and trust in their ability to talk openly and directly about each other's performance. It also must fit with the organization's basic approach to management.

Employment Contract

Organizations make a variety of contracts or "deals" with the people they hire. Here I am not referring to a legally binding contract between an individual and an organization but to a mutual understanding or psychological contract regarding how the organization will treat its members. Contracts usually cover job security, personal treatment, how financial rewards are distributed and handed out, development opportunities, and the type of work that individuals will be asked to do.

Some organizations have formal statements that cover their policies and practices with respect to how employees will be rewarded, dealt with, and treated. The majority, however, do not have a clearly stated philosophy or set of practices but an understanding that has developed between the employees and the organization. The understanding is usually the product of the organization making a number of decisions about how elements of their reward system will work and dealing with employees in a particular way over a period of years.

The last decade has seen a well-publicized change in the type of employment relationship that most organizations establish. This change involves the area of employment security but goes beyond it. The traditional employment contract is highlighted in Figure 2.1. This is essentially a paternalistic loyalty relationship in which the organization assumes some responsibility for taking care of the employee and, in return, expects the employee to be loyal to the organization. With the downsizing activities of many corporations in the 1980s and 1990s, this traditional loyalty-employment relationship has been on the wane. When all is said and done, it did produce dull organizations but not safe ones because it did not create

Figure 2.1. Loyalty Contract.

If you:

- Are loyal
- Work hard
- Do as you're told

We'll provide:

- A secure job
- Steady pay increases
- Financial security

And you'll be part of:

- A dull, safe organization

organizations that could compete effectively in the business environment of the last quarter of the twentieth century.

In many organizations the loyalty contract was replaced by one that many employees have found to be negative (see Figure 2.2). In some organizations this so-called crisis contract is increasingly being replaced by one that recognizes the importance of human capital. This contract, which is presented in Figure 2.3, is frequently called an employability contract. It essentially states that the organization will help individuals gain skills and abilities and pay them well, but it offers no guarantees with respect to employment stability and expects individuals to develop their own career and worry about their personal development.

A fourth contract has become popular in a number of large corporations—a more temporary one than the contract cited in Figure 2.3. It covers the contingent workforce, that is, its part-time, contract, and temporary employees. This employment relationship asks that individuals perform effectively while they are doing a particular job or task and offers nothing in terms of a long-term relationship.

There is an important connection between the type of employment relationship an organization has and the types of capabilities and competencies it can develop. For example, to develop

Figure 2.2. Crisis Contract.

If you:

- Stay
- Do your job plus someone else's
- "Volunteer" for task forces

We'll provide:

- A job if we can
- Gestures that show we care
- The same pay

And you'll be part of:

- An organization in crisis

Figure 2.3. Employability Contract.

If you:

- Develop skills we need
- Apply them in ways that help the company succeed
- Behave consistently with our new values

We'll provide:

- A challenging work environment
- Support for your development
- Rewards for your contribution

And you'll be part of:

- A high-performance organization

---

complex or difficult-to-master competencies, organizations may need to establish long-term employment contracts with at least those employees who are vital to the development and maintenance of the competencies. Also closely related to the employment relationship are reward system practices. The types of rewards that can be used to motivate performance are, to some degree, limited by the type of employment relationship and the competencies and capabilities that need to be developed. The obvious conclusion is that an effective organization design needs to create a fit among the reward system, the employment contract, and the competencies and capabilities that need to be developed.

Design Strategy

Figure 2.4 depicts one way of thinking about the reward system. It follows the Star Model by showing that the design must be congruent with the basic organization design and the management style of the organization, which, in turn, needs to be strongly influenced by the organization's strategy. Finally, the figure shows that the reward system, in combination with the organization's design, drives the performance of the organization because it influences critical individual and organizational behaviors. Not shown

Figure 2.4. Role of the Reward System.

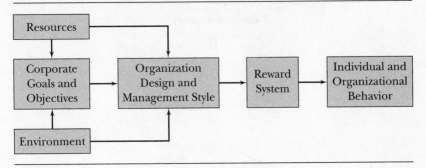

in the figure are the specific behaviors that the reward system influences. The research evidence provides some clear answers to the question of what reward systems influence. As I will discuss in the next chapter, they can affect the performance motivation of individuals, as well as their organizational membership behaviors. They also can serve to reinforce key organizational capabilities such as lateral coordination, customer focus, and quality.

Figure 2.5 makes essentially the same point as Figure 2.4 but with a slightly different flow. It depicts the design process an organization should use in creating a reward system and in testing its effectiveness. It shows that business strategy should be the foundation for identifying the organizational behaviors that are needed. This, in turn, is shown as driving the design of the reward system. The challenge here is to correctly identify the features of a reward system that will produce the individual and organizational behaviors that are needed to make the strategy come alive.

Three critical elements of the reward systems are identified in this figure. The first is the set of core principles that the organization holds. These principles may be stated or simply implicit in the way the organization operates, but they are part of every organization and its reward system. Examples of core principles are a commitment to pay for performance, a commitment to secrecy about pay, and the other fundamental, relatively long-term reward system design features that I have discussed in this chapter.

The reward system is shown in the figure to be made up of process and structural practices. Typically, the structural practices

Figure 2.5. Design Process.

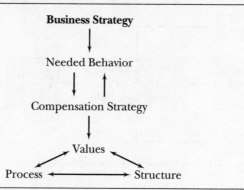

I reviewed in this chapter are the features of reward systems that get the most attention. Although often not receiving as much attention, communication and decision making are often as important in determining effectiveness.

Reward systems are assumed to be effective to the degree that their core principles, processes, and practices are in alignment. This is depicted in the figure by the arrows among the three elements. Fit is critical because organizations need to be consistent in what they say and do. Violations of this consistency always lead to misunderstanding about how the reward system works and failure to motivate the proper or needed behavior. As I will discuss in the next chapter, attracting, retaining, developing, and motivating excellent employees is not simple; it requires rewards systems that reward the right behaviors and satisfy the right individuals.

Chapter Three

Motivating and Satisfying Excellent Individuals

The organizational behavior research on how reward systems affect individuals has focused on two topics: motivation and satisfaction. These two topics need to be well understood and effectively managed in order for a reward system to motivate excellent behavior and satisfy excellent employees. The literature is vast; thousands of studies have been done on employee motivation and employee satisfaction.[1] At the risk of oversimplifying the vast and complex literature on these topics, I will briefly review what is known about rewards as motivators and what is known about the causes and consequences of satisfaction with rewards.

Pay for Performance

In an increasingly competitive and capitalistic world, few disagree that individuals who contribute more should receive greater rewards. There is also universal recognition that motivation is critical to organizational effectiveness and nearly universal recognition that an effective pay-for-performance system can increase motivation.

It is, of course, one thing to say that pay for performance is a great idea; it is another to develop an effective pay-for-performance system. The devil is in the details—the details of the design and management of the delivery system. It is probably an understatement to say that pay-for-performance systems are complex to design and that they often have difficulty living up to the hopes and expectations of the employees who are paid by them and the organizations that create them.

For the past century, work organizations have primarily used two approaches to paying for individual performance. The first is strongly associated with factory work and scientific management and flourished during the 1920s and 1930s. Often called incentive pay or piecework pay, it involves paying employees directly for the amount of work they produce. Engineers study jobs and determine what an employee should be paid for various steps in the manufacturing process. Employees are then told that they will be paid a fixed amount of money each time they complete a particular operation. Incentive pay is also a common way to pay salespeople. They are paid a predetermined amount of money for each product or service they sell.

The incentive-pay approach to paying for performance has produced an enormous research literature that details its advantages and disadvantages.[2] There is little question that it typically increases the amount of rewarded work that an employee does; there is also little question, however, that the systems are difficult to design, maintain, and manage. Over time, they often collapse from their own bureaucratic weight or are sabotaged by clever workers who figure out ways to beat the system.

The second major approach to paying for performance is merit pay—the "standard" approach to paying for performance in most of the developed world (Japan was one of the last holdouts, but in the 1990s many major Japanese firms, including Toyota and Honda, adopted it). Unlike incentive pay, which peaked in popularity in the first half of the twentieth century, merit pay continues to be popular.[3] Also unlike incentive pay, it typically covers most of the employees in an organization, except perhaps those in non-management positions and those who are covered by incentive pay. It typically involves employees getting an increase in their pay as a result of a subjective performance rating by their boss. The pay raises become an annuity for the employees who receive them because their regular pay is permanently increased.

Like incentive pay, merit pay has been the subject of a considerable amount of research.[4] The results suggest that merit pay does a poor job of relating pay to performance and, as a result, does a poor job of motivating employees. Its faults, which I will discuss in more detail later, typically include poor performance measures and relatively small rewards for performance.

At this point, it may seem appropriate to conclude that pay for performance is a great idea that cannot be effectively implemented and therefore cannot be an effective motivator of performance. This is just what has been concluded by some critics of the idea.

Perhaps the most visible and vocal critic for a number of years was W. Edwards Deming, the world-renowned expert on total quality management.[5] Deming spoke strongly against individual pay for performance and management by objectives. He correctly pointed out that they often produce dysfunctional competition among employees and are bureaucratic and administrative nightmares. He strongly emphasized the importance of eliminating merit ratings and the "evils" associated with them. Interestingly, my research shows that even companies that adopt total quality management on a wide scale still maintain pay-for-performance systems.[6] Apparently, either hope springs eternal when it comes to pay for performance or managers simply don't believe their systems are as dysfunctional as Deming thinks they are.

A second group advocating the elimination of pay for performance focuses on the research literature concerned with motivation, in particular on findings concerned with intrinsic motivation— the type of motivation that comes from the pleasure of performing a task.[7] Research in this field suggests that pay for performance can cause people to stop finding intrinsic pleasure from doing work, and as a result, cause employees to do things only when they are paid for doing them.[8] Therefore, they suggest concentrating on creating work that is challenging and motivating and not worrying about using money as a motivator of performance. They are particularly critical of the type of piecework incentive plans that were popular in the thirties and forties. They also reject the theorizing of behavioral psychologist B. F. Skinner, who emphasized reinforcing individual behaviors in order to get people to perform in a particular way.

Pay as a Motivator

I agree with many of the criticisms of merit pay that Deming makes. The problems with it are well documented, and he is not the first person to criticize merit-pay systems. I also agree with many of the intrinsic motivation theorists' arguments that intrinsic motivation can be an important driver of behavior and that extrinsic rewards such as pay should not interfere with it. But I do not agree that the best route to organizational effectiveness is through abandoning pay for performance. Rather, I believe the best route is through developing pay-for-performance systems that fit modern organization designs and business strategies. Given the potential power of pay to motivate performance, the best solution is not to eliminate pay as a motivator, thereby losing an important driver of performance, but to get it to motivate the right behavior.

Unfortunately, critics such as Deming and the advocates of intrinsic motivation do not provide viable alternatives to the traditional pay-for-performance approaches; they only provide compelling criticisms of them. Deming, for example, suggests "paying everyone fairly," instead of paying for performance. This is obviously not an adequate alternative to pay for performance because, among other things, in many societies pay is deemed fair only when different amounts are paid to workers who make different contributions. Deming also fails to acknowledge that motivation can be created by effective pay-for-performance systems. Ironically, evidence to support the argument that pay can be a motivator is embedded in his criticisms of existing pay-for-performance systems. If pay were not a motivator, it could never cause the many dysfunctional behaviors that he and others ascribe to it.

The intrinsic motivation advocates, for their part, also fail to provide an adequate alternative to pay for performance. They talk about the importance of intrinsic rewards and how they can be powerful drivers of performance. So far so good. The research evidence leaves little doubt that intrinsic rewards can be important motivators. What the advocates of intrinsic motivation do not recognize is that, in most cases, intrinsic rewards are not sufficient in and of themselves to motivate all the behaviors that are needed to make most organizations successful. In the absence of pay-for-performance systems, it is hard to imagine, for example, how an organization can motivate people to work effectively on tasks such as chicken processing or making cold sales calls for telephone services and credit cards. Further, they fail to recognize that intrinsic rewards sometimes motivate the wrong behaviors. Unfortunately, what is fun and interesting is not always what is best from an organizational effectiveness point of view.

Intrinsic motivation theorists also do not deal with the issue of fairly distributing the profits and value that corporations create as a result of the efforts of the individuals who have invested their human capital. In order to have a fair and just organization and a fair and just society, there needs to be a division of the profit that is made from the collective efforts of organization members.

Perhaps the most compelling argument for creating pay-for-performance systems rests on the fact that money is a unique commodity. It is relatively easily distributed, is valued by most individuals, can be given in a wide variety of forms, and exists in every organized society. Further, it is something that everyone expects to get when they work for a business organization. Indeed, business organizations cannot operate without distributing money to their employees. This distribution does not have to be based completely or even partially on performance or, for that matter, on the value of human capital, but the research evidence suggests that distributing at least part of it based on performance contributes to organizational effectiveness. Specifically, when pay is based on performance, it is seen as fair and motivating.

Pay for performance is sometimes presented as a silver bullet that can be easily shot and can yield large improvements in performance. As my discussion so far clearly indicates, this is a naive view. Nevertheless, it is true that pay for performance can have a large positive impact on organizational performance.

Creating an effective reward system takes a substantial understanding of the kind of impact that pay can have on employee behavior and on the business strategy of an organization, its structure, its information systems, and its performance. Thus, before I talk about specific reward systems, it is important to look at how rewards affect individual motivation and behavior. In later chapters I will discuss the effectiveness of different pay-for-performance approaches.

Motivation and Rewards

Psychologists created motivation theories and studied work motivation for most of the twentieth century. The research was marked by controversy, competing theories, and sometimes conflicting research results. Some argued that the work of Abraham Maslow, a well-known need theorist of the sixties and seventies, showed that money is not a motivator once individuals have achieved a minimum level of financial security.[9] Many still hold this view, even though Maslow never made this statement, nor is there research evidence to support it.

Others argued that the work of Fredrick Herzberg showed that pay and other extrinsic rewards can never be motivators, only a source of dissatisfaction.[10] Interestingly, many still hold this view, despite the fact that it is not consistent with Herzberg's research results or with the research of most who have followed up on his original work.[11] The research clearly shows that pay can be a source of motivation when it is tied to performance and seen as a form of recognition.

I cite Maslow's and Herzberg's theories to make the point that the field of motivation is full of conflicting points of view and misinformation. At the risk of falling completely out of favor with my academic colleagues who, like myself, have written entire books on the subject of motivation, I will summarize what is known about motivation and satisfaction in the rest of this chapter. Although not every theorist would endorse my summary, I think it represents a good overview of the thousands of research studies on motivation that are available and should be helpful in understanding how rewards can be used to motivate individuals in work organizations.

Reward Importance

Organizations can directly give a variety of rewards such as recognition, fringe benefits, cash, titles, and a host of other items. Indeed, a best-selling book in the 1990's was *A Thousand and One Ways to Reward Employees*. The rewards offered by corporations today are truly diverse. Private rodeos with mechanical bulls, fly fishing on western ranches, flying in a fighter plane, river rafting, and a lifetime supply of Ben and Jerry's ice cream are all rewards that have been given by corporations. The key questions about any of them are, How great is their appeal? and Are they valued more than their cost?

The starting point for most theories of motivation is the concept of reward importance. The argument is that to be a motivator a reward needs to be important to the person receiving it. The importance of a specific reward, in turn, is said to depend on at least two major determinants: (1) how much the individual values the particular type of reward being offered and (2) how much of the reward is being offered. The more an individual values the type of reward and the more of it that is offered, the more motivation potential there is in the reward.

One behavioral example of the importance of reward size can be observed by anyone who lives in an area that has a lottery with varying sizes of payouts. As the size of the prize goes up, the number of participants playing the lottery increases dramatically. A $100 million payoff attracts many more players than a $1 million payoff. People will stand in line for hours to buy a ticket when the payoff is large. In the case of a lottery, the probability of winning is extremely low and gets even lower as more people play. Nevertheless, when the reward is big enough individuals will endure quite a bit just to play.

A common question that managers ask me is, How much money has to be offered in order for it to be important enough to motivate behavior? Unfortunately, there is no precise research-based answer to this.[12] Generally, the amount needed to achieve a motivating level of importance is best thought of as a percentage of the amount somebody already has. Thus, in the case of salaries, in order to understand how important a $500 bonus will be to a group of employees, it is necessary to take their salaries into account. If $500 represents less than 1 percent of their annual salary, it will probably not be important enough to influence motivation. But if it is 5 percent or greater, it may well be important enough.

I feel some anxiety about mentioning the 5 percent figure, because it may be taken as a minimum amount that will automatically motivate people. Unfortunately, the situation is not that clear cut. In most cases, 5 percent probably is enough to be an important reward to the typical individual, but, depending on how strongly an organization wants to influence motivation and on the needs of the individual, 10, 15, 20 percent or more may be needed.

To make the importance of rewards a bit more complex, it is also true that small amounts of money can sometimes be important, particularly when the money is given in a way that involves recognition, goal achievement, and status. Just as small amounts of money can be a positive reward, and therefore a motivator, so can other forms of recognition. For example, employees can sometimes be motivated by the opportunity to become the employee of the month, to get a letter of commendation from their manager, or to receive a simple "thank you" from their supervisor.

Before it merged with BankAmerica to form the new Bank of America, NationsBank gave a reward that was highly prized by its employees. NationsBank's corporate culture dripped with military metaphors; thus, it was not too surprising that its major recognition reward was a crystal hand grenade modeled after a real one that the CEO kept on his desk. One of many cultural mismatches between NationsBank and BankAmerica involved this type of reward. The San Francisco–based BankAmerica executives saw the crystal grenade as a joke and characteristic of the overly autocratic, top-down culture of NationsBank. Nevertheless, it was an important reward in NationsBank and therefore worked as a motivator there.

The crystal hand grenade, like many symbolically important rewards, had a series of identifiable characteristics associated with it. A brief review of those will highlight what must happen to make nonfinancially significant rewards important.

- *The rewards are public.* Because symbolic rewards rely heavily on recognition for their value, it is particularly important that they be public. This can happen as a result of the way they are given and through publicity that is associated with their reception. Further, they can be visibly in the possession of the recipient. In the case of the crystal hand grenade, for example, the winners proudly placed them on their desk.
- *The rewards are given infrequently.* Symbolic rewards tend to lose their value if they are given too frequently; their recognition value and significance tend to decrease. Instead of being special rewards that denote status, they become entitlements and everyday occurrences.
- *The reward process is credible.* The selection of recipients for symbolic rewards must be done by a highly credible process. It is particularly important that it be done by respected individuals who have good information about the performance and accomplishments of potential winners.

- *The rewards are associated with winners.* Symbolic rewards gain their importance and their status, in part, by who has received them in the past. It is crucial that winners (particularly early winners) have high status and be well respected in the organization. Without this, symbolic rewards can become rewards that no one wants to be associated with.

- *The rewards are meaningful in the culture.* The nature of the reward can sometimes make a difference. Picking the right artifact or symbol can provide a tremendous boost to the visibility and meaningfulness of the reward. The crystal hand grenade is a good example; it worked in the culture of NationsBank because it was tied to a respected CEO. As became clear when NationsBank merged with BankAmerica, it is not a reward that works everywhere. Other companies give similar types of idiosyncratic and symbolic rewards that work because they fit a particular historical event in the company or a characteristic of the company's leader.

The nature and amount of the reward are only part of the equation that determines how important a reward will be to a particular person. Also important are the person's needs and desires. Much of the early research on motivation focused on determining and influencing individuals' needs. This research establishes that most people have the same basic needs. Maslow did a reasonably good job of identifying them when he put forth his theory, arguing that people have certain physiological survival needs, as well as needs for social interaction, respect from others, self-esteem, and personal growth and development. He also made the point, as have many other need theorists, that there are tremendous individual differences in need strength. This, of course, is what leads individuals to attach different degrees of importance to rewards such as money and recognition from a supervisor.

A number of factors influence people's needs and desires. Maslow made the point that unless the basic physiological needs for security, food, and water are satisfied, the higher-order needs (growth, esteem, self-actualization) are not likely to come into play. This point has been generally accepted in the field of psychology as valid. Beyond this point, a number of factors seem to help determine the importance of needs. The cultural and environmental conditioning that individuals experience is clearly one important determinant; age and maturity also seem to be factors. Finally, as needs become satisfied they tend to become less important. For example, people seem to need only so much food, water, and social interaction.

A whole industry has grown up around the study of the importance that people place on different kinds of rewards. Visible products of this industry include regular reports on how generations differ in what they value. The current focus is on Generation X. It may well be that members of Generation X are somewhat different from those of other generations—they did grow up in a world very different from the one my generation experienced—but the differences are most likely small. Like any other generation, the most significant point about this one is likely to turn out to be the differences among the members of the generation rather than the differences between this and other generations.

There is also a constant stream of studies on what the latest research has shown about how important different rewards are to employees. Pay, career, family time, interesting work, and having a good boss are among the factors that researchers frequently argue are the most important. Most of this research is of poor methodological quality and shouldn't be taken seriously. Often the major reason that studies obtain different results is that the questions they ask are worded differently. For example, studies that ask about the importance of fair pay often find pay rated as one of the more important, if not the most important, feature of jobs. However, the results of studies that ask about the importance of getting rich or having high pay often show the importance of pay to be less than the importance of career opportunities and the challenge that a job offers. All I can do here is issue a blanket warning: be very suspicious of any study that claims to report on what "employees really want from their jobs," particularly those arguing that one thing is much more important than others.

Perhaps the best general conclusion that can be reached about the importance of needs is that the needs of individuals differ substantially—so much so that when it comes to rewards, an organization that wishes to motivate its members needs to proactively take individual differences into account, particularly when the workforce is diverse and global and when different kinds of employment relationships exist within the organization.

In many respects, it would be easier to deal with employees if they could say accurately what they value. Many attitude surveys that I have seen distributed in organizations try to tap into individual differences in need strength by asking employees what they value. Unfortunately, the accuracy of self-report data about reward importance is highly questionable. For a variety of reasons, it is difficult for most people to state what is most important to them. First, they may not know themselves well enough to respond to the question effectively. Second, in some cases, social desirability and what seems to be appropriate can prevent people from reporting their feelings accurately. This is particularly true in the case of money. In many societies it simply isn't good impression management to say, "I work for money"; as a result, individuals sometimes understate its importance.

CEOs and other senior executives are often the most adamant about the fact that money is not a powerful motivator for them. They go on to add that they deserve to be paid a large amount because of their tremendous contributions but that the amount they earn is not that important to them. At first blush, this argument makes a lot of sense, particularly given how much they make. But something must account for the tremendous increase in CEO compensation over the last decades in the United States. Somebody seems to be working awfully hard on increasing the amount of CEO compensation. Pay levels don't just double or triple or quadruple without some effort being put into it.

Based on what I have seen in a number of corporations, CEOs share at least part of the blame (or credit) for the fact that their compensation has increased so dramatically. They are often very tough negotiators when it comes to dealing with corporate boards. Particularly when they are hired from the outside, they often make extremely high compensation demands and get boards to meet their demands. CEOs are also skillful at selecting compensation consulting firms that will support their claims for high pay by effectively lobbying boards. In short, CEOs seem to put a lot of effort into being sure they are well compensated. On the surface, this suggests that the amount of money they make is important to them, even though without any special effort most could make more money in a year than most people make in a lifetime.

The effort that CEOs put into determining their compensation leads us to ask why they do it. Perhaps the best explanation concerns their need to achieve and to receive recognition for their achievements. CEOs are highly competitive, achievement-oriented individuals, and their compensation is a clear, objective, and highly visible measure of their level of achievement.

Given that people are not good reporters of the importance they give to money, how can reward preferences be determined? Often the best way is to offer individuals a choice and see what they choose. As I will discuss later, this should begin with the hiring process, when by offering a particular package of rewards to potential employees, organizations can help determine the kinds of needs their employees will have. People often choose to join an organization based on whether it offers the rewards they value. Once individuals join an organization, giving them opportunities to choose among rewards is another way to understand what they value most. Once this is established, the most valued rewards can be used to motivate their performance.

In several respects the difficulty of knowing what individuals desire argues for using financial rewards as motivators. Although money may not be the most important reward for some, it usually is important to most. Money has a certain universality about it because purchasing power and status are attached to it in every society. Money is also easily quantified into and allocated in varying amounts.

Money can be converted into other commodities such as the clocks, vacations, and the many other items that some companies give instead of money. However, before giving noncash rewards, companies should explore whether in fact they are good purchases, that is, whether their cost is more or less than the value that recipients attach to the dollars used to purchase them. Clearly, if an item is not more valued than the dollars, it doesn't make sense to convert the dollars into the item. The first key to a motivating reward system is to use only rewards that are valued.

Expectations and Motivation

Currently, the most widely accepted theory of work motivation is expectancy theory.[13] It emphasizes that individuals act in ways they believe will lead to rewards they value. Expectancy theory argues that individuals are mostly rational decision makers who think about the consequences of their actions and act in their own best interests. The theory doesn't deny that individuals sometimes have misperceptions about reality, make mistakes in their estimates of the likelihood that things will happen, or badly misread the realities of situations. It does argue that they try to deal rationally with the world as they see it and to direct their behavior in ways that will meet their needs. In that sense, it views people as proactive, future-oriented, and motivated to behave in a particular way when they feel there is a good chance that the behavior will lead to valued rewards.

Part of the reason expectancy theory is so popular is that it is useful for understanding how to motivate individuals in most aspects of their lives. This is particularly true with respect to their work lives. Simply stated, expectancy theory suggests that the rewards organizations give out should be tied to individuals behaving in ways that support the organization's basic business strategy and performance needs. In essence, it says that pay for performance is a viable motivator if performance can be measured and if valued amounts of pay can be tied to performance.

The connection between performance and rewards is often called the line of sight. Perhaps a better term would be *line of influence* because it refers to the fact that, in order to be motivated in an organizational setting, people must see how their behavior influences a performance measure that, in turn, drives the allocation of a reward. Expectancy theory argues that if valued rewards are clearly seen as being tied to a particular performance behavior, the organization is likely to get more of that behavior. Unsaid but also important to remember is that if a particular behavior is not rewarded, the organization is likely to get less of that behavior.

Expectancy theory can also be used to explain people's job choices. It is particularly useful in this respect because it leads to a simple valid conclusion: people choose to join and remain members of organizations that offer them the best mix of the rewards they value. Thus, the issue of attracting and retaining employees becomes a relatively "simple" matter. Organizations need to offer a very attractive mix of rewards to people they particularly want to join their organization and to those they want to retain.

Expectancy theory clearly does not argue that individuals are motivated only by extrinsic rewards. To the contrary, it argues that

individuals may reward themselves for certain kinds of performance because they feel they have accomplished something that
is worthwhile, achieved a personal goal, learned a new skill, or were
intellectually stimulated and excited. Thus, in the framework of
expectancy theory, individuals can be motivated both by organizationally given rewards and by intrinsic rewards they give to themselves. Further, it does not see a cancellation or interference effect
between the two kinds of rewards. Rather, it argues that the greatest amount of motivation is present when individuals are doing
tasks that are intrinsically rewarding to them when they perform
them well and that provide important financial and recognition
rewards for performance.[14]

Expectancy theory places great emphasis on the importance of
goals—an emphasis that is supported by the research on goal setting. Research evidence shows that when individuals commit themselves to a goal, they become highly motivated to achieve it because
their self-esteem and sense of self-worth get tied to accomplishing
that goal.[15] Of course, they may also be motivated to achieve a goal
because a financial reward is tied to achieving it.

Goal difficulty is an issue that often comes up when goals are
discussed; expectancy theory provides an interesting way of thinking about it. The theory argues that if goal difficulty gets too high,
individuals may see a low probability of achieving the goal. This in
turn will destroy the connection between their effort and the re-
ceipt of a reward. This doesn't necessarily mean that individuals
will never try to achieve hard goals. It does suggest, however, that
if they are going to be motivated to achieve hard goals, two conditions need to exist. First, the connection between achieving the
goal and the reward needs to be clear. Second, the amount of reward, either intrinsic or extrinsic, that is associated with goal accomplishment needs to be large. When there is a low probability
of achieving a goal or the rewards are small, it is almost certain that
individuals will not put forth the effort to try to achieve the goal.

Goal difficulty is an interesting issue with respect to the combination of extrinsic and intrinsic rewards. Some evidence from
the research on the desire to achieve suggests that as goal difficulty
rises, people feel a greater sense of accomplishment and achievement when they actually reach a goal. Thus, under certain conditions individuals may be more motivated to achieve difficult than

easy goals, even though the line of sight between trying and achieving the goal is weak. In essence what happens is that the intrinsic rewards associated with accomplishing something significant and difficult become so large that individuals are willing to try to achieve difficult goals, even though the probability of accomplishing them may be relatively low. This is like the lottery example, except that in this case the rewards are intrinsic.

To summarize, motivation is a function of reward importance and the degree to which rewards are tied to a particular kind of performance or behavior. The implication of this is that organizations can motivate individuals to perform in particular ways if they develop a line of sight between important rewards and performing in that way. The kinds of performance that can be motivated this way include learning new skills and abilities, developing new competencies, dealing courteously with customers, producing a certain number of products per hour, increasing sales volume—in short, any behavior that is measurable and therefore can be related to organizationally given rewards.

There is no reason to make a trade-off between designing interesting work and motivating through extrinsic rewards. Nor is there a reason to debate the relative importance of recognition rewards versus financial rewards, and so on. Any reward can be a motivator, if it is important. The key in any particular work situation is to identify what rewards are important to the employees involved and emphasize them in a reward-for-performance system.

Job Satisfaction

One of the long-standing myths in the field of management is that job satisfaction is an important determinant of motivation and performance. As expectancy theory points out, it is *anticipated satisfaction* rather than *present satisfaction* that drives motivation because anticipated satisfaction is what reward importance is all about. Satisfaction comes about as a result of individuals receiving valued rewards and feeling good about it. Thus, satisfaction is best thought of as being determined by an individual's reward level. Indeed, performance may indirectly cause satisfaction if it causes rewards that, in turn, cause satisfaction.

Causes of Satisfaction

Satisfaction is strongly influenced by the amount of reward an individual receives but is determined by more than simply the quantity of the reward. Individuals compare the amount of reward they receive with a standard. When the reward level meets that standard, they are satisfied; when it falls short, they are dissatisfied. On those few occasions when it exceeds the standard, they feel guilty or overrewarded.

The research evidence suggests that feelings of being overrewarded tend not to last long.[16] Individuals usually quickly rationalize the situation they are in and decide that they are, in fact, fairly paid or even underpaid. On rare occasions they actually reduce their reward level by declining rewards or giving them away. The same is not true when individuals feel underrewarded. In this condition, they tend to try to obtain additional rewards in order to improve their situation, thus reducing their uncomfortable feelings of dissatisfaction.

The key to understanding how satisfied individuals will be with a particular reward level lies in understanding how they set the standard against which they compare reward amounts. The research literature on this topic suggests that they set their standard by looking at what others who are similar to them receive.[17] They then use what "similar others" receive as the basis for comparison.

What do individuals consider in choosing with whom to compare their rewards? The answer seems to be a variety of things, including performance, training, and background; in short, it can be any characteristic they think is important. They are particularly likely to think that those attributes of themselves that are particularly outstanding should be the basis on which they are rewarded. For example, if they are well educated, they think education should be very important in determining the amount of their rewards, and they compare themselves to individuals who are well educated. If they perceive themselves to be high performers, as most people do, they tend to compare their pay with the pay of "other" high performers.

Reward comparison choices are sometimes upsetting to those responsible for reward allocation, because individuals tend to pick reward comparisons that make their own reward levels look low.

For example, if they are highly paid compared to others in their own organization, they may look at other organizations for their comparisons in order to find individuals who are paid more. They also tend to rate their own performance very highly and, as a result, to compare their rewards with those of the best performers in their organization and indeed in other organizations as well.

The tendency of individuals to make remote connections in establishing what their reward level should be is clearly exemplified by CEOs who sometimes compare their reward levels to those of star athletes and entertainers. Time and time again, I have heard CEOs and senior executives say, "Well, I'm worth at least as much as Michael Jordan or Michael Jackson." This is an apples and oranges comparison to say the least. Interestingly enough, they don't compare their pay with that of Michael Jordan's coach or with that of the president of the Chicago Bulls. Similarly, they don't compare their pay with that of Michael Jackson's business manager. In many respects these would be much better comparisons because these lower-paid individuals are doing administrative, leadership, and coaching activities that are more similar to what CEOs do than what Jordan and Jackson do. The reason they make their comparisons to Jordan and Jackson is, of course, not because of the similarity of their work or skills but because of their very high rates of compensation.

One final point: although the pay comparison processes that individuals go through are oriented toward producing a high standard, they typically are not completely irrational. Production workers typically do not compare themselves with CEOs, and sales representatives typically do not compare themselves with vice presidents of human resources. Thus, it is possible to find sales representatives and production workers who are just as satisfied with their rewards as are CEOs and vice presidents of human resources, even though they are paid much less.

In addition to focusing on the amount of reward, individuals also focus on how rewards are distributed. The perceived fairness of the method of distribution can influence satisfaction.[18] It is difficult to state exactly what will lead to a perception on the part of employees that "distributional or procedural justice" exists, but some factors usually contribute positively to perceptions of fairness and satisfaction.

Openness about the decision process is one way to build trust and a perception of a fair process. A second key is having the "right" individuals involved in the decision process—in this case, those who are trusted because they have integrity, as well as valid information on which to make reward distribution decisions. Third, reward distribution is likely to be seen as fair when clearly stated criteria are used for the distribution. Fourth, individuals are more likely to feel fairly treated when they have a chance to participate in the decision process. Finally, perceptions of fairness are more likely when an appeal process exists that allows individuals to safely challenge decision making that they feel is unfair, uninformed, or unreasonable.

It is precisely because individuals often choose very high comparisons when they set their reward standard, and because they expect procedural justice, that pay satisfaction is often low in organizations. In many attitude surveys that I have done and seen, pay is an area of great—indeed, often the greatest—employee dissatisfaction. The level of pay satisfaction typically does vary from company to company, and it is related to how well organizations pay relative to the external marker.

When interpreting pay dissatisfaction survey data, it is important and valid to focus on changes in pay satisfaction over time and to compare satisfaction scores for different parts of an organization and for different organizations. The time to be concerned is when my satisfaction drops and when it is low compared to other organizations. Comparing pay satisfaction with satisfaction in other work areas such as job security and supervision often leads to the false conclusion that pay is a more important problem in an organization than it actually is. This occurs because pay dissatisfaction is high even when the best pay practices are used and pay is high.

Typically, 50 percent or more of all employees in an organization report dissatisfaction with their pay. Given the types of comparisons they make, this is probably inevitable. Even when pay is high, employees can always find comparisons that make their pay look lower than it should be. If they can't find these comparisons within their organization, they can always look outside and find people who seem to be contributing less and have less value but are making more.

It is often useful to compare the pay satisfaction of high performers with that of low performers and to track the satisfaction of those who are key sources of the organization's core competencies and organizational capabilities. These comparisons are important in determining how well an organization is managing its key human capital and can give an organization an early warning that it is about to lose key human capital since pay dissatisfaction is an important cause of turnover.

Most theoretical approaches to job satisfaction make no definitive predictions about which facets of the job (for example, pay, supervision, or work) are the most important in determining overall job satisfaction. Instead, as is true with motivation theory, they argue that large individual differences exist and that, as a result, what is a satisfying job situation for one person may not be so for another. What is true is that over time, individuals tend to gravitate to work situations that meet their needs; as a result, their satisfaction often goes up over time. This point argues that it is futile to debate whether, for example, money, recognition, interesting work, or promotion opportunities is the most important determinant of employee satisfaction. For some there is little doubt that money is the most important; for others the work itself is key. For still others it is the social relationships or maybe the opportunity to learn new skills.

The implication of individual differences in reward importance is relatively straightforward. It is imperative that an organization employ individuals who are satisfied by the rewards that the organization has to offer. In short, just as is true with motivation, organizations need to put hiring and development processes in place that do a good job of matching individuals to the reward and work systems that exist in the organization. For example, it can be very expensive and foolish to try to motivate and satisfy with money a scientist who is driven by making an important discovery. Similarly, it is foolish to try to motivate and satisfy with interesting and challenging work a production line worker who cares only about off-the-job activities.

Satisfaction and Performance

Simply increasing job satisfaction is unlikely to have a positive effect on performance; rather, it may have a negative effect because, at least temporarily, people will cease to seek additional rewards. It is the anticipation of rewards and satisfaction that motivates, not being satisfied. However, the fact that satisfaction does not drive motivation and performance does not mean that it is unimportant.

Study after study has shown that job satisfaction is strongly related to individuals' membership behavior and organizational commitment, that is, their willingness to continue to work in a particular setting and, indeed, their willingness to show up for work on a daily basis.[19] This finding is predictable from expectancy theory.

What employees are indicating when they say they are not satisfied with their job is that they do not see positive consequences associated with coming to work and remaining part of an organization. Satisfaction with the current situation is the major determinant of an individual's anticipation of how satisfied he or she will be in the future. Thus, it is hardly surprising that dissatisfied employees typically begin to look elsewhere for employment and ultimately leave if they find a situation that offers a better mix of rewards. If they don't leave, they become disgruntled employees who seek to change the current situation by organizing and voting for a union, becoming an activist within the organization, filing lawsuits, and engaging in other actions that they think will improve their situation.

Even though pay satisfaction does not have a direct impact on the job performance of most individuals, it can have an important impact on organizational performance because of its effect on turnover and absenteeism. Turnover can be a particularly costly item for organizations. It is relatively inexpensive to replace unskilled labor, but knowledge workers and highly skilled employees can be very costly to replace. Estimates vary considerably, but a reasonable estimate is that replacing skilled employees can cost anywhere from the equivalent of six to twenty times their monthly salary. Costs rise as the level of complexity of the work the individual does rises and as the scarcity of their skills increases.

Job satisfaction can be particularly important in service organizations. In addition to its impact on turnover, which can disrupt effective customer service routines and capabilities, it also may affect customer retention in a second way. A significant amount of research has shown that people prefer to do business with organizations that have satisfied employees because the experience is more enjoyable.[20] Thus, even though satisfaction does not directly affect the performance of individual employees, it does affect customer retention and therefore the long-term profitability and viability of the business. Because of this, retailers such as Sears, Nieman Marcus, and Nordstrom focus on having satisfied employees. They regularly measure employee satisfaction and evaluate store managers on the basis of how satisfied their employees are.[21]

Research on service organizations suggests that job satisfaction is particularly important in organizations that wish to develop a relationship with customers, that is, organizations wanting customers to feel a sense of commitment to a particular service provider and a certain amount of confidence in that provider. In service situations that are primarily transaction-oriented, job satisfaction is much less important and may not be important at all. Apparently, customers going into 7-Elevens do not particularly want to make friends with the cashier; they simply want to be served by a person who quickly completes their transaction. The same applies to many fast-food restaurants, as well as to toll takers, parking lot attendants, and a host of other transaction-oriented sales situations.

The implications of the research on satisfaction for attracting and retaining human capital are straightforward. If organizations want to attract and retain the best human capital, they have to create work environments that are satisfying and attractive to the investors of that capital—the people who have those skills. This is more easily said than done because the rewards that need to be offered may be costly. Further, because of individual differences, there are likely to be many variations in what individuals want. Nonetheless, in order to attract and retain excellent employees, organizations have to give rewards that are at least equal to what other organizations are giving to people with similar skills and knowledge. Organizations must also distribute rewards internally in a way that is generally seen as fair and just. If they fail to do these two things, they will have high levels of dissatisfaction and will fail to attract and retain the best human capital. Thus satisfaction is important, even though it is not a direct determinant of job performance.

Concluding Thoughts on Motivation and Satisfaction

Motivation and satisfaction are at the same time complicated and simple topic areas—complicated because of the enormous individual differences that exist and the complexity of human beings;

they are simple in that there are some key "truths" that can be used to guide the design of effective reward systems. These are worth repeating here because they are fundamental to the remainder of this book:

- Rewards must be important to be motivators.
- Individuals differ in the importance they attach to rewards.
- Individuals are motivated to perform when they believe they can obtain rewards they value by performing well.
- Individuals are attracted to jobs and organizations that offer the rewards they value.
- Job satisfaction is determined by how the rewards individuals receive compare to what they feel they should receive and how the rewards are distributed.
- Satisfied employees are unlikely to quit and be absent.

Part Two

Attracting, Developing, and Retaining Employees

Chapter Four

Attracting and Selecting Excellent Employees

Attracting the right applicants is the first step in creating an organization that has excellent employees. Research on the selection of new employees clearly indicates that a precondition for selecting people with the right motivation, competencies, knowledge, and skills is having a large number of good applicants.[1] Even the most effective selection system is limited in its impact on organizational performance when it is faced with a small number of job applicants. The implication of this for organizations is clear: they should create reward systems that attract a large number of talented, qualified, and properly motivated job applicants.

Decades of research and experience have shown that organizations offering the greatest quantity and quality of rewards end up with the most job applicants.[2] Thus, one way to become an employer of choice is to offer a high level of rewards. This is hardly surprising in light of my discussion of motivation and rewards in Chapter Three. Financial rewards appear to be particularly important in attracting job applicants. I believe there is an obvious reason for this: they are easy for job applicants to assess and very visible during the recruiting process. Many other important features of a particular job and company only become apparent after a person has done a job for a while.

If anyone doubts the importance of financial rewards, I suggest watching the job choices people make. In sports, free agents in virtually every major sport tend to select the team that makes them the highest financial offer. They often say they did not take the offer just because of the money, but, lo and behold, the offer they take is almost always the highest. Three examples illustrate this point.

The twenty-two-member Dutch squad for the 1998 World Cup was made up of eighteen players who played professionally for teams based outside of the Netherlands. The reason: soccer is a global business in which the Dutch teams have a relatively low salary structure, and the country has a relatively high tax rate. Thus, rather than play in their home country, the vast majority of Dutch soccer players choose to play in countries like England and Italy where they can earn and keep a great deal more money. Even in this case, money is not everything; Dutch players leave their country for other reasons. The Dutch leagues tend not to be as high-profile and as competitive as those in Italy and England; as a result, the players do not get as much attention and play in as many challenging games if they stay at home.

Athletes do not always go for the money. In about 10 percent of cases, athletes accept a somewhat lower pay rate in order to be on a winning team, live in a city they prefer, be close to their family, or gain some other outcome that is important to them. Just as it is silly to say that financial rewards are unimportant, it is silly to say that money is the only factor that determines job choice.

I have regularly had the chance to observe one group as they make job choices: M.B.A. students. I frequently read articles in the press saying that M.B.A.'s do not consider pay to be a very important determinant of the job they pick. The articles usually go on to discuss opportunities for growth, learning, and other factors that are undoubtedly important influences on the job choices of newly minted M.B.A.'s. However, as I look at the choices M.B.A.'s make, they, like professional athletes, almost always end up taking the highest-paying job. Indeed, over time the career preferences of M.B.A.'s at leading schools have shifted as different sectors have offered the highest pay rates. At the moment, consulting firms seem to be the high payers, and not surprisingly, a large number of M.B.A.'s have decided that at least for the first few years of their career, consulting is the way to go.

Lincoln Electric, the Cleveland-based firm that is known for its high pay, has so many job applicants that it has trouble processing them, whereas my university, which is not known for high pay, commonly has open positions and few if any applicants.

The best advice to any organization that wants a talented work force: offer pay and benefits that are at least equal to those offered by organizations competing for the same employees. Although this conclusion represents a partial answer to the question of how rewards should be used to attract the right employees, it is only part of the answer. The rest of the answer is suggested by the Star Model and the importance of the fit between the rewards and people points of the star.

Attracting the Right Applicants

Simply offering great rewards can result in several problems. First, it may not attract the right kind of employees, and second, it may be an extremely high-cost strategy that puts the organization at a competitive disadvantage because it is committed to higher fixed costs than its competitors. Therefore, an important step in attracting the right individuals to an organization is identifying what "right" means.

Four major factors need to be considered when identifying the right employees. The first two, discussed in Chapter One, are key to an organization's design: (1) the core competencies of the organization and (2) its organizational capabilities. The next two are related to motivation and satisfaction: (3) the type of rewards that the organization uses to motivate performance and (4) the type of employment contract that the organization wishes to establish with its employees.

To be useful in attraction and selection, core competencies and organizational capabilities need to be translated into specific competencies and capabilities that job applicants should have when they are hired or be able to develop after they are hired. In the case of core competencies, this typically means technical knowledge and skills that individuals need to have before they join the organization. In the case of organizational capabilities, it is a matter of identifying the skills and competencies that support the development of particular organizational capabilities. For example, organizations that use employee involvement and total quality management as their way to develop organizational capabilities may need to attract individuals who are particularly effective at working in teams, making decisions, and solving problems.

I mentioned in Chapter Three that a number of different rewards can be used as motivators by tying them to performance. The major types include financial, intrinsic, recognition, and social rewards. I also mentioned that if an organization is to motivate its employees, the employees must value the rewards that are based on performance. A sure recipe for poor organizational performance is relying on money to motivate performance but being staffed by people who are, for example, more interested in learning and developing technical competencies or in socializing and having a good time than they are in money.

In many cases, an organization's business strategy and the kind of work it does determine what motivators it can use. For example, government agencies often have great difficulty using financial rewards because of the restrictions they are under. The same is often true of volunteer and charitable organizations, which simply do not have the budget to use financial rewards. They may, however, be able to use recognition rewards or the intrinsic rewards that come from being part of a mission- or values-driven organization. If, for whatever reason, the organization cannot create interesting and challenging work, opportunities for personal growth, or a compelling mission, it may have to rely on recognition or financial rewards to motivate individuals.

Organizations need to develop a profile that specifies their approach to motivating employees.[3] The motivational approach that an organization chooses to use is important, but it is not the only part of the employment contract that an organization establishes with an individual. Other important parts include job security, type of work, and career opportunities. In determining its attraction strategy, an organization needs to take into account the type of overall employment contract it wishes to establish. It needs to establish itself as a brand-name employer, that is, to develop a reputation as an organization that provides a particular set of rewards and expects a particular type of performance from its members. In short, it shouldn't try to be an all-purpose employer; it should be an employer of choice for those employees who fit its employment contract.

For example, it makes no sense to attract individuals who seek secure jobs to an organization that does project work and wants to have an employability or a contingent workforce contract with its employees. An organization must attract and hire people who are motivated by the types of rewards that the organization can offer them. If this is not done, the inevitable result is dissatisfaction and turnover.

Reward System Design

The ability of the reward system to attract the right kind of employees is a function of several of its characteristics. I've already discussed one of these: the reward level in the hiring market. As I pointed out, in order to attract a large number of qualified applicants, an organization must at least equal the market with respect to the rewards it offers and perhaps slightly exceed it. As I will discuss next, this is often most easily accomplished by focusing on the market value of individuals rather than on jobs. Although position in the market is the most obvious and perhaps the most critical decision in designing a reward system for the purpose of attracting employees, the type of rewards offered can also have an important influence. A discussion of this point follows the discussion of market value.

Market Value

The traditional approach to determining what an individual should be paid is rooted in job evaluation–based pay. A job opening is noted, the job is priced in the market, and individuals are offered a starting pay rate that is appropriate for the job they are to fill. In essence, this approach assumes that the worth of an individual is equal to the worth of the job he or she will be doing.

Historically, job-based compensation has been a reasonable way to determine pay. In traditional organizations, jobs are usually carefully described, allowing performance to be monitored and controlled. As a result the amount of value that individuals add is relatively predictable and often does not vary greatly from person to person. This is not true in today's more involvement-oriented, lateral organizations. Jobs are often loosely defined or not defined at all, and individuals have great latitude to add value. This is particularly true as work complexity increases and the knowledge and skills needed to do the work grow. As I stressed in the Introduction, individuals who are particularly talented and effective may add many times more value than those who are average contributors. This runs directly counter to the traditional job evaluation–based approach to compensation, which has relatively narrow pay bands and tends to generate relatively homogeneous pay rates for individuals doing the same job or kind of work.

As I mentioned in Chapter Two, a viable alternative to job-based pay has emerged over the last several decades. It started in manufacturing plants where it is called skill-based pay. In the 1990s, it spread to other parts of organizations where it is often called competency- or knowledge-based pay. This approach is fundamentally different from job-based pay in that it assesses the skills, knowledge, and abilities of individuals and determines what they should be paid based on what the market pays similar individuals. As I will discuss further in the next two chapters, there are many differences in the approaches that organizations are using to measure and pay for competencies. One popular approach is broad banding—an approach that increases pay ranges so that more of the variance in individual performance can be reflected in a person's pay.

The reality is that the hiring market is clearly a market of people, not of jobs. Individuals change jobs and decide where to work. Jobs do not change organizations. There is no market for jobs. Thus, the critical issue in hiring is not correctly pricing jobs in the market but correctly pricing individuals. Pricing a job for hiring purposes misses the whole point of human capital. It assumes that individuals are worth what the job they are going to take is worth. The important thing to remember with attraction is that the market matters and what matters about the market is how much an individual is worth, not how much a job is worth.

Even organizations with job-based pay systems often end up having to pay individuals rather than jobs when they hire new employees. When they hire, they are competing with other organizations, and as a result the market price of individuals is and should be the major determinant of what potential employees are offered. This is particularly clear for M.B.A.'s and new college graduates, where job offers clearly reflect the market value of the individual more than the type of work or job they will take once they join the organization. Engineers, for example, are paid much more than liberal arts graduates, just as M.B.A.'s are paid more than individuals with master's degrees in education and psychology or bachelor's degrees in business. Industry differences do exist and need to be taken into account. For example, consulting firms typically pay more than manufacturing organizations. Nonetheless, the focus at the time of hire is typically on what the individual is worth, not on what the job is worth. The job, however, comes into play once the individual is hired and put into the salary structure of the organization. I will discuss the desirability of this in the next chapter. At this point, my focus is on hiring and the importance of offering wages based on people's market value. Failure to do this can result in either a compensation level that is too high and therefore too costly or is too low and therefore is inadequate to attract and retain excellent employees.

One final point about pricing: the key in pricing individuals accurately in the market is determining what the hiring market actually is for the skills and knowledge of the individuals being hired. Relatively low-skilled employees, for example, often are hired in a local market that covers a limited geographic area; thus, they need to be priced in that market. However, Ph.D.'s in chemistry, senior executives, and technical employees often are in a national labor market, so they need to be priced according to what the national and sometimes the international market pays for people with these skills. And in every skill and knowledge area there is variance in how well job applicants can perform. Some have average or poor skills and thus have an average or below-average market value, whereas others are highly skilled and command a premium in the hiring market.

Finally, it is important to remember that markets change, both in how highly they price skills and knowledge and in the degree to which they are international. Shortages appear, and this can push the market up for certain skills. Skills also may become international in their supply and demand. For example, this has happened recently with software engineers and some senior managers. When this occurs, pricing needs to reflect the more global perspective. Similarly, skills sometimes move from being local to national in their labor markets.

Pay as a Motivator

The level of total compensation, as well as the mix of different compensation elements that are used to attract applicants, should reflect the degree to which pay systems are used as an important motivator by the organization. As I mentioned earlier, not all organizations can or should rely on compensation as an important driver of behavior. Those that do, however, need to be sure that their employees value compensation. The best way to ensure this is to offer a pay and reward package that emphasizes pay so that individuals who value pay will be attracted to the organization. One way for an organization to do this, of course, is to be a relatively high payer. Another way is to offer a distinctive package of pay-for-performance programs in order to help define its "brand identity" as an employer and to attract people who are concerned about financial rewards. Organizations that do not wish to depend on pay and other extrinsic rewards as important drivers of performance may be better off emphasizing features other than their pay package to prospective employees.

A strong argument can be made that if an organization wants to attract people who will be motivated by pay, they should include some variable pay in their initial job offer. This has two signaling effects to prospective employees: (1) it indicates that performance is important, and (2) it may help eliminate employees who are low on trust and unlikely to believe that an organization will deliver on its pay for performance commitments.

Managers sometimes tell me that one of the problems with offering prospective employees a bonus plan as part of an initial job offer is that some are suspicious and are not willing to trust that the bonus will be fairly determined. One answer to this is to guarantee the bonus for a year or two in order to make the initial offer more attractive. Another alternative, however, is to simply eliminate applicants who are not willing to make this leap of faith because they are a bad fit for the organization. If a person is unwilling to accept the credibility of the organization's pay-for-performance system, that person is likely to be difficult to motivate in an organization that relies heavily on pay for performance. To be motivating, pay-for-performance systems require that individuals trust the organization to deliver on its reward system commitments.

Reward Mix

A number of key decisions must be made about the reward mix an organization offers. These include how compensation will be divided between cash and benefits, the amount of emphasis that will be placed on financial rewards, and the degree of choice that individuals will be given in determining their reward mix.

The traditional employment relationships in large corporations often involve a mix of cash and benefits that includes a large, costly benefits package. The value of benefits typically exceeds 35 percent of the value of the cash compensation. In some companies it is over 40 percent. Benefits are also typically seniority-driven. As employees gain more seniority they get better retirement, more vacation time, and so forth. A combination of expensive benefits and reliance on seniority in determining the amount of benefits received very much fits with the traditional, paternalistic, long-term employment relationship that organizations have historically preferred.

Not surprisingly, the benefits-heavy approach to rewarding and attracting employees tends to attract those who look for security and are in personal situations that place great importance on benefits like medical coverage and retirement pay. Examples are people who have children and are over thirty. The benefits-heavy approach to rewards may not, however, fit well with the young technical expert who is more interested in personal development and learning opportunities than in a long-term relationship with a company and developing a high level of job security. It also may not fit an individual with whom the organization wishes to establish a short-term relationship that is tied to a particular project or a particular series of tasks or services that it needs to have performed. Indeed, the best fit for many of these employees may be a compensation system that is based almost totally on cash payments.

All-cash compensation is frequently used by engineering firms and others that hire individuals for project work. It is also appropriately used in situations of temporary employment and sometimes in the case of part-time employment. The key point is that it is important to develop a mix of cash and benefit compensation that fits the type of relationship an organization wants with an individual. It makes no sense—in fact it is misleading—to offer a heavily seniority-driven benefit package to employees who are viewed as short term. All this will do is frustrate them, and it is not optimal in attracting the right kinds of individuals to this employment relationship.

Given the importance of attracting talented individuals, a number of companies have started programs that are intended to make them "employers of choice." They take pride in being listed as one of the best companies in the United States to work for and offer their employees a number of attractive perquisites. These include such things as gourmet meals, concierges to run errands, exercise clubs, flexible working hours, and a host of other benefits that some employees value highly.

Sun Microsystems, the very successful computer company, offers sunrooms, pool tables, basketball and volleyball courts, fitness equipment, and showers. In essence, it offers all of the accouterments and environment of an Ivy League campus or a country club. Another technology firm, Adobe Systems, gives employees a three-week paid sabbatical every five years, and everybody in the company has an office with a door. Finally, Excite, Inc., an around-the-clock Internet company, encourages technical people to telecommute and to work outside standard business hours.

There is little doubt that "enriching" the rewards an organization offers its employees will increase the number of people interested in working for that organization. The key question is whether the mix attracts the right employees. I recently heard a CEO express considerable skepticism about the advantages of offering Silicon Valley technology workers a large array of perks. He noted that he had no intention of offering the perks that are becoming increasingly common in Silicon Valley because he did not want employees who would be attracted by them. He thought it was great that employees who were concerned about flexible hours, concierges, work and family balance, and parties went to work for his competitors. He did not want those people; he wanted employees who were primarily interested in the nature of the work to be done and willing to work the outrageous hours that it takes to be successful in high-technology businesses. His point is probably correct, although perhaps a bit overstated.

There is no doubt that offering too many perquisites of a nonwork-related nature can attract the "wrong" kind of people, individuals who are not looking for a demanding job and are attracted by extra vacation days and company-sponsored recreational activities. But it is also likely that some perks free people up to spend more time thinking about and doing work (as when the company offers child care or food service). The challenge is to put together a package of rewards that establishes the organization as a brand-name employer and makes it the employer of choice for the types of employees it needs.

Mary Kay Cosmetics has been particularly effective at using the nature of a reward package to influence who is attracted to and who stays with the organization. Mary Kay's highly visible incentive rewards clearly do not appeal to everyone. The top sales reward each year is a pink Cadillac and a trip to Dallas where the lucky winner is crowned by Mary Kay herself at an award ceremony. One of the effects of this and other company policies is that few males want to work for Mary Kay.

Perhaps recognizing that the reward package it offers is too narrow, Mary Kay has recently become a bit more diverse in its recognition program. Now employees can get a white GMC Jimmy as an alternative to the pink Cadillac that has been the mainstay of Mary Kay for decades. A pink Pontiac Grand Prix still goes to the next best, and a red Pontiac Grand Am still goes to the third-tier winners. Interestingly, in Russia the top sellers get a Volvo, not a Cadillac.

Choice in Reward Mix

Since the 1970s there has been an increasing use of "flexible benefit" plans.[4] As I mentioned Chapter Two, with these plans individuals are allowed to choose the mix of benefits that fit their situation. Cafeteria or flexible benefits plans have become increasingly popular for a number of reasons. Research years ago showed that many people do not value the benefits they get because they are not relevant to their personal situation.[5] Indeed, a good estimate is that the average employee believes his or her benefits to be worth only about 70 percent of what they cost an organization to provide. This leads to the no-brainer, mass-customization recommendation that I made in Chapter Two. Given a choice, it stands to reason that people will only choose the benefits they value, so organizations can be sure that their benefit dollars are well spent.

Unfortunately, many flexible benefit plans do not allow the translation of benefit dollars into cash compensation dollars; this defeats some of the potential advantage of a flexible benefit plan. It ensures that the employee who is not particularly interested in benefits will be receiving something that he or she doesn't value. Of course, this can be corrected by allowing people to take cash instead of benefits.

When I interview organizations about why they don't allow employees to substitute cash for benefits, they report that they feel a responsibility to be sure that everyone has a certain level of benefit coverage. This view reflects a kind of paternalism that may make sense in the case of some benefits, given the potential ramifications of individuals having no health care coverage or no life insurance for example, but it does not make sense for benefits such as dental insurance and vacation days.

In my experience, most organizations can be much more flexible than they are with the benefit mix they offer. But is flexibility always desirable? It is, in the sense that organizations will be getting maximum reward value for their compensation and benefits dollars, but it may not be from a targeted attraction and retention point of view. Flexibility means that a reward package will appeal to a much more diverse set of employees than one with a fixed combination of benefits and cash. Thus, if an organization wants to be sure that a certain type of person is attracted to it, a highly flexible, choice-driven plan may have the wrong effect. Instead of increasing the homogeneity of the workforce, choice is likely to increase diversity.

For example, if an organization wants only employees who are interested in developing a long-term, traditional relationship with their employers, giving them a great deal of choice may work against this. It may lead to some people joining the organization because they can take minimal benefits and, for a short period of time, enjoy high cash compensation. In the case of an organization that does not want long-term employees because it wants to employ individuals only as long as their skills are relevant and world-class, choice may attract individuals who want a longer-term relationship because they can get good retirement plans, medical plans, life insurance, and so on.

Part of the answer to the question of how much choice to give should be determined by the size of the organization and the diversity of its staffing needs. Some large organizations simply need to attract so many employees that they have to offer reward packages with wide appeal. If an organization needs a diverse staff, it may have to use a flexible compensation system simply to attract the variety of individuals it needs to attract. However, an organization that is predominantly looking for one type of employee to fit a particular situation may be well advised to carefully structure the mix of benefits and cash to reflect the type of employee it wishes to attract, for example, by using largely cash compensation when it wants to attract short-term, highly skilled individuals to work on particular projects. Using larger amounts of at-risk cash compensation to attract entrepreneurial individuals is another example.

Variable Rewards for New Hires

Particularly with respect to hard-to-recruit "hot talent," it may be desirable to give new hires a one-time payment or signing bonus in order to motivate them to join the organization. There are a number of advantages that one-time payments have over a higher salary. Salaries are annuities that may make it too expensive to offer future rewards, whereas a one-time bonus, when combined with a lower base pay, leaves the option open to have significant amounts of variable pay as part of an individual's long-term package. It also leaves room for future merit-pay increases and for keeping pay low if the person is not effective. If there is concern about an individual taking the bonus and then leaving, the bonus can be prorated over a period of employment that fits the type of employment relationship that the organization wants with the individual.

Giving signing bonuses is becoming a more common practice. They have often been used to attract senior executives as well as athletes. Recently, however, bonuses have been used to attract business school graduates and burger flippers. Even the U.S. Department of Labor has gotten into the game by offering $4,000 bonuses to attract young economists. Instead of offering cash, some companies are offering money for home purchases and other types of one-time financial incentives to attract employees.

Xerox is among the companies that have used signing bonuses with contingent workers. Xerox pays $100 or more to its former workers when the company wishes to use their services again. This policy makes sense in situations where the company can avoid making a significant training and start-up investment in a contingent worker by attracting people who already know how to do the work. Xerox sometimes goes beyond a signing bonus and gives its returning temps a bigger title, a better desk, and even a sweatshirt that says, "I'm Back."

An interesting alternative to a cash bonus plan is the granting of stock options and the making of stock grants. They can often be powerful attractors, particularly when the company's stock has performed well. Stock can also be used as a retention device by delaying the vesting period of the stock until a year or more after the individual joins the organization. With this approach, stock serves the dual purpose of both attracting and retaining people. It also signals to individuals that their pay will be based on performance and that they are expected to become involved members of the organization. Stock fits best when an organization is particularly interested in establishing a several-year relationship with its employees—a relationship that is based on involvement in the business and major contributions to the business's success.

The degree to which hiring bonuses and stock are used by organizations is partly related to the unemployment rate and the scarcity of talent. When unemployment is low and individuals possess a scarce talent, hiring incentives are an obvious way for an organization to differentiate itself. That said, incentives may still be useful when unemployment is relatively high. Particularly in technology and knowledge-work organizations, there are always skill shortages, and incentives are an attractive alternative to base pay in attracting hard-to-recruit talent. They also help establish the organization as a brand-name employer in the pay area.

Selecting the Right Employees

There are two basic ways to effectively select individuals: self-selection and organizational selection. Self-selection involves making it absolutely clear to job applicants what the nature of the job and work situation is and letting them decide whether it is one they are attracted to. It views attraction and selection as one and the same; thus, it tries to design the attraction process so that it will only attract "good hires." Historically, this has been a powerful strategy with respect to selecting employees who represent a good fit for motivational purposes and is the reason I have been emphasizing the creation of reward packages that attract the right employees. It works particularly well when individuals have a number of job opportunities. In these cases they tend to pick jobs that best fit their needs.

Individuals will make the right choices, of course, only if they are aware of their needs and have a clear idea of what the organization is offering. The issue of self-awareness is hard for organizations to address. As I pointed out earlier, some people don't know what they want and what motivates them. As a result self-selection will never be 100 percent accurate. This is true even when individuals get perfect information about what the job they are being offered is like.

Organizations can have a strong impact on the amount and kind of information individuals get about what it is like to work for them. Study after study in the research literature on selection emphasizes the importance of "realistic" previews.[6] An organization typically gains little, if any, advantage by presenting a false image—or no image—of what the work situation will be like for individuals once they join. However, they can gain a tremendous advantage in two respects if they give a clear picture of the work situation to all job applicants. First, they can get a head start on the socialization process so that employees start work with an accurate understanding of the organization's employment contract and of what it takes to be an effective employee. This can reduce disappointment and turnover. Second, they can improve the success rate of the selection process by helping individuals make good decisions about whether to join or not.

It is hard to make too many generalizations about what makes for effective realistic preview situations but I can make some suggestions. First, it is extremely important that job candidates talk to those they are expected to work with. If applicants are to be part of a team, they should meet with the team in a team setting and experience what that is like. If at all possible, candidates should actually do some of the work that is involved in the position they are being offered. The feasibility of this varies greatly according to the workplace, but in many factory situations that I have studied, employees can be given a meaningful sample work experience. It is usually best if the sample lasts several days and is set up as temporary employment. Work sample experiences are particularly good at giving individuals a chance to learn what intrinsic rewards and social relationships are associated with the work.

As far as the financial rewards of the work are concerned, it is important that they be discussed with the potential employee both by management and by employees who are subject to the same type of pay and reward system. This begins the socialization process and also facilitates the selection process.

In addition to offering realistic previews of work, organizations need to gather as much data as they can about job applicants in order to determine whether they will fit the organization's reward and motivation structure. It is one thing to assess the technical and knowledge assets that individuals bring to the work situation; it is quite another to assess their motivational orientation and determine how they will respond to the organization's reward systems.

Three approaches are possible here. The first is to rely on the judgment of those who interview the job applicant. If the interview process is relatively structured, it is possible that the ratings of the interviewers will be valid predictors of success.[7] In a team environment, for example, the opinions of potential team members who do interviews can often predict the success of a new hire. This may partly come about as a result of self-fulfilling prophecies because individuals want people they like and recommend to be successful. Thus, they help the new hires that they help select to learn and fit in once they join the organization.

The second approach is less direct but potentially quite useful. It is to look at the individual's work history and determine, as closely as possible, the kinds of reward systems and employment contracts they have worked under and how they have responded. This may, of course, involve contacting previous employers and gathering data from the job applicant. Often an analysis of an individual's employment history can provide helpful information about what the person values. For organizations that use variable compensation plans, it is important to see whether the person has experience with a variable compensation plan and, if so, how the person responded in those situations.

Finally, a number of psychological tests claim to be able to measure the motives and personality characteristics of job applicants.[8] The tests vary all the way from very simple, easily distorted and faked personality tests to relatively complex, standardized personality tests that try to assess underlying psychological dynamics. Projective tests are also used to assess the need for achievement and power by having people look at a picture and describe what they see in it. My advice on all personality tests is to use great caution. There are numerous problems concerning their validity, so I recommend their use only when it is difficult to get other approaches to selection to work effectively or when good validity data exist or can be gathered to establish that they are a valid predictor of how individuals will perform in a particular work situation.

Conclusion

Attracting and selecting the right employees from a reward system point of view is always a difficult and potentially error-filled activity. However, by using a realistic preview of the reward system practices and the nature of the work, along with an analysis of the individual's work history, the odds of success can be greatly improved. Realistic previews can lead to better decision making on the part of applicants. Also, applicants' work histories and their responses to certain interview questions can help determine whether they will respond effectively to the work situation that the organization has to offer. As we shall discuss next, a good selection process is the first of many actions that need to be taken in order to retain and develop excellent employees.

Chapter Five

Job- and Seniority-Based Approaches to Development and Retention

Organizations must selectively retain and develop individuals if they are to develop the competencies and capabilities they need to effectively implement their business strategy. The reward system can be an important contributor to the development and retention of people who have the skills and abilities that form the basis of organizational capabilities and competencies. The reward system can also be an important source of support for organizational change as the business environment and strategy of an organization change. The key to accomplishing both—retaining key people and supporting change—is to retain employees who already have the right skills and abilities and to encourage others to learn them.

How the reward system should be designed to accomplish the twin objectives of development and retention is no mystery. The answer has already been given in earlier chapters, but it is worth repeating here. In the case of development, the system needs to offer valued rewards to employees who develop themselves in strategically important ways. To facilitate retention, the reward system needs to position the reward levels of excellent employees favorably with respect to the external market.

As is true with attraction, the key point for retention is how an individual's reward package compares to the market. In an era of free agency and weakened bonds between organizations and individuals, the market makes the difference. Individuals stay with organizations as long as they receive rewards that represent a better deal than they could receive elsewhere. In other words, an organization needs to offer its employees a more attractive value proposition than the ones that are offered to them by other organizations. Because pay rates and reward practices in the external market change regularly as skills become more or less scarce and more or less valuable, rewards for employees must change to keep up with the market. Further, individuals change and develop new skills, often because an organization encourages them to do so. When this happens, their rewards need to change to reflect their new value.

It is important to consider retention and skill development together because in many respects they are opposite sides of the same coin. In a changing business environment there are essentially two ways for organizations to modify their competencies and capabilities: (1) change their employee populations by buying (recruiting) new talent and removing old talent or (2) build from within by developing their existing employees. With a buy strategy the emphasis needs to be on the attraction dimension; with a build strategy it needs to be on the use of rewards to motivate skill development. Of course almost no organization can or should operate with a pure development or a pure buy approach. Most need a reward system that both selectively attracts new employees and selectively retains and develops existing employees.

Regardless of the strategy an organization has, it is virtually never desirable to retain all employees. The emphasis needs to be on retaining those who have the right motives, skills, and abilities to be successful in the organization. In many respects this is similar to the situation with respect to selection and attraction; the key issues there are also selectivity and fit.

In an era of free agency, the line between attraction and retention is at best fuzzy. Particularly with respect to employees who are in high demand, the attraction activities of an organization should never end; excellent employees need to be re-recruited on a regular basis.

As I noted in Chapter Four, a poorly focused emphasis on being an employer of choice and retaining employees can be dysfunctional. An organization should not try to be the employer of choice for all employees but should concentrate on being the employer of choice to "the right kind" of employees. This often involves making some tough choices about what rewards to offer and how to structure the reward system. Organizations that do not selectively retain employees can end up with a significant number who do not fit its current strategies but who are locked into the company because of the reward system.

Microsoft has an interesting strategy with respect to retaining employees. It tries to offer great work, great people to work with, and great managers. It does not claim to offer a balanced lifestyle—quite the contrary. It argues that people have to work extremely hard but that if they perform well and the organization performs well, the opportunities for financial gain are tremendous. Microsoft offers this particular employment contract because it feels that its business requires extraordinary effort on the part of employees. The markets and technologies Microsoft deals with change rapidly, and the CEO, Bill Gates, believes the company can only be successful if its employees are very focused and very committed to their work.

Turning to employee development, the issue again is selectivity. Organizations need to reward the development of the right mix of skills and abilities so they can develop the right core competencies and organizational capabilities. It usually does not pay to reward employees for developing skills and abilities they cannot use because they do not fit the organization's technology, design, or business processes. A possible exception is a situation where, as occurred with United Technologies, an organization wants to build a learning culture.

It is, of course, much easier to state that reward systems should reward skill development than to develop operational systems that accomplish it. As I will show, developing operational reward systems requires the development of clear maps of the knowledge and competencies that specific functions and business units need in order to be aligned with the business strategy. This can be particularly difficult to accomplish but is often most important when the business is changing rapidly and when technical skills quickly become obsolete.

The rest of this chapter will review the two approaches to rewards that are most frequently used for retention and development. I will begin with the job-based approach to reward management and follow by considering the impact of seniority-based rewards.

Job-Based Systems

The basic building block of the human resource management systems in most organizations is the job. In traditional bureaucratic organizations, jobs are carefully designed and constructed to fit the business activities that an organization needs to perform in order to be effective. The job-based approach to management starts with a job description that contains a detailed specification of the activities individuals are supposed to perform. Job descriptions form the basis for reward system practices that include job evaluation and several other approaches to managing rewards.

Job Evaluation

Job evaluation is a well-established, well-developed approach to determining the pay of individuals in bureaucratic organizations.[1] It scores jobs on dimensions such as responsibility and then uses the score to determine the pay rates for jobs. The most popular system by far is the Hay system, which has been sold for decades by a large consulting firm of that name. The Hay system is the most commonly used approach for determining pay and reward levels in large organizations, although numerous other evaluation systems have also been developed. There is a real question, however, about whether Hay or any of the others is the best approach in today's business environment.

The most important test that any management practice has to meet is the value-added test, that is, whether its adoption adds to the organization's effectiveness because its benefits outweigh its costs. In some cases the evidence suggests that job evaluation does pass the value-added test, but in an increasing number of cases it does not. The advantages that are claimed for job evaluation tend to be present only when it fits the basic approach that an organization takes to organizing and managing employees. Job evaluation fits a traditional bureaucratic approach to management that relies heavily on control through job descriptions, standardization of work, and hierarchical levels of management.

Even when job evaluation is used in conjunction with a traditional top-down approach to management, it has a number of problems. These have been extensively discussed elsewhere so they warrant only brief mention here.[2] Most criticisms focus on the fact that job evaluation systems measure the size of jobs in order to determine job worth and pay levels. These criticisms include the fact that the concept of job worth can be hard to communicate and that people find the value system that underlies job worth difficult to accept because they think of *themselves* as having value to the organization, not the work they do.

Job evaluation systems do not have to be used to determine the distribution of rewards other than pay, but they often are. Because they provide a quantitative measure of status in the organization, they are often used to determine a number of features of how people are rewarded. For example, they are often used to determine office size, office furnishings, travel policies, access to executive dining facilities, and an almost never-ending list of benefits that organizations give to their employees. They are also sometimes used to determine who is invited to meetings and who gets certain kinds of information.

The message that tying perquisites and benefits to job size delivers is clear: higher-level individuals who hold highly evaluated jobs are the ones who matter; thus, the key to being a success is moving to bigger and bigger jobs. This message may be highly appropriate and fit the culture of a traditional, hierarchically managed bureaucracy. It does not fit the culture that needs to be developed in organizations where some of the most valued employees do not have highly evaluated jobs because they do not supervise a lot of people or have a large budget. Instead, they are doing critical technical work that is part of the organization's core competencies or serving as functional experts who support an organizational capability.

In one company I studied, having a cellular phone was directly tied to a person's position in the management hierarchy. Lower-level employees were not allowed to have one at all. At each succeeding level above the first few, managers could get more expensive phones. The problem with this policy was simple. Many lower-level employees, particularly those in sales and distribution, were constantly out of their office and as a result needed a cellular phone much more than those higher up in the organization. Because of their lack of status, however, they were unable to get one and as a result missed calls from customers and spent too much time trying to find pay phones.

Job evaluation systems also lead to internal bureaucracies. Often a large staff is needed to develop job descriptions, score jobs, and constantly update and keep current the job evaluation system. Further, once job descriptions are put into place, employees may try to add to their responsibilities and duties to make their jobs larger and more important. This in turn can raise an organization's costs.

A focus on job size can also discourage managers from giving up some of their budget and areas of responsibility, even when it is in the best interest of the organization. For example, in a period of downsizing, individuals often hesitate to permit reductions in their area because it might mean a reduction in their job size and therefore their pay and prerequisites. Focusing on job size can also cause managers to resist restructurings that lead to their operations being split into new divisions or business units. This can be a particularly serious problem in an organization that is growing rapidly and needs to create new business units in order to develop new products and serve new markets.

One of the secrets to the growth of Dell Computer is that it has created a pay system that rewards managers for breaking up their divisions in the service of growth. It allows their pay to grow even when the size of the business they lead decreases. Thus, managers at Dell are rewarded for developing new business units that spring from the division they manage. In order to do this, Dell had to abandon the practice of basing pay strictly on job size.

Job evaluation systems tend to lead to a focus on internal equity. It becomes the most important focus because individuals are told that their job is measured relative to others in their organization, and a common metric (usually points) is used to evaluate the worth of all jobs in the organization. This allows employees to compare the size of their job and its pay rate with the job size and pay rate of others in the organization.

For a number of reasons it is important for organizations to have an external and not an internal equity orientation. As organizations find themselves in increasingly competitive business environments, the key issue is not internal equity; it is external equity and competitiveness. Organizations get in trouble when their pay is out of line with that of their competitors and when they lose touch with how effectively they are competing for the best human capital.

Some additional problems with job evaluation occur because it measures the worth of jobs, not of individuals. This can lead to an internal culture in which key individuals feel unappreciated and not valued as human beings. It may also put in place the wrong incentives for learning and development, as it tends to reward the learning of only those skills that lead to higher-level jobs. Horizontal learning is not rewarded, nor is developing greater expertise in a specialty. Finally, it may price individuals incorrectly in the labor market (remember that the market is what counts) if, in fact, their skills happen to be out of alignment with the job or work they are doing at the moment. This can result in costly turnover; individuals with the most skills leave because they have the highest market value and the most to gain from leaving.

Matching the Market

Inadequately matching the labor market is particularly likely to happen with individuals who add a great deal of value and are critical to organizational success. As I noted earlier, traditional job-based pay systems assume that individuals doing the same job add approximately the same amount of value. Those systems allow for the best employee to earn 30 to 40 percent more, but no more than that, regardless of their market value and contribution. In many knowledge-work situations, starting with many lower-level technical jobs and culminating at the CEO level, the variability in the contributions of employees doing the same work can be enormous. As is true with athletes, the best employees are often worth several times more than other employees. Sometimes they are worth more because their performance is many times better. In technical sales work, for example, the best often outsell average performers by 400 percent or more. In software development, the best may write ten times more usable lines of code than average performers. Other times the best are worth more because they are a little better at something that is very important to corporate performance or the organization's bottom line. In technology firms, a new product development manager who can cut just a few weeks off the development time of a new product may be extraordinarily valuable.

Employees with superior knowledge, skills, and performance are increasingly valuable because they make the vital difference between having the best product and having the second, third, or fourth best or between getting a project done on time and not quite getting it done on time. In today's highly competitive business environment, advantages of this kind can make enormous differences in corporate profit performance.[3] For example, in technology businesses, product profitability is often determined by which products get to the market first, and weeks can make a big difference in terms of brand identity and market share.

If a reward system is to support organizational excellence, it must recognize the different amounts of value that individuals doing the same job add to an organization's performance. Organizations need to recognize the true market value of those who make the difference between a company being the best in its business and those who make a solid but not differentiating contribution. Reward systems that focus on jobs, like those that provide concierge services, gourmet meals, and other amenities in the workplace, do not meet this need. They may cut down the overall turnover rate and attract some employees, but they cannot effectively target the most valuable employees. These people must be satisfied with their rewards, and this means rewarding them at least as well as other organizations are willing to—in short, rewarding them according to their external market value.

Whole-Job Pricing

Some of the disadvantages of job evaluation can be dealt with by simply taking whole jobs to the market and pricing them accordingly. Often, this alternative is much less expensive than a formal job evaluation system because it requires less bureaucratic time and effort to develop and maintain. It can also more clearly focus the attention of individuals on the external labor market and how highly it pays particular jobs. Because no job evaluation score is developed, not as much focus is placed on internal equity and how one job in the organization compares with others. Because of this, individuals are less likely to focus on what others in their organization are paid and more likely to focus on what their type of job gets paid in the external market.

Taking whole jobs to the market and pricing them by comparing them to jobs in other organizations in some ways is a "lower" level of technology than is a sophisticated point-factor job evaluation system. In the past many organizations have moved from whole-job market-pricing systems to point-factor job evaluation systems as they have become larger and more sophisticated. Indeed this is often seen as a sign of organizational growth and maturity by human resource managers. It may well be a sign of growth and maturity, but there is a real question as to whether it is a value-added move. It may be one of the many reasons that large bureaucratic organizations lose their sense of excitement and purpose and develop a focus on maintaining an internal bureaucracy. Thus, it probably is a move that should be avoided and one that should be reversed by many of the organizations that have made it.[4]

Although taking whole jobs to the market avoids some of the problems with point-factor systems, it stays within the same paradigm, that is, it assumes that the best thing to measure to determine pay is the market value of the job. In this sense it stays within the traditional, bureaucratic paradigm of how work should be organized and conceptualized. It assumes that jobs are the best building block for an organization and that individual behavior and organizational effectiveness can best be managed through a focus on jobs as the fundamental building block of the organization and its HR management systems. Thus, although whole-job pricing often is preferable to job evaluation, it has many of the same problems.

Broad Banding

One relatively new approach to structuring pay systems does solve some of the problems with job-based reward systems and makes it possible to respond better to the fact that some employees contribute significantly more than others. The approach is called broad banding. It typically reduces the many pay grades that a traditionally structured organization has to a relatively small number of wide or broad bands, hence the name. With a broad-band approach the pay difference between the bottom and the top of the pay grade is often 100 percent; so the top of the pay range is twice as high as the bottom of the range. Northern Telecom (now Nortel Networks) was an early adopter of broad banding. Today it is used by many large organizations, including General Electric and PepsiCo.

There are several advantages to broad banding. It allows for easy job pricing or slotting. Often there is a single pay grade associated with each level in the organization, thus, it is a no-brainer to decide where jobs fit. Broad banding also allows individuals who are outstanding in their skills and performance to move to a relatively high level of pay without being promoted or, in some instances, changing jobs. In theory, this kind of flexibility should allow organizations to do a better job of matching individuals' pay to the market.

It is hard to argue with the objectives of the broad-banding approach to pay, and in fact it does reduce some of the dysfunctions of traditional pay systems. However, the challenge that must be confronted concerns how to place and move individuals within the bands. In many organizations that I have studied, this issue was not adequately addressed before broad bands were put into place. The move was made without a clear statement as to why some individuals should be high in their band and others low and, most important, how individuals could move up in a band.

Broad-band systems can be particularly problematic when they are installed in organizations in which little money is provided for pay increases. Even though individuals are told that they are now in a broad-band system, they see no opportunity to advance their pay and to improve their situation because there is no budget for increases. Indeed the new pay system looks like the same old pay system, with some individuals getting 3 percent increases, others getting 4 percent, and some others getting 5 percent, but with no practices that facilitate the development and retention of the best employees.

In some companies after a few years of trying to explain why individuals are in various positions in the new broad bands, zones are created within the bands. These often end up looking like new pay grades that are nested within the broad bands. At this point, it can be unclear what the difference is between the old narrow-band system and the new broad-band system, with its zones.

The following are two examples of the problems that can develop with broad banding. In one company, dissatisfaction with a complicated forty-plus-level pay-grade system led to the creation of a new broad-band system. In the new system just nine bands covered employees from the bottom of the organization to middle management. Within a year, complaints were heard about the system because of a lack of clear guidelines and controls; particularly troubling was the issue of how much new hires should be paid. The organization responded by creating three zones within each band. In essence, they went back to the original system that had proved to be so cumbersome and bureaucratic.

In another organization, the director of compensation championed the move to a broad-band system. He did a great job of marketing the system and of explaining to everyone how it would create a more flexible pay system and allow the organization to better recognize the talents and performance of individuals. The plan met with an initial favorable reaction, but within a few months most concluded that there was really no change in their opportunity to get a pay increase or control their own pay. After about a year, the dissatisfaction was so widespread that the compensation director was fired and the system scrapped.

Despite its problems, broad banding often is an improvement over the traditional approach of having many narrow pay grades. It is significantly less bureaucratic and allows for differentiating more among individuals. However, it often functions more like a Band-Aid that temporarily keeps job-based pay systems alive than a new technology that reinvents the way individuals are paid.

Future of Job-Based Approaches

In earlier chapters I discussed the changes that have occurred in the business environment during the last several decades. Without question the business environment is more competitive, more global, and more dynamic; as a result, organizations need to be more flexible, more innovative, and more cost-effective. In the United States and other developed countries, many traditional types of manufacturing work are disappearing because of the labor costs involved. Increasingly, the workforce is doing knowledge, service, and white-collar work. Organizations are operating with fewer levels of management and different types of supervisory relationships; in many cases they have pushed power and responsibility to lower levels in the organization. These changes raise important questions about the appropriateness of job-based approaches to management in general and to reward management in particular.

In a job-based approach it is assumed that there are specifiable, regular duties that an individual performs and that these can be captured in a job description. For this system to be valid, a certain integrity and stability must exist in the tasks individuals are asked to perform. To the degree that there is little stability in what people do, the whole idea of using jobs as a basic building block and control device in an organization can be challenged.[5] Rather than thinking of individuals as having jobs, it may be more effective to think of them as having areas of responsibility, team memberships, and assigned tasks.

To keep this discussion from deteriorating into an argument about what a job is, I must make a point. I'm not contending that people will stop having an ongoing relationship with an organization that hires them and pays them to do work. I am arguing that to an ever-increasing degree they will not have jobs in the traditional, bureaucratic sense of a set of fixed responsibilities and duties that can be reasonably captured in a job description and evaluated for the purposes of determining a rate of pay.[6]

The dangers of focusing on jobs as the basic building blocks of an organization's management systems are particularly apparent when the issue is determining how much individuals should be paid. People have market value; jobs don't. Jobs are simply microstructures in a bureaucratic framework that can be used to estimate the market value of individuals. Jobs do not quit organizations, and jobs are not hired by other organizations. Individuals leave because, given their skills, knowledge, and human capital, they can earn higher pay elsewhere. Jobs are not excellent or poor performers; individuals are. Individuals decide where to invest human capital; jobs do not. Therefore, the key compensation issue concerns what an individual is worth, not what a job is worth.

Job-based compensation programs often have the wrong impact on development. It is precisely because organizations pay individuals based on their jobs that individuals often try to obtain larger and larger jobs. Virtually every job-based pay system rewards moving to a higher-level job but does not reward lateral moves that lead to cross-functional learning or learning to do one's present job better.

Thus, job-based reward systems often result in individuals developing in ways that are optimal for organizational effectiveness if the organization needs more hierarchical managers. However, they do not if the organization is de-layered or if it wants to operate with lateral teams or does not need more managers.

Increasingly, organizations need individuals to learn skills that are not rewarded by the job evaluation system because they are not skills that will lead to being promoted to a more highly evaluated job. They are, however, skills that are critical to the organization being able to develop needed competencies and capabilities. An example of this is the skills that are needed to be a good team member. Team effectiveness is aided by having team members who have knowledge of several different functions. This in turn often requires lateral job moves, something that is not rewarded by job-based pay systems because cross-functional moves often do not entail any change in job size.

Boeing is an example of a company that for years provided the wrong motivation for skill development. The best engineers were very limited in the kinds of rewards they could get as long as they did just "engineering work." For example, getting a private office and parking in a favorable location, even getting a high-status identification badge, required that they take on managerial jobs. This was true even for engineers who provided a critical core competency to Boeing—the design and engineering of aircraft wings. The impact of the system was predictable; in many cases the best engineers became managers, and, I might add, often not the best managers because they sought management jobs for the wrong reasons.

In traditional, hierarchical structures it makes a great deal of sense to motivate a large number of individuals to get to the top of the organization. These structures depend on the best and the brightest ending up in the senior management positions because they provide the overall direction and focus for the organization. Quite a different mentality needs to exist with lateral, more team-oriented approaches to organizing. To be effective, these approaches depend on individuals being willing and able to develop knowledge about several functions and to exercise leadership and self-management skills, even though they may not be in a hierarchical position in the organization.[7] In a traditional, job-based system, this is not rewarded. Indeed, it may even lead to a lower job evaluation score. All too often this causes individuals to avoid learning these skills, even though learning them might be quite desirable from an organizational effectiveness point of view.

The alternative paradigm to using jobs as the basic building block of an organization is to focus on individuals. In many respects this approach fits better with the argument that an organization's capabilities and competencies rest in its human capital. When individuals are the basic, value-added component, they are the key to organizational effectiveness, so it makes sense to focus the reward system on them. Focusing on jobs rather than on individuals sacrifices effectiveness to obtain efficiency. Precisely because there are important individual differences, any system that tries to deal with a large number of people in a similar way simply because they are doing similar work must be suboptimal from an effectiveness point of view. Most people will end up being treated wrongly whether in the area of pay, skill development, or retention. This has to have negative repercussions for an organization that depends heavily on its human capital.

Overall, the argument against job-based reward practices rests primarily on the fact that they don't do a good job of either retaining or developing excellent performers. The more dynamic, less bureaucratic organizational models of today require a focus on individuals and what they need to do if the organization is to be effective—in short, management systems that focus on individuals and what they can do, not on jobs and what they involve.

Seniority-Based Rewards

Many organizations tie important rewards to one employee characteristic: seniority. The traditional employment contract calls for mutual loyalty and a long-term, sometimes a lifetime, relationship between individuals and their organizations. This is reinforced by reward systems that reward seniority. The longer somebody works for an organization, the more opportunities they have to get pay increases and promotions; therefore, high-seniority employees almost always end up with a higher salary. But the advantages of continued membership do not stop with higher pay. A number of time-based rewards are used to lock people into an organization. Probably the most financially significant of these in many organizations is the retirement program.

Most large organizations have lucrative retirement plans that require at least five years of service before an individual can collect from them. The amount of retirement pay individuals receive increases significantly for each year they work, until they reach a targeted retirement age. When companies have defined-benefit retirement plans, the rewards for an employee who stays until a designated retirement age are particularly great. In these plans employees are guaranteed a certain retirement amount. The amount of the guarantee typically increases with each year of service so that all an employee has to do to increase his or her retirement benefits is continue to work.

For decades it was said that once you spent ten years at AT&T you had a bell-shaped head and could not leave. This partly reflected the psychology of the Bell system and the ability to think outside that logic, but it also reflected the many benefits employees received after ten years of service. Not only did high seniority employees get a very attractive retirement program, they got more vacation days, lower-cost health insurance plans, service recognition awards, and a host of other small rewards (at the University of Southern California it's better football tickets and parking spaces) that say, "We value long-term service, and if you stay around you will be rewarded more and more."

Virtually every major corporation in the United States and Europe rewards seniority, and rewards for years with the firm are particularly prevalent in Japan and some other Asian nations. In fact, rewarding seniority is such an accepted practice that until recently it was rarely questioned. However, the pattern of extensive layoffs and downsizing that began in the 1980s has led some organizations to reduce the degree to which they give special awards and recognition for long service. It seems inconsistent to be laying people off and offering early retirement buyouts and, at the same time, to be rewarding individuals for long service.

Perhaps the greatest annuity in most organizations is the annual pay increase. Simply by doing an adequate job, individuals tend to receive pay increases that are compounded annually. The net result is that staying around for a number of years leads to individuals being relatively highly paid, in fact, often overpaid with respect to the outside market. Study after study has shown that the second-best predictor of the pay rate of individuals is the length of time they have been in their job.[8] High seniority leads to high pay. Of course, the best predictor of individuals' pay is the size of their job because that determines what pay grade they are in. Taken together, job size and seniority are far more important in determining an individual's pay than is performance.

Union contracts often specify automatic raises for each year of seniority. A good example of this is the airline industry; regardless of performance, the pay of flight attendants and pilots goes up each year. By the time employees have twenty or more years of seniority, they are paid two or three times more than new employees doing the same job. Of course in some cases, longer seniority leads to better skills, but skills are not what determines pay; simple seniority does. The same phenomenon operates in the teaching profession. In the United States, union contracts for teachers in grades K–12 typically call for an automatic increase for each year a teacher is employed. The result is much higher pay for high-seniority teachers, regardless of whether they are better teachers.

Particularly for nonmanagement employees, many organizations have developed pay systems that are similar to the ones specified in union contracts. They too simply give automatic raises each year so that the more senior employees receive higher pay regardless of whether they have greater skills or perform at a higher level.

When seniority-based pay is combined with the other privileges and benefits that go with seniority, the longer-tenure employees in many organizations are often paid and rewarded at much higher levels than they would be anywhere else. The result is that they wear "golden handcuffs" that keep them from departing the organization. This phenomenon is even more extreme when stock options are given to everyone in a corporation, and several years of membership are required in order for them to vest. In essence, individuals know that if the company does well and they stay around for three or four years they will do well, too.

The large U.S. automobile companies for years had bonus systems that paid out the bonuses managers earned over a multiyear period. This resulted in individuals having large future bonus payments due them if they stayed as members of the organization.

Needless to say, few of the average or poor performers left under these conditions. Occasionally an outstanding individual would leave because another organization would buy out the bonus dollars that were due.

There is little doubt that rewarding seniority is one way to retain employees. As time passes it is harder and harder for an employee to quit when extra vacation, retirement pay, recognition rewards, promotion opportunities, and pay increases all depend solely or partly on staying with the organization for a longer period of time. In essence individuals earn so many automatic rewards simply for their seniority that they are hesitant to leave because it means starting all over somewhere else.

The key question, of course, is whether the seniority approach to retention is functional for organizations. Clearly it best fits the "develop and build from within" human capital approach to keeping organizational competencies and capabilities current. It also fits businesses that are relatively stable and need to have a long-term, stable workforce. An example is capital-intensive businesses that need to make long-term investments—businesses like natural resource companies in oil and mining. Often they correctly emphasize stability of employment and long-term employment relationships. They need employees who develop an in-depth understanding of the business and take a long-term approach to it.

The seniority approach does not fit organizations that face rapidly changing business environments; this is particularly true for those that take a buy strategy with respect to developing new competencies and capabilities. The seniority approach is likely to retain all employees, not just those who are needed to deal with new technologies, markets, and businesses. Finally, it does nothing to facilitate the departure of employees whose skills and knowledge are no longer needed.

Seniority-based rewards generally do not fit contingent workers. Particularly with temporary workers, it makes little sense to reward them on the basis of how long they have been with a company. One exception is when there is a particular performance period that an organization has identified, during which it wants to retain a temporary employee. In this case it may make sense to offer a completion bonus that is tied to satisfactorily performing a job for the contracted period of employment. With the exception of this type of seniority-based reward, it is hard to see any reason to use seniority as a criterion for determining the reward package of temporary employees.

Seniority-based reward systems can turn out to be a negative, even for high-seniority employees. All too often they make high-seniority employees overpriced human capital and, as a result, high-seniority employees become prime candidates when layoffs and downsizings occur. They are obvious targets in cost-cutting drives because their salaries are high and they may not be more important contributors than are less senior, lower-paid employees. Of course there is a solution to this problem short of layoffs and dismissals: salary and benefit reductions. Unfortunately, most organizations do not take that approach. It is seen as too risky because it may retain an employee but create a bitter, nonproductive employee. Thus, most organizations usually make the decision to eliminate overpaid employees rather than reduce their salaries.

In many respects eliminating high-seniority employees serves neither the organization nor the individual well. It often creates a difficult situation for the employees because they have trouble finding a new job, given their age and lack of experience with other employers, and it can cause the organization to lose valuable resources, even if they are overpriced.

The incidence of high-seniority, overpaid employees is likely to increase in the United States over the next several decades. Because of age discrimination legislation, U.S. companies cannot force anyone except corporate officers to retire simply because of their age. Thus, organizations are increasingly likely to find themselves in situations where employees continue to work into their seventies and perhaps eighties. Because of seniority-based pay and reward systems, these older employees are likely to be highly compensated and potentially significantly overpaid in companies that have seniority-based reward systems.

Some companies have taken dramatic steps to solve the problems that have developed as a result of their long-standing, seniority-based reward systems. For example, Ford, which for years had policies that led to high-seniority employees being highly rewarded regardless of their performance and knowledge, recently identified its lowest-performing employees. Many were highly paid and as a result were not interested in leaving the company. Like many companies, Ford decided it couldn't afford the high pay that it was committed to for its poor performers. Whereas most companies have attacked this problem by offering early retirement packages to all high-seniority employees, Ford took a different approach. In order to prevent good performers from leaving, Ford offered large bonuses and generous retirement packages to only the lowest-performing 5 percent of its employees. Ironically, it meant that the individuals who were already overrewarded relative to their performance and market value were given one more reward—provided, of course, that they were willing to exit Ford.

Ford's effort to correct the problem with its reward system was dramatic and proved to be a significant intervention into the culture of the organization. It sent a clear message that Ford would be more performance-oriented in its reward system in the future. It might not have gone far enough, however, because it did not eliminate many of the seniority-based rewards (such as merit salary increases) that led to poor performers being highly rewarded and hesitant to leave.

Conclusion

Overall, seniority-based rewards appear to be a poor way to develop and retain excellent employees. In virtually every respect they are a blunt instrument when it comes to retention and development. They serve to retain everyone. They make the assumption that all employees are more valuable the longer they are with an organization. Especially in today's rapidly changing business environment, seniority often does not equate well with value.

In essence, seniority is a one-size-fits-all solution when it comes to retention. It does not distinguish between the employees who have twenty years of valuable experience and those who have one year's experience twenty times over. Neither does it distinguish between employees who have the skills that are critical to the key competencies and capabilities of the organization and those who do not. What is needed is to more precisely relate rewards to the importance of retaining individuals rather than to how long they have been with the organization.

Finally, seniority-based rewards do nothing to motivate or develop specific skills and abilities, and they serve to retain all employees, not just those who have the right skills and knowledge. Taken to the extreme, they can be significant contributors to an entitlement-oriented culture in which individuals feel they are owed something simply because they are long-tenure employees and have in the past made significant contributions to the organization. As we shall consider next, the alternative is to reward individuals on the basis of what they can do.

Chapter Six

Developing and Retaining the Right Individuals

The alternative to job- and seniority-based development and retention systems are systems that focus more on the person. In the area of pay and rewards this means paying people for what they can do and what their market value is. The difference between person-based systems and job- and seniority-based systems is enormous. Paying the person requires significantly different human resource management practices and produces dramatically different results. The most important outcome difference is that focusing on rewarding the person instead of the job has the potential to create organizations that are much more effective at developing and retaining the right people. The challenge is to develop practical, person-based reward systems that reward employees for developing the right skills and that can price them in the market in a way that will retain but not overpay them.

Paying the Person

Paying people for what they can do is growing in popularity in part because more and more organizations are adopting flat, team-based approaches to organizing that require individuals to develop new skills.[1] These new-logic approaches to organizing place a premium on organizations being able to develop and retain those highly skilled and knowledgeable employees who are critical to an organization's key capabilities and competencies.

In one respect, paying employees for skills, knowledge, and competencies is not a new idea; organizations have done it for decades. For example, most technical ladders in organizations and most faculty pay structures in universities are based on this concept. What is new is the idea of paying individuals *throughout an organization* based on the skills and knowledge they have.

Person-based pay is not a substitute for a carefully thought out approach to organizing and managing the work to be done. Indeed, in important ways it places greater demands in this area than does a job-based approach. If an organization does not determine what skills and knowledge it needs and how many people need to have them, it can end up with a tremendously bloated payroll because its workforce is overqualified or wrongly skilled. The challenge from an organization design point of view is to figure out the mix of skills and knowledge an organization needs in order to be optimally effective.

One way of looking at pay that is based on skills and knowledge is that it uses the money and other rewards that would otherwise have been spent to reward employees for promotions and greater seniority to motivate skill and knowledge acquisition. Typically, when individuals get larger jobs or get promoted, they are given a pay increase automatically. When pay for skills and knowledge is in place, money is not automatically given out; it is saved until individuals demonstrate that they have acquired the skills and knowledge that are needed to perform the new work. Thus, as with a job-based pay system, money is spent, but it is spent only when it can be justified in terms of an individual's being able to perform effectively.

Organization Design Considerations

A focus on the individual is highly consistent with management approaches and business strategies in which individuals are a key source of competitive advantage. When people are an organization's key resource, it is logical to focus on them and what they are worth. It also makes sense to focus on their growth and development so they can add more value to the organization's products and services. If, because of the management style or technology of an organization there are few opportunities for most employees to add more value, encouraging them to add skills and knowledge will not increase organizational effectiveness. It will only increase costs.

Some kinds of products and services require repetitive, low-value-added human labor. Call centers, traditional production lines, and toll collection booths are among the work areas that immediately come to mind as fitting in this category. When low-value-added labor is needed, a focus on individual worth and skill may not be productive. Indeed, it may simply add costs to the organization rather than value to the product or service. In these situations the performance differences between the best employees and average employees are often very small and can be handled by a traditional reward system.

The situation is quite different in the kind of new-logic organizations discussed in Chapter One. In order for this management style to be effective, organizations need considerable amounts of knowledge development to occur at all levels. They often need individuals who are with the organization long enough to gain a good understanding of its business model and who have good technical skills that support its core competencies. In many knowledge-work organizations, individuals are constantly assigned and reassigned to projects and tasks. They are asked to do a considerable amount of lateral process integration and self-management in order for the organization to operate effectively without extensive overhead and management costs.

A key management task in project-based organizations, such as professional service firms, is matching individuals to the projects that need to be performed at a particular time. In a dynamic environment, these organizations must operate as a giant matrix of individuals and tasks in which skills are matched to a constantly changing mix of work. Given the dynamic nature of projects, making this fit often requires that a number of individuals have multiple skills because it is impossible to predict exactly what mix of skills the organization will need at any given time. Some employees may not directly use all of their skills all the time, but having them is a critical asset for the organization. Not only does it make employees flexible so they can be assigned to a variety of different projects, often they are better at managing and doing a particular project because they have skills that allow them to put the task they are performing into a larger perspective. This can increase their ability to self-manage. In addition, individuals may not have all of their time assigned to any one project. If they have multiple skills, they can work on several projects at once—projects that use the same or somewhat different skills.

Managing Change

A focus on individuals' skills and knowledge fits very well when organizations need to constantly change or update their core competencies and organizational capabilities. An important key to being agile is the ability to change the skill mix of employees. When it comes to managing a change in the skills and knowledge of a workforce, a reward system that focuses on what individuals can do is a much better basis to operate from than one that focuses on jobs. The former allows an organization to identify the skill and knowledge shortages that exist with its current workforce and to motivate current employees to develop new skills and knowledge. It can also help identify when new employees need to be hired in order to build new core competencies.

A focus on jobs does little to produce an understanding of the new skills and knowledge individuals need, or for that matter what new individuals are needed in order for the organization to develop new competencies. It also typically offers employees little or no incentive to develop the new skills and knowledge that will help the organization change. As a result, when organizations with job-based systems need to change their capabilities and competencies, they usually end up either failing to change or replacing most of their existing workforce.

From Jobs to Roles

The term *role* is increasingly being used to describe the work situation of individuals in new-logic organizations. The term replaces *job* because it typically refers to a much less well defined and specific set of activities that an individual is supposed to perform. It is probably a better word to describe many knowledge-work and rapidly changing situations, particularly if it is taken to mean that individuals have general responsibilities within a particular area of the company and that within that area they may be called on to do a constantly changing mix of activities. What determines their assignment is not so much a job description but their ability to perform and act effectively and the type of work that needs to be done.

In a work situation in which people have roles, paying the person is much more suitable than paying the job. Indeed, paying the job is essentially impossible because of the constantly changing nature of the work. And paying the job is not a high-leverage approach to change because it does not create the correct incentives for individuals to learn the new things they need to learn in their ever-changing roles. Finally, it runs the risk of mispricing them in the market because the tasks they are doing at the moment may not represent their total capabilities and as a result may not reflect their market value. Thus, the recommendation is clear: when organization designs require the flexible allocation of individuals, employees should be paid on the basis of what they can do rather than what they are doing at the moment. The challenge is to develop pay systems that do this effectively.

The best-developed person-based pay system is the skill-based pay approach that has been used for several decades to pay production and service employees in high-performance organizations. I will discuss that approach next in order to provide a general introduction to the idea of paying the person instead of the job. I will then turn to the challenge of paying management and technical employees for their skills, knowledge, and competencies.

Skill-Based Pay

In skill-based pay systems, individuals are paid according to the number and kind of skills they have mastered. Skills usually are identified as the ability to perform very specific work tasks. More skills lead to higher pay.

The self-managing work teams that have grown up in many manufacturing plants are a good example of where skill-based pay fits particularly well.[2] As I mentioned earlier, in these situations individuals need to learn a number of skills in order to create a self-managing work team that can operate with a minimum of supervision and external control.[3] They differ somewhat from a typical project team in that their task is often a long-term task rather than one with a predetermined life expectancy. As such, the particular skills they need are often more predictable and the teams are more easily managed. Work teams, however, can end up as dynamic entities that need to change because of a particular product ending its life cycle or a particular customer no longer needing a service.

Skill-based pay has been used frequently in organizations that use self-managing work teams. It was first applied in the late 1960s in both the United States and Europe and continues to be the pay system of choice in manufacturing and service environments that use self-managing teams.[4] Because there is so much experience with the use of skill-based pay in self-managing teams, it is possible to specify in detail how a plan should be developed for a team-based environment and what the typical outcomes are of putting in a skill-based pay plan. I will review briefly the major development steps and outcomes that are involved when skill-based pay is used. I do not intend to provide a detailed outline of how to develop a skill-based pay system; instead I will highlight the issues that are involved in establishing one in order to add greater depth to our discussion of paying the person instead of paying the job.

Establishing a Skill-Based System

Setting up a skill-based pay system is not an easy task. It can be as labor-intensive and cumbersome as setting up a job-based plan. Indeed, it may be even more cumbersome and require more administration because it lacks some of the efficiencies of a job-based system. In essence, each person must be treated and recognized as an individual. Thus, some of the volume efficiencies, which are inherent in a job-based system that treats large numbers of individuals the same because they hold the same job, are lost. The trade-off here, however, is a potentially positive one if an organization ends up with a more flexible and highly skilled workforce.

Effective skill-based pay systems are usually founded on a core principle stating that individuals are paid only for skills and knowledge the organization needs them to have and that they are willing and able to use. It is up to the organization to determine what skills it needs and to determine whether an individual has a particular skill.

The typical steps in developing a skill-based pay system for an organization are as follows:

1. *Identify the skills needed for effective operation.* Skills are usually identified by analyzing the tasks that need to be performed in order for the organization to operate effectively. Once the tasks are identified, the specific skills needed to perform them are specified.

A second approach is to focus on the core competencies and organizational capabilities that an organization wishes to develop. Once an organization does this, it needs to design a reward system that will reward individuals for developing the types of skills and knowledge that will lead the organization to have the desired set of competencies and capabilities.

For example, if an organization wants to develop a core competency in a particular area of software engineering, it needs to establish the details of what kind of language people need to know, at what depth they need to know it, and so on, until a clear skills map is created that can be used to develop the pay system and be presented to individuals to facilitate their learning and development. Such a skills map, of course, is also critical when the time comes to change the skills and knowledge that an organization has. It can point out where the organization is invested in obsolete skills and help it make decisions about whether to recycle the existing employees or to hire new employees with the needed skills and knowledge.

2. *Identify optimal skill profiles for all individuals.* Organizations need to specify not just what skills they need but how many individuals they need with each skill. The answer to this question can only be determined once the organization has a good sense of how it intends to operate. If, for example, it intends to operate with self-managing work teams that are constantly facing new and different demands, it may need to place a great emphasis on cross-training and flexibility. However, if it is operating in a relatively stable environment and needs high levels of expertise in certain functions, it may wish to emphasize skill profiles that encourage people to become more and more expert in a particular area.

3. *Price each skill and skill set.* Setting pay levels requires determining the market value of the skills individuals have. This can be difficult. Salary survey market data can certainly be of aid here, but often it is an imprecise guide because job-based systems are the dominant approach to setting pay rates and to gathering market data. Thus, it can be difficult to find what the market is willing to

pay for the unique and unusual skill sets that individuals develop in skill-based systems. Often estimates must be made of what the addition of specific skills does to individuals' market value and the skills priced accordingly.

4. *Develop access rules.* Rules are needed to specify what sequence and at what rate individuals can learn new skills. This is a critical component of any skill-based system because in a skill-based system the major way individuals gain additional pay is through learning additional skills, thus they naturally are concerned about what skills they can learn and what they need to do to acquire those skills.

The answer to what rules an organization should establish rests in part in its approach to managing and organizing. This is a key area where, as the Star Model specifies, the reward system needs to fit the structure. If the organization wants a team environment in which cross-training is critical, it may want to put a strong emphasis on individuals learning horizontal skills. Not only should individuals be told that they can learn horizontal skills, it may make sense to require them to learn these skills in order to maintain employment. If an organization wants to operate with a flat structure, an emphasis on vertical skilling in which employees learn management and administrative skills is needed. If it simply wants to be sure it encourages some individuals to develop depth of expertise in key areas, a technical ladder approach, in which a few people are rewarded for being experts, may be appropriate. Ultimately, access rules that specify when skills can and should be learned need to be developed.

5. *Develop ways to determine whether an individual has acquired a skill.* In many cases, assessing skill mastery can be the most difficult part of a skill-based system but is particularly critical if the system is to be effective and defensible. Typically, the best approach is a work sample test; the employee performs the task that is relevant to the skill and is certified based on how well the work sample is done. As I will discuss further in Chapter Eight, it is important to identify who is best able to assess the skills and knowledge of those who want to be certified as having learned a new skill. In some cases the best person to do this is the supervisor; in other cases it may be peers, technical experts, or a combination of several individuals.

6. *Develop policies concerning obsolete skills.* Policies and practices need to be developed with respect to situations in which individuals will no longer be paid for certain skills. This can occur because changes in technology or products make skills obsolete. It can also occur because individuals move from one work area to another, thereby eliminating the need for them to have a particular kind of skill. Usually, change in skill needs is dealt with by a grace period, during which individuals are paid for their old skills until they have a chance to learn new ones.

Overall, effectively paying for the skills people have requires a considerable amount of thought and system development. If the needed design and development work is not done, the system can end up as a giveaway. Employees are paid in a chaotic manner for virtually any skills they possess, or worse yet, they get pay increases simply because they have acquired more seniority and therefore "must have learned something."

Effectiveness of Skill-Based Pay

The following are the major conclusions that come from the research on skill-based pay:[5]

- Paying for skills can be an effective approach to determining the base pay of individuals.
- Skill-based pay systems are relatively complex to develop and require a good understanding of the organization's management style and the tasks that need to be performed.
- Skill-based pay systems are relatively high-maintenance because they require continuous updating as the technology and structure of an organization changes and as individuals change their ability to perform tasks.
- Individuals generally like skill-based pay systems better than they like job-based pay systems, at least in part because they end up feeling in greater control of their pay and they make more money.
- Skill-based pay systems have their greatest impact during the first few years they are in place because during this time period they lead to tremendous increases in people's skills.

- Because they don't pay for ongoing performance, skill-based pay systems are often best combined with pay-for-performance systems that reward individual, group, or plant performance.
- It is critical to pay only for skills that people are willing to perform and that the organization determines it needs.
- Skill-based pay systems are effective only when reliable and valid measures can be developed of a person's ability to perform key tasks.
- Skill-based pay systems are most successful when they involve those who will be affected by them in their design.
- Skill-based pay systems help retain the most skilled employees because they are highly paid relative to the external market and because individuals develop organization-specific skill sets that cause them to be worth more to their organization than to any other. As a result they rarely are offered higher pay by other organizations, and they rarely leave.

Organizationwide Person-Based Pay

Skill-based pay systems are usually seen as successful when they are used to pay members of work teams, but in most cases they have not led to similar person-based pay systems for employees who are not in teams. Plant after plant that I have studied has had a skill-based pay plan in place for employees in production teams but a traditional job evaluation plan in place for managers and other employees. I have long argued that this is an undesirable inconsistency because it creates a "seam" in the organization between production employees and others and because it misses the opportunity to apply a successful pay approach to employees who are not in teams. This situation is changing, however. We seem to be in phase two of the evolution of person-based pay.

Phase two is likely to last ten or more years, and I expect it to be marked by the successful development of organizationwide, person-based pay systems. But before it can be successful there needs to be considerable development work done on how to pay the person in managerial and technical jobs. The person-based pay approaches that many organizations are currently using cause me considerable concern.

Most person-based pay systems for managerial and professionals start with the premise that, particularly in knowledge-work situations, there are tremendous gains to be had from paying the person rather than the job. Gains are said to include a better strategic focus and competitive advantages that come from superior organizational capabilities and competencies. It is hard to disagree with this argument, but it fails to answer the key question: How do you pay the person when that person is doing management or knowledge work? That is, what characteristics of the individuals do you focus on to determine their market value and their value to the organization?

Competency Approaches

Increasingly, organizations are choosing to use competency models in order to determine how much to pay their employees. Doing this requires converting competencies into measurable characteristics that allow for the reliable and valid determination of pay rates. This is where many of the competency models that I have seen fall short.

One study showed that similar lists of generic competencies have been adopted by a number of organizations—hardly a way to gain a competitive advantage.[6] However, my problem with using generic competencies is not just the fact that it fails to differentiate. My concern is more fundamental and begins with the definition of a competency. According to Spencer and Spencer, the authors of an influential book on competencies, a competency is an underlying characteristic of an individual that causes effective and superior performance in a job.[7] They add that "underlying characteristic" means that the competency is a fairly deep and enduring part of a person's personality.

Spencer and Spencer provide a dictionary of competencies that includes leadership, adaptability, innovation, team orientation, communication, customer focus, achievement orientation, and flexibility. For each of these competencies, they provide scales that describe different levels of competency. They also present an iceberg model that shows competencies as below the water line and consequently hard to see and measure. It depicts knowledge and skills as above the surface and therefore more easily measurable.

Spencer and Spencer briefly mention that individuals should be rewarded for the development of competencies "by merit pay for skill." This raises an obvious point. Given that organizational effectiveness is about task performance, why try to measure and reward competencies that are below the surface and therefore difficult to measure and relate to the organization's core competencies and organizational capabilities? Is it not likely to be more effective for pay purposes to focus on what is most easily measurable and directly related to organizational effectiveness—knowledge, skills, and task performance?

If competencies can be converted into skills and knowledge that are observable and related to task performance, paying for them has a number of potential advantages. If, however, paying for competencies is about trying to measure and pay for individuals' personality traits and attributes, then I have a major problem with the idea of paying for competencies.

I was studying performance appraisal and pay systems in the 1960s and 1970s when it was popular to rate individuals on traits like leadership, cooperation, and reliability and to use these ratings as a basis for determining merit pay.[8] Thus, I am all too aware of the many measurement problems with these ratings. They tend to produce invalid data that, because of their subjective nature, are particularly likely to discriminate against those who are not like the individual(s) doing the rating. Unfortunately, some organizations still use trait-rating scales as part of their performance appraisal process. They ask managers to rate the performance of individuals in terms of innovation, dependability, communication skills, and the like in order to determine whether they should get a favorable merit review and a "merit" pay increase. As I will discuss further in Chapter Eight, this is not the way to do performance appraisals, nor is it the way to determine market value for the purpose of setting a person's pay.

Some organizations have made the trait-rating approach a bit more sophisticated when they evaluate competencies. They add descriptive anchors to different points on rating scales (instead of just using high-low or good-bad), but this does not address the fundamental problem. Rating traits is an extremely subjective process, and a great deal of research over the years has shown that it tends to lead to unfair, invalid, and discriminatory outcomes. It was for this very reason that during the 1960s numerous studies were highly critical of trait-based performance appraisal forms. As a result of legislation and numerous court cases, standards have been developed concerning the validation of tests and what should be contained in a performance appraisal form. These standards emphasize the importance of measuring only the job behaviors that are related to successful task performance. This brings us back to what has been found in studies of skill-based pay in production plants.

Skill-based pay plans work best when they are tied to an individual's ability to perform a particular task and when good measures are available of how well an individual can perform a task. When good measures are available, then and only then can effective skill-based pay systems be developed. This critical point is neglected in competency-based systems that pay for generic personality traits that are not clearly related to task performance.

Despite what I have said so far, I believe there is often a role for competencies in the human resource management systems of organizations. If a competency is a basis for successful task performance because it is related to the development of the skills and knowledge that are needed to perform the task, then measuring it may be very helpful. It can be used in making job assignments and hiring decisions and in selecting candidates for training and development. Assessment of competencies is still an issue here, so it is important to test the validity of the measures used and, where possible, to use established competency measures that are available from consulting firms. It is also important that organizations establish which competencies are needed for each role or job. All too often organizations simply assess everyone on the same list of five to ten competencies, ignoring the fact that the importance of having a competency may not be the same for all jobs.

Once a person has performed a job, his or her task-related skills and knowledge can be determined and measured. At this point, I believe knowledge and skills, not underlying competencies, are the most useful basis for setting pay, because they most directly determine what work an individual can do and will do well, which of course is the key determinant of their value to the organization and their market value.

Beyond Competency-Based Pay: Knowledge-and-Skill-Based Pay

To pay the person in most knowledge-work and managerial roles, a *person description* that specifies what the person should be able to do needs to be developed. It should specify the task or tasks to be performed and the performance or mastery level required. This description should be used as the basis for determining whether individuals have the necessary work-related skills and knowledge and as the fundamental building block of an organizationwide, knowledge-and-skill-based pay system.

For example, instead of saying the person needs to have communication skills, the person description should specify exactly what kind of communication tasks the individual needs to engage in, as well as what level of performance on each of these tasks represents an acceptable level of mastery. It should establish measures that distinguish between successful and unsuccessful task mastery so that individuals can be certified as having the necessary communication skills. A version of these same measures may, of course, be useful in measuring ongoing job performance. But that is not what we are talking about here. In certification, the focus is on what individuals *can* do rather than on what they actually do in their day-to-day work performance.

As a general rule, I believe there are three areas of skill and knowledge that each person description should focus on. The first is the set of technical skills that are needed to do the work. These skills are likely to be radically different for someone in human resources and someone in engineering. In both cases certain function or discipline-specific knowledge must be mastered, which can be done at different levels of expertise, depending on the kind of work the individual is likely to be assigned. Knowledge in this area is often best identified and assessed by experts in the function and is frequently specific to the core competencies of the organization.

The second kind of knowledge involves the business model of the organization, that is, its financial measures and business strategy and how these relate to the work that employees do. To master this, individuals need to understand the marketplace, competitors, and of course the organization's financial model and measures.

Again, the depth and kind of knowledge needed will vary considerably from one work role to another.

The third and final area in which employees need specific knowledge and skills involves organizing, leading, and managing. This area is shaped by the management approach and design of the organization. Organizations that use teams, for example, need individuals to develop good team skills and communication skills. Those who are expected to lead the organization clearly need to be evaluated on their leadership skills and their ability to communicate a sense of mission and vision for the organization.

Overall, the types of knowledge and skill individuals need in order to perform effectively are determined by the strategy, processes, and structure points on the Star Model and by the kind of work individuals are expected to do. Given this reality, it is important that all employees have a person description for their role that tells them what they need to learn in order to perform effectively and that can be used to determine their pay level.

A good example of an organization that has developed specific person descriptions is the Fiat Company. Fiat has defined three types of knowledge that everyone in the organization needs to master, as well as seven types that are related to the fundamental professional areas and business processes that an individual is engaged in. The three general knowledge areas are (1) the company and its business, (2) the management practices of the company, and (3) the operations and economics of the business. The seven types of basic professional knowledge are defined specifically by each business unit in Fiat and are based on the area of professional knowledge that is the focus of each individual's work. For example, in marketing and sales, knowledge concerning sales networks and channels, competitive market structure, and three other general areas are identified as being important parts of the knowledge base.

Hallmark is another company that has spent considerable time and effort developing person descriptions. Success profiles are composed and used to identify each individual's knowledge and skills, focusing on the specific skills needed for that person's position. A competency assessment worksheet is used to establish development objectives for individuals. Managers turn these objectives into performance objectives, which are ultimately used for performance appraisal purposes as well.

The consulting business of PricewaterhouseCoopers has use the company intranet to leverage its person description system. The system contains a person description for every consultant in the business. It profiles the extensiveness and type of technical content knowledge and industry-specific knowledge of each consultant. This profile is used for development, compensation, and staffing purposes. It is available on the intranet for managers who need staff for projects and provides a clear image of the strengths and weaknesses of the technical knowledge available within the organization. The process helps managers staff their projects, determine the firm's recruiting and development needs, and support its knowledge management efforts.

Admittedly, creating person descriptions that specify what tasks a person needs to be able to perform and how task performance mastery can be measured is likely to be considerably more work than simply picking competencies from a list provided by a consulting firm. But I believe it is the only effective way to pay the person in knowledge-work situations. The alternative of paying for underlying competencies is likely to produce invalid measurements, discriminatory decision making, and, ultimately, the downfall of the idea of paying the person rather than paying the job.

Information technology can assist in developing, maintaining, and communicating person descriptions, but there is a lot to be done that requires individuals to make judgments and translate strategies into behaviors. It is crucial that organizations get on with the challenging work that is involved in specifying what they expect people to be able to do and how well they expect them to do it. Only then can they reasonably expect to create high-performance organizations that provide a competitive advantage.

Market Pricing

There is no well-developed way to gather market data on the value of skills and knowledge. Because salary surveys are usually based on jobs, organizations that choose to pay the person rather than the job face a challenge. They need to determine the market value of individuals in the absence of generally available market data. This presents a challenge but for several reasons it does not represent a compelling reason for not paying the person.

It is often possible to make a good estimate of the worth of individuals by looking at salary survey data that are based on jobs. At the very least it can give an indication of which broad bands individuals should be slotted into, along with some idea of the value of the role an individual is expected to fulfill in the organization. This is, in fact, precisely the way jobs have been priced in manufacturing settings when skill-based pay is used. A general assessment of the local market is made, and from it a starting rate and a highly skilled rate is determined. Between those two rates, pay amounts for skills are established, based on how long or how difficult it is to learn particular skills. In this case, market data are used in combination with judgment.

In addition to traditional salary survey data, one other kind of data is particularly useful in establishing the market value of individuals. Job offers are constantly being made to individuals and are being accepted or rejected. These transactions are perhaps the best available indication of the worth of individuals, so they should be carefully monitored by any organization using person-based pay.

Hiring-market data are generally available when companies are hiring technical experts and recent college graduates. They look for individuals with certain skill sets and make offers accordingly. As I mentioned in Chapter Four, typically these offers are independent of the job that individuals will be assigned when they join the organization. The reason for this is very straightforward: organizations are not hiring someone to do a specific job so much as they are hiring an individual with particular skills, experience, knowledge, and competencies. Thus, it makes sense to pay the market value for these individuals.

By monitoring hiring pay rates, organizations can adjust their existing wage rates to reflect individuals' true market value. Organizations that are frequently hiring new employees can do this easily; those that are not can monitor information that is available from the professional groups that gather data on hiring rates. They can also monitor the tremendous amount of information on pay rates that is available on the Internet, including auction data on individuals with specific skills. Finally, they need to look carefully at the success rates of the job offers they have made and at situations in which they have lost employees.

In the absence of true person-based salary information, firms may have to rely partly on internal comparisons to determine pay rates. This should be a temporary approach. It moves away from a market-based approach and runs the risk of duplicating the same problems that exist with traditional job evaluation plans, that is, a focus on internal comparisons rather than on the external market.

As organizations develop more systematic descriptions of the skill and knowledge sets they want individuals to have, it should be relatively easy to begin to do salary surveys that focus on the value of individuals rather than jobs. This should allow organizations and individuals to get a good sense of what particular skill and knowledge sets are worth and, as a result, what the market value of individuals is.

Value-Based Retention

The alternative to seniority-based retention is to focus on retaining the individuals who represent the most important human capital. This is much easier said than done. Nevertheless, some key steps can be taken so that reward systems will be targeted to retain the right individuals rather than every high-seniority individual.

Seniority

The first step is to eliminate seniority as a driver of most rewards. One obvious area where this can and should be done concerns merit pay. As will be seen in succeeding chapters, variable pay amounts can be substituted for fixed pay increases. This has two advantages: (1) it can increase the effectiveness of pay as a motivator, and (2) it can avoid annuity situations in which individuals are rewarded for years of seniority rather than for present performance and present market value.

Retirement plans are another major retention device that are not well focused. There is a simple solution. Eliminate defined-benefit plans that guarantee increases in retirement pay for each year of service. They simply do not make sense from a number of perspectives. The obvious alternative here is a defined-contribution program in which individuals and their organization make annual contributions to a plan that pays out based on the actual dollar amount that is in the plan at the end of the person's employment. These plans also can be structured to encourage individuals to stay but do not have to be structured that way. They can vest early and be made portable.

AT&T and Owens Corning are among the corporations that have dropped their traditional retirement plans in favor of cash balance plans that neither reward tenure nor penalize job changes. A number of technology firms, including Apple, have no employer-funded retirement plans. They allow employees to contribute to their own plans, but they make no company contributions to a plan that serves to "lock in" everyone. The rationale for this is simple. They are not sure they want to encourage employees to stay around long enough to retire. Their strategy is one of churning the workforce in order to get the best young technology talent for whatever technology is hot at the moment.

Matching the Market

Eliminating the features of a reward system that serve to lock in all employees is only the first step toward establishing a system that retains the right employees. Accomplishing this also requires rewarding high-value individuals at levels that match or exceed their market value. This is particularly important in the case of employees who are crucial to the core competencies and capabilities of the organization.

A number of reward approaches can be used to retain key employees; all of them require that the organization identify individuals who have critical skills and key knowledge and who perform at levels that make them excellent employees. This creates an obvious synergy between a knowledge-and-skill-based pay system and the retention of key employees.

A well-developed knowledge-and-skill-based pay system should move individuals up in the market based on their becoming more and more valuable. If skills are of short-term value to an organization because the organization's strategy or technology may be changing, knowledge-and-skill-based bonuses can be given instead of pay increases. However, when areas of knowledge and skill have a long-term market value, it makes sense to raise the individuals' pay when they acquire them so they will be appropriately positioned in the market.

One way to pay for skills and knowledge is to use a version of broad banding that allows individuals to move through bands based on skill acquisition. Bands need to be priced in terms of the kind of role or position that an individual has in the organization. With broad banding, it is possible to reward depth knowledge as well as knowledge in several functional and technical areas. Tying rewards to knowledge and skill acquisition can solve one of the major problems of broad banding: how to move people through the bands in a flexible and value-added way. An alternative to broad banding is to give fixed pay increases to individuals for learning and developing specific skills. This is exactly the way skill-based pay operates. As employees learn additional skills, they get a base wage increase.

Performance-Based Rewards

Often simply raising base pay through a knowledge-and-skill-based system is not sufficient to retain key individuals. Various kinds of stock and cash bonus plans need to be used to selectively retain key employees. Performance-based bonuses are particularly attractive because, when they are well administered, they can target employees whose retention is critical.

Stock option plans are another powerful approach to the retention of outstanding performers. There is one qualification here. These plans are effective only if during the period before they vest—before individuals can cash them in—the stock goes up appreciably. If the stock does not go up they will have little value and as a result hardly serve as an effective retention device. Because stock options are risky, in many cases it is best to supplement them with restricted stock that is given to individuals based on their staying with the organization for a certain period of time and accomplishing certain performance goals. Stock has value, even if the company's stock price does not improve, so it is more dependable as a retention device than options.

A carefully structured program of rewards that are tied to the continuing membership of key employees can be much more effective at retaining the right employees than one that relies on seniority-based rewards. The simple fact is that in today's business environment some employees get much more valuable as time passes, and it is important to retain them. Other employees become much less valuable, and the objective should be to replace them or increase their value, not to reward them for staying.

Conclusion

In today's business environment, reward systems that recognize employees for years of service send the wrong message. It is better to send the clear message that an employee's value to the organization varies, depending on the strategic goals of the organization and the skills, knowledge, and performance of the individual. The message should go on to say that this will be recognized in reward systems that are targeted at retaining the organization's most valuable human resources by rewarding them at or above market levels.

Part Three

Rewarding Performance

Chapter Seven

Rewarding Individual Performance

It is hard to argue with the practice of paying excellent performers better than everyone else. Since Frederick W. Taylor made individual pay for performance an important part of scientific management in the early 1900s, it has been a basic principle in most approaches to management. Pay for performance fits with the values and beliefs of individuals in most Western countries and resonates particularly well in the United States and Australia, where there is a strong emphasis on individualism and the importance of rewarding and recognizing individual excellence.

In addition to fitting well with the national cultures of many countries, individual pay for performance has the potential to create a number of positive outcomes. Without question, the major one is employee motivation. In Chapter Three, I stressed that the key to using rewards as motivators is the line of sight between the behavior of individuals and their rewards; with individual pay for performance it is possible to establish an almost perfect line of sight. At least in theory, how well people are rewarded can be put completely under their control. Thus, with an effective individual pay-for-performance system, the potential exists to create a highly motivated workforce in which employees see a close relationship between how well they perform and how much they are paid.

With individual performance reward systems, it is possible to tailor the rewards offered to the preferences and motives of individuals. If one person is particularly motivated by large cash payments, they can be offered; if another is particularly motivated by a vacation trip to Hawaii, it can be offered. Admittedly, tailoring rewards to individual preferences can get complicated, but it can also ensure that the rewards offered are powerful incentives for those who receive them.

Individual pay for performance can have an extremely positive effect on the retention of excellent employees. As I have stressed throughout this book, it can be difficult to retain outstanding performers because they have a higher market value than average to poor performers. Paying outstanding performers highly enough to retain them requires either paying everybody a high wage, hardly a financially wise thing to do, or identifying the best performers and being sure they are well compensated. Individual pay-for-performance programs take the latter approach. They create the possibility of giving significantly higher rewards to good performers; this in turn can ensure that high performers are at or above market, whereas poor performers are at or below market.

An effective individual pay-for-performance system can help remove poor performers from an organization. When large amounts of pay are effectively tied to performance, the result can be a reduction in the pay of poor performers until they cannot afford to remain as employees. The key is having enough pay dependent on performance so that poor performers end up under the market. This frequently happens in sales work, but it need not be limited to it.

Requirements for an Effective System

The research literature clearly indicates what it takes for individual pay-for-performance systems to be effective motivators. Essentially, it establishes that comprehensive measures of individual performance need to be developed, standard levels of performance established, and a pay system developed that clearly ties pay to how the performance of individuals compares to the performance standards. Stated this way it sounds simple to do, but often it is not. A brief review of what is involved in establishing the elements of an effective individual pay-for-performance system will serve to highlight why it is often difficult to do a good job of paying for individual performance.

Basic to the measurement of individual performance is the existence of identifiable, regularly assigned work activities. In other words, an employee needs to have a well-defined job. As I noted earlier, in a traditionally managed and designed organization this situation often exists. Elaborate job descriptions can be developed that describe in great detail the activities that individuals are supposed to perform; indeed, when they are well done, they often specify what the outcomes of these activities should be and how they can be measured.

For decades, IBM was a master at creating job descriptions and individual accountability "contracts" with their employees. Individual accountability was at the core of its much admired approach to managing this large and successful corporation. Job descriptions were well maintained and carefully specified, and they formed a good basis for measuring individual performance. Individual performance was carefully measured with a well-developed performance management system that influenced promotions and merit-pay increases.

IBM is not alone in emphasizing the importance of individual accountability and of assigning tasks to individuals. Many large corporations operate with this model and, as a result, have the potential to create an effective individual pay-for-performance system.

In any pay-for-performance program it is particularly critical that all key elements of performance be measured. Things that get measured and rewarded get attention; those that do not get ignored. This point is particularly appropriate when individual pay-for-performance systems are used.

As I will discuss further in Chapter Eight, identifying and developing good measures can be an extremely difficult and challenging process. It is difficult to do because it means translating an overall business strategy into measures that capture what each person should be doing in order for the business to accomplish its strategic goals. Large organizations must take their corporate strategies and translate them into measures for thousands and thousands of individuals. Unless this is done well, it can mean that employees are motivated to behave in the wrong ways with respect to the strategic agenda of the business.

In addition to being strategically aligned, performance measures and standards need to be sufficiently objective and credible so that employees feel they are being measured fairly. In the absence of the perception of fair and valid measurement, there is little hope of establishing a clear line of sight between individual performance and rewards.

A good example of the importance of measurement is provided by what has recently happened to the work of information operators. Historically, information services were offered by local telephone companies, and operators were paid by the hour. Operators may not have been highly productive in these environments, but the accuracy of their responses to customer requests was reasonably high. Since deregulation, information services are more and more often being delivered by large, centralized banks of operators who are rewarded for the quantity of calls they handle. This has resulted in both a higher level of productivity and a great many more wrong numbers being given out.

Errors have increased simply because measuring operator accuracy isn't easy and operators aren't penalized for giving out incorrect information. Because the failure to give out a number is easily measured and can be grounds for dismissal, operators are giving out wrong numbers and being rewarded for doing so! For example, if somebody calls up to get the number for a store that is part of a chain, often the easiest thing for an operator to do is simply give the first phone number that pops up on the screen for that chain of stores. Of course, it may not be the store the caller is interested in contacting, but it completes the call as far as the information operator—and the incentive-pay plan—is concerned.

Valid measurement of individual performance is feasible only when the work that individuals do is relatively independent of others' work. Independent work allows for the direct measurement of an individual's productivity without having to be concerned with the complexities of what they are responsible for and what other people are responsible for in the production of a product or delivery of a service. When the work of individuals becomes highly interdependent, it is often difficult to sort out who is responsible for what; as a result, the performance management of individuals becomes much more difficult.

Individual measurement is particularly difficult when individuals work in team settings. In a team environment, the work often requires extensive cooperation and mutual support so that the impact of individual performance on output is often difficult to establish and measure. Often cooperation and teamwork can only be measured by other members of the group and in a subjective manner. In an increasing number of organizations individuals are on multiple teams; as a result, it is difficult to identify individual accountabilities and responsibilities for them during a particular time period.

As I mentioned earlier, W. Edwards Deming and others in the quality movement have frequently criticized individual pay-for-performance systems because of their focus on individual performance.[1] They correctly point out that individuals are rarely responsible for quality problems. System breakdowns and bad process designs are usually responsible. As a result, they argue, it is important to focus on the systemic causes of low quality rather than on individual performance and its relationship to quality. Those in the quality movement are particularly effective in pointing out that focusing on individual performance runs the risk of suboptimizing collective performance. Individuals can work in a high-quality way but still produce products and services that are of poor quality. This occurs because the cumulative effects of individual performance do not automatically create processes that are in correct alignment.

Finally, it is important to remember that individual pay for performance is not right for every individual. As I pointed out in Chapter Three, not everyone values financial rewards enough to make them a significant motivator of performance. Some of the early research on piecework makes this point clearly. It shows that certain individuals respond enthusiastically to financial payments for individual performance, whereas others do not.

In a classic study of incentive-pay plans, W. F. Whyte found decades ago that individuals who respond positively to incentive plans tend to be loners who do not join in group activities and more often than not are Republicans who own their own homes.[2] They see making money as a mark of virtue because it is a sign that they work hard. Those who do not respond well tend to be more collectivist-oriented; they belong to more social groups and in general place a higher value on social contacts and egalitarian friendship networks than on financial rewards.

It is a reasonable guess that incentive pay is right for a decreasing number of work settings. Nevertheless, when it fits and is done correctly, it can be a major contributor to organizational effectiveness, so it is important to consider in more detail how it can be done well.

Approaches to Paying for Individual Performance

The thousands of different ways to pay for individual performance can be divided into two general types. The first type provides merit-pay increases based on individual performance; the second provides a one-time payment or bonus for accomplishing a particular objective or reaching a particular performance level. These two approaches have been extensively studied and have very different effects, so it is important to consider them separately and to reach some firm conclusions about how effective each one is.

Merit Pay

The many different merit-pay plans that organizations use follow the same general model: individual performance is appraised, usually by a supervisor, and as a result of that appraisal an adjustment (usually upward) is made to a person's salary. How large that adjustment is depends on the favorableness of the appraisal and the size of the salary increase budget, which is usually strongly influenced by the labor market and inflation. In high-inflation periods, large budgets exist and therefore large increases can be given, whereas in low-inflation times, small budgets only permit small adjustments.

The size of raises is also often influenced by how well employees are already being paid compared to others doing the same kind of work. If they are highly paid relative to others and to the market, they are likely to get a relatively small raise, even if they are good performers. If they are paid less than others and below the market rate, they are more likely to get a relatively large raise. The rationale for this approach is based on the argument that good performers only need to be paid so much in order to retain them; a large raise therefore isn't necessary if they are already highly paid. However, good performers who are poorly paid relative to the market do need large raises if they are to be retained.

Given its popularity, merit pay must be effective—right? Wrong! The evidence is clear that in most cases it does little to motivate performance and often does not even retain the right employees.[3] There are a number of reasons for the neutral to negative effects of merit-pay systems, but two stand out and need to be looked at separately: (1) performance measurement and (2) pay delivery.

Performance Measurement

Performance measurement is perhaps the most obvious and the most frequently cited problem with merit pay. Often, adequate measures of individual performance do not exist, so valid performance judgments cannot be made. As I mentioned in earlier chapters, this is especially true when teams are used and organizations face dynamic environments.

Faced with ambiguous jobs and collective action, organizations rely on supervisors to sort out how well individuals perform and determine what their pay should be. The hope is that supervisors can disentangle the effects of job changes, collective action, luck, and their own likes and dislikes to make accurate and valid judgments of how well individuals have performed over a period of time. This hope is rarely realized. Managers bring their own biases and information-processing problems to the task of performance appraisal, thus the appraisals are often flawed.[4] Instead of creating sense out of a very complex situation, they add to the confusion and complexity of identifying and accurately measuring individual performance.

The challenges supervisors face are compounded by the fact that most people think they are performing well. Particularly in successful organizations, employees are frequently told that they are a carefully selected elite. Most have been successful at the things they have done in life, otherwise they would not have been hired by a good corporation. The result is that about 80 percent of employees think they are above average in performance and expect to be treated accordingly. Statistically, 80 percent may be above average in terms of the national workforce, but it is impossible for 80 percent to be above average in their company. Thus, many employees end up disappointed and in conflict with their supervisors over their performance ratings.

As I will discuss in the next chapter, it is possible to create performance management systems that can help supervisors do a reasonably good job of evaluating individual performance. However, this can only occur when the right work structures and measures are available and when supervisors are trained and required to do a good job of performance evaluation. Often when merit pay is used, these conditions do not exist and as a result the supervisor evaluations of performance that form the basis for the merit-pay actions are full of errors and bias. Thus, they are an extremely poor foundation on which to base pay for performance.

Pay Delivery

The challenges involved in operating an effective merit-pay system do not end with finding good performance measurers and measures. Even when they exist, merit pay may not be an effective motivator or retainer of excellent employees. There is a fundamental flaw in merit systems that relates to the annuity feature I mentioned in Chapter Five.

Merit salary increases typically become a permanent part of an individual's pay—an entitlement or annuity that may not reflect current performance. Instead, merit pay reflects performance over a number of years of organizational membership. This is not an enormous problem if an individual's performance is stable from year to year. For some it is, but individual performance often varies considerably over a person's working life.

As a result of performance changes, poor performers can end up with very high pay and outstanding performers with very low pay. This often occurs when a new employee performs outstandingly well and a longer-term employee performs poorly.

As I mentioned earlier, to try to compensate for the annuity problem and its impact on total compensation, many pay systems create merit increase policies that cause the amount of increase an individual gets to vary as a function of how highly paid they are and how well they have performed. High performers who have low salaries get larger increases than those who have high salaries. This well-intentioned policy often ends up delivering a very confusing message. In essence, it tells highly paid, good performers that continuing good performance will not result in particularly large merit increases because they are already paid well. In order to make this palatable they are told to look at their total compensation level, not their merit increases, to see the relationship between their pay and their performance. Conversely, highly performing new employees are told that they should not look at their total compensation but at their merit increase because it indicates how well they are performing. Obviously, at this point, the simple idea of rewarding better performers with bigger merit increases has been lost, and the organization has shifted to a complex relationship between the amount of an individual's pay increase and how well he or she performs.

The annuity problems with merit increases are closely related to a second major problem with pay delivery in merit-pay systems: the size effect. As I mentioned in Chapter Three, there is no ultimate scientific answer to the question of how large a pay change needs to be in order to be a significant motivator of performance. Sometimes very small changes in pay can be powerful motivators if they are seen as a form of recognition and accomplishment. The same can be said for some nonfinancial rewards that have a low monetary value. For example, reward ceremonies, certificates, letters, and even crystal hand grenades may be valued highly by individuals, even though they are relatively inexpensive. That said, a good guess is that in order to be meaningful from a financial and lifestyle point of view, merit-pay increases must reach at least the 5 percent level and may need to exceed 10 percent in order to be truly motivating and energizing.

In low-inflation environments, pay increase budgets of even 5 percent are difficult to justify. Indeed, during the 1990s pay increase budgets in the United States averaged around 4 percent. This meant that the very best performers were getting maybe 6 or 7 percent increases, whereas average performers were getting 3 or 4 percent. The difference between 4 and 6 percent is not the kind of difference that is likely to produce a high level of motivation based on the importance of the financial reward. Of course, a recognition factor may come into play so that individuals who get the highest raises feel significantly rewarded simply because they are told that they are top performers and got the top raise.

Ironically, the recognition effect of pay increases is often diluted or diminished by pay secrecy policies. Instead of announcing that Joe or Mary is an outstanding performer and got the highest raise, most organizations caution employees not to talk about their raises. In many cases organizations do not even indicate what the top raises were, so it may be difficult for those who got the top increase to establish that in fact they received truly special recognition.

Merit-pay systems have the potential to work better in times of high inflation. One of the things a high inflation rate does is create large pay increase budgets, and, as a result, it is possible to give large amounts of money to outstanding performers. In times of high inflation, merit salary increases become more like bonuses. Because of inflation the previous year's increase disappears, and in order to maintain the same market position a large increase needs to be given. Of course, most corporations need pay systems that operate effectively in high- and low-inflation conditions. It is quite possible for inflation to change yearly and for both high and low inflation to occur at the same time in an organization that operates globally. Thus, it is hardly wise for organizations to count on inflation to aid their merit salary plans.

One final comment on the effects of merit salary increases: they tend to enhance the importance of promotion in one important respect. Typically, the only way to get a large increase in merit pay systems is to get a promotion because there is a separate budget for promotion increases. Promotion also has a second desirable effect; it moves people into the lower end of a new and higher pay range, thus making them eligible for larger merit increases if they perform well in their new job.

As I pointed out earlier, there is nothing wrong with the idea of promotion being a positively rewarded and motivating event. However, it is one with limited potential as a motivator. Particularly as organizations are flattening and more and more organizations want individuals to make lateral career moves, it is dangerous to rely on promotion as a major source of motivation. It is simply not that available and as a result may not be a reward that many individuals feel is worth pursuing. It also may be a reward that organizations do not want many employees to pursue. They may want people to stay at their current level or move laterally and simply perform well there. Finally, it may motivate individuals to learn the wrong skills because it rewards upward movement rather than the development of the skills individuals need to have in order to support the organization's core competencies and capabilities.

Despite the fact that merit pay is not effective, most organizations spend large amounts of time every year deciding how to distribute merit increases. For many companies the annual merit-pay activity has become kind of a corporate rain dance: there is great ceremony, noise, and activity. Like a rain dance, large amounts of time and resources are used trying to influence something that cannot be influenced through this vehicle. Unlike the rain dance, however, sometimes the corporate activities around merit pay actually have a negative impact on the things they are intended to affect positively. Employees often come away from merit-pay reviews concluding that performance and rewards are not related and that the organization does not deal with them fairly. As a result of their experience they may be more likely to quit and perform poorly than if there weren't a merit-pay system.

Incentive Pay

A variety of approaches to rewarding individual performance with one-time payments or bonuses exist. Without question the two most popular are piecework and sales incentive or commission plans. Both pay individuals a prescribed amount for each unit of work they do. Like merit pay, under some conditions these plans can be quite successful. The problems that develop with them are in some ways the opposite of those occurring with merit pay. They frequently become too powerful motivators of what is rewarded and measured. In essence, it is a case of needing to correctly choose what is rewarded. A company may get more of it but less than it wants of things it doesn't reward.

Individual incentive plans focus on establishing a clear line of sight between a particular kind of performance and a significant amount of money. This can happen when incentive plans are applied to jobs that involve independent work that can be measured accurately and when the plans make a one-time, variable payment. The one-time payment is critical because it means that large amounts of money can be paid without creating an annuity effect. Effective piecework bonus plans require not only good measures but also standards and a specification of payment amounts for performance at different levels.

Piecework plans in manufacturing settings once were very common but have become less popular as the nature of manufacturing work has changed and the plans' weaknesses have become better known.[5] All too often they create conflict between employees and the managers who set piece rates. What constitutes a fair and reasonable standard is almost always a difficult call and, as a result, the subject of contention and negotiation. Conflicts can result in a variety of dysfunctional behaviors by employees on piecework plans.[6] They can, for example, cause them to join unions and to restrict their production in order to get a lower piece rate. In extreme cases it can cause them to hide new work methods that allow them to work more effectively because, if they become known, management will increase the expected performance level. The same situation often exists with sales incentives. There is constant negotiation between individual salespeople and management about how much commission should be paid, what kind of sales they should be paid for, and how each new product and customer should be handled.

The payments that are made in piece rate and sales incentive plans are often large enough to focus individuals on those behaviors that lead to bonuses. In a comprehensively measured work situation, this is not a problem because all relevant behaviors will be motivated and rewarded. In many situations, however, it is difficult to measure everything an employee needs to do. This can be a major downside when key things are not measured or when a number of subtle things are difficult to measure. For example, passing on information to another employee, training another employee, and working cooperatively on a problem-solving team are typically not measured and are often important.

I recently saw an interesting example of the kind of dysfunctions an individual pay-for-performance system can produce. In this case, much of the work was best done by individuals, so an individual incentive plan fit the work, but there were significant measurement problems with respect to what constituted adequate performance of the tasks. The employees were doing telephone installations in a wide variety of homes and businesses, so their work was not observed by a supervisor. Each installation had unique characteristics, so it was difficult for management to judge how long the installation should take and therefore to determine what was successful performance. The employees, however, were often able to identify the easy jobs, and they tried to get them in order to maximize their incentive pay. When this failed they sometimes created easy jobs by making faulty installations; this would generate a recall order, which they could easily correct because they had created the problem in the first place. Because they knew exactly how to fix it quickly, they earned a significant bonus.

The effect of this incentive system was a dramatic increase in productivity, at least as measured by the number of work assignments completed by the average employee. Of course, a productivity increase was desperately needed because of the service calls that resulted from employees' creating problems. An in-depth analysis of the situation determined that, as a result of this misdesigned and poorly aligned pay system, the organization ended up raising its labor costs for little or no improvement in performance.

The sales incentive plan at EMC Corporation provides a good example of just how motivating an individual sales incentive plan can be. EMC is a successful manufacturer of corporate data storage systems. The EMC sales incentive plan has no cap on compensation; most sales representatives get 65 percent or more of their pay in commissions, compared to 25 percent for most of their competitors. EMC sales executives have been quoted as saying that its six hundred or so representatives earn an average of $250,000 a year, making them among the best-paid salespeople in any industry. In 1998, according to the *Wall Street Journal,* the five top performers earned more than $1 million.[7]

The EMC plan sets ambitious sales goals for its representatives—goals that are driven by the company's business strategy. Making their sales goal is an absolute necessity for salespeople. Failing to consistently meet the sales goal means being fired. In 1997, more than fifty sales people were discharged because they failed to make their goals. Thus, in the EMC plan there are both positive rewards attached to high performance and punishments attached to poor performance.

EMC's plan is more aggressive than the typical plan because it puts so much at risk and has no cap. All too many sales incentive plans put a cap on employees' earnings and thus fail to motivate them once they have reached a relatively high performance level. Further, many plans do not offer a large enough incentive to excite

individuals, which clearly is not true with EMC. One of the most fa-
mous cases of a cap actually driving an employee out of an organization concerns Ross Perot—the founder of Electronic Data Systems
and Perot Systems. He left IBM when he reached his salary cap early
in the year and saw no reason to continue working for IBM.

A microcosm of the behavioral impact of sales commission
plans can be seen in the many stores that pay their salespeople on
commission. Typically, they are paid a percentage of all the sales
they make. The impact of this is multifaceted and variable. Nordstrom, the large department store chain, has turned the customer
focus that is produced by their individual incentive plan into an
advantage. It uses extensive customer satisfaction measures and
tries to establish a long-term relationship between a customer and
a salesperson.

Commission plans can be highly motivating with respect to encouraging salespersons to meet and greet customers when they enter
a sales area. They are also effective at encouraging salespersons to
sell expensive upper-end products, especially when a higher commission rate is paid on sales of the most expensive models.

Individual systems tend to discourage salespeople from helping
out with "somebody else's customer" or handling returns and refunds. This often results in interesting behaviors, for instance, a
salesperson trying to identify whether a customer has already talked
to somebody else in the department. If the customer has done so,
he or she is told to deal with that person. This occurs because the
norm among salespersons is that the first contact between a customer and salesperson establishes ownership. After this point, no
other salesperson will service a customer because sales credit goes
to the person who first talked to the customer. In many respects this
system works well because it strongly motivates the salesperson to
complete the sale. However, it can create dysfunctional situations
such as when a customer stops by a department two or three times
in the process of making a purchase and must deal with a different
salesperson because the original one is not available.

Individual sales incentive plans clearly do not fit situations
where team behavior is needed. For example, in technical sales,
people with different functional specialties and product knowledge
must work together to explain products and help customers make
the best purchasing decision. Therefore it is not advisable to give

sales credit to just one person. It is much better to give an incentive payment to the entire team because, as I will discuss in Chapter Nine, this leads to greater cooperation and team effectiveness.

Discretionary Bonuses

An increasingly popular form of variable pay uses the results of a performance appraisal process to determine the amount of bonus that is paid to individuals. In essence, this approach has the potential to eliminate one of the major failings of merit pay: not enough money being available to motivate individuals. It does this by eliminating the annuity feature of merit pay, thus freeing up dollars to be used for variable pay. Often, bonus plans are installed in organizations by gradually decreasing the merit budget and increasing the amount of money that is paid out in variable bonuses to individuals. Kodak did this several years ago, and the result was that some employees earned significantly higher pay than they did before; others earned less. Similar plans have been installed in America West Airlines and a host of other American and European organizations.

With a discretionary bonus-pay approach, changes in base pay typically result from promotions or perhaps from changes in the value of jobs in the marketplace. In the case of person-based pay, they come from changes in the person's skills, knowledge, and competencies. Rewards for performance are given strictly in terms of a variable bonus amount. The amount of bonus pay is often relatively small for lower-level jobs (5 to 10 percent) but can be 100 percent or more of salaries for higher-level management and key technical jobs.

A bonus-pay approach can be an effective way to reward individual excellence as well as to retain excellent performers. It is particularly effective at retaining new employees because they can almost immediately be given pay at a high level; they do not have to wait for a series of merit increases. It also has the advantage of quickly reducing the total compensation of poor performers. Finally, it can make very clear the relationship between a performance appraisal judgment and the amount of someone's pay.

What the bonus approach doesn't do is ensure that supervisors do a good job of judging the performance of their subordinates, which they must do in order for this approach to be effective. Indeed, if performance is not appraised accurately, the approach may be much more destructive than merit pay because in this approach the appraisal makes a real difference in how much people are paid. Thus, it puts a great deal of pressure on what is often the weak link in many companies' performance management system—the appraisal. As I will discuss in the next chapter, it is not easy to design and administer a performance appraisal system that effectively drives pay, but it can be done if an organization is willing to make the investment and the situation is right.

Overall, it is hard to argue with the point that piecework, sales commissions, and bonus plans have both significant downsides and upsides. In this respect, the plans are different from merit-increase plans. The incentives offered by most merit-increase plans are sufficiently small that many of the dysfunctional behaviors that are discussed by the critics of individual pay for performance are relatively unlikely to appear. Similarly, many of the positive results that are hoped for also typically fail to materialize. In essence, merit plans often do measure the wrong things and have poor measures, but because the rewards they offer are so small, they don't often cause dysfunctional behavior; they "just" waste time and resources.

Quite the opposite is true with incentive pay. With incentive pay the reward is often relatively large, thus it does make a difference what is measured and what kind of work situation exists. The literature on piecework has example after example of bonus plans that have caused increases in measured performance but simultaneously have caused major dysfunctions.[8] Not surprisingly, in most of these cases, poor or incomplete measures were used or the work involved required the cooperation and teamwork of individuals. Therefore, the optimization of one person's performance was not sufficient to produce high organizational performance.

Lessons Learned

Our discussion of individual pay for performance leads to some clear conclusions about when and how it should be used. Two important situational factors determine whether individual pay for performance makes sense. The first is the nature of the work. It needs to be measurable and independent. The second involves the nature of the individuals doing the work. Individual pay for performance works best when individuals not only desire money but tend to be oriented toward achievement and control. Individuals with a collectivist orientation do not respond positively to individual rewards.

Our discussion clearly establishes that merit pay, despite its popularity, should not be used, even in situations where individual performance is a proper focus and good measures can be developed. It is not appropriate because it does not have significant incentive value and suffers severely from the annuity problem.

The evidence on variable payment plans that reward individual performance is more positive, although mixed. The issues here concern using them appropriately and selectively, as well as designing them correctly. If they are designed and administered well and they fit the situation in which they are used, there is clear evidence that they can affect performance positively. The following are the key elements that must be present:

- Independent work
- Achievement-oriented individuals
- Individuals who value money
- Significant amounts of variable pay at risk
- Comprehensive measures of performers
- Objective measures of performance
- Clear connections between performance measures and payment amounts
- Performance standards at achievable levels

Conclusion

Clearly, there are places for individual pay for performance plans. However, their number is likely to diminish because of the way work is changing. Simply stated, work is becoming more dynamic and more interdependent, and, as a result, individual rewards for performance are less and less likely to be appropriate. Merit pay seems to be the odd man out. It is not an effective incentive, and it does not fit the way organizations are likely to operate in the future. Bonuses are useful as rewards for individuals if performance can be measured adequately. In the next chapter I will explain what steps need to be followed in order to ensure accurate measurement of individuals' performance.

Chapter Eight

Appraising Performance

Performance appraisal has been one of the most praised, criticized, and debated management practices for a number of decades. It has also been the subject of a great deal of research that has provided a considerable amount of information about the impact of performance appraisal on organizational effectiveness and how appraisal can be done effectively.

Recently, discussions about performance appraisal have changed as a result of the increased adoption of total quality management practices, the increased use of teams, the popularity of employee involvement strategies, and the development of skill- and competency-based pay systems and the growth of company intranets. These trends have focused attention on some new and some old problems with performance appraisals and to the use of the term *performance management* instead of *performance appraisal.* Before considering the new issues concerning performance appraisal, I would like to provide some background information.

Performance Appraisal Challenges

There are some good reasons to do individual performance appraisals. They can help a supervisor define the work of direct reports, measure their performance, and reward them in a way that will create motivation. As part of the process of setting goals and evaluating and rewarding performance, supervisors can also counsel individuals on their skill deficiencies and help guide them in the development of new skills and knowledge. Clearly, these are all worthwhile objectives, and no one can be too critical of a performance appraisal system that accomplishes them. Indeed, any system that accomplishes them is best referred to as a performance management system because it does more than just score performance. It manages performance.

The problem—and it is a well-documented one—is that most performance appraisal systems neither motivate nor effectively guide the performance development of individuals.[1] Instead, they often end up causing conflict between supervisors and subordinates, which leads to dissatisfaction and dysfunctional behaviors. The dysfunctions are most common when performance appraisals are tied to traditional merit-pay systems. They are particularly severe when the performance appraisal system forces supervisors to compare subordinates with each other and to evaluate some favorably and some unfavorably—the classic forced-distribution rating approach.

In some organizations, performance appraisal is such an onerous activity that supervisors and subordinates alike avoid it. I have found company after company where phantom and vanishing appraisals "take place," that is, there is paper documentation of an appraisal event but no meaningful discussion has taken place between a supervisor and a subordinate. Interviews often reveal that supervisors felt as though they had a discussion with their subordinate, but it was so casual that the person being appraised did not think it was a formal appraisal.

In many respects, the occurrence of phantom and dysfunctional appraisals is not surprising. In most cultures it is difficult for one adult to sit in judgment over another. The person judging often feels uncomfortable about giving feedback and finds ways to avoid it. The person receiving the feedback suffers from simultaneously wanting to get feedback and fearing that it will be negative. When asked, employees almost always say, "Yes, I would like to get feedback about my performance," but what they really mean is they would like positive feedback about their performance. This, combined with the fact that most employees think they are performing at an above-average level, creates many situations in which individuals receive a more negative appraisal of their performance than they think is fair and just. After several experiences in which this occurs, individuals become a bit gun-shy about their next performance appraisal.

General Electric is one organization with a long-term concern about the effectiveness of its performance appraisal system. It has clear policy guidelines that require managers to appraise their subordinates for both development and reward practices. GE has also sponsored a considerable amount of research on performance appraisal. The most visible study they conducted was published in 1965 in the *Harvard Business Review.*[2] It received a considerable amount of attention because of its conclusion that it is dysfunctional to talk about pay increases and development in the same meeting. The study found that when pay and development are talked about at the same time, individuals who are appraised tend to remember the pay discussion but not the development discussion. This led to the recommendation that pay changes and development should be discussed at separate meetings.

In the 1970s, GE invited my research center at USC to study the performance appraisal systems in most of its major business units. Given the results of the earlier studies at GE, we expected to find that most of the business units would have appraisal systems in which pay increases and development were discussed separately. However, that is not what we found. Appraisal systems at GE varied greatly with respect to the timing of appraisals, the relationship between the performance discussion and the pay increase discussion, and when and how development was discussed. Some parts of GE still combined the pay discussion with the development discussion. Others separated the two by holding a performance review and development discussion at one point during the year and announcing the pay raise six months or so later. Still other parts discussed pay increases and performance at one time and development at another.

Different parts of GE also used widely varying performance appraisal forms. Some used traditional trait-rating forms; others had extensive management-by-objectives formats. One of the most interesting practices we saw was the use of a book that contained ten different appraisal forms; supervisors could pick the form they felt best fit the appraisal situation they were in. One thing that was common across GE: all the units we studied took performance appraisal seriously and made it a major responsibility of all managers. As a result appraisals got done, even though a wide variety of approaches were used.

Approaches to Appraisal

Given the many valid criticisms of performance appraisals, one conclusion seems clear: most organizations should either significantly alter the way they are done or abandon them. But what should replace them? It is one thing to point out what is wrong with performance appraisals but quite another to create an effective system. Coming up with one that is motivational and that contributes to skill development requires a good understanding of an organization's design and business strategy and a well-developed and articulated approach to performance management. One thing is clear: doing a poor job of appraising performance is worse than doing nothing. Doing nothing, however, is not an option in a highly competitive world in which organizations must constantly improve their performance, so I will describe four alternatives that organizations might adopt with respect to performance management and then consider when each is appropriate.

Traditional Appraisals

The first alternative is to do a traditional performance appraisal correctly, that is, to have a supervisor and perhaps others appraise each employee's job performance on a regular basis and to consider skill development during a separate session. The results of this appraisal can be tied to a pay-for-performance system and, if appropriate, to a knowledge-and-skill-based pay system. As we will discuss further in Chapter Nine, if cooperation among employees is desired, the pay increase budget should not be a zero sum or fixed pool.

The traditional approach is appropriate in many hierarchical, bureaucratic organizations. It was developed to support this type of organization, and it still fits. Appraisals do not have to be negative experiences when done correctly and when they fit the organizational context. As I will show later in this chapter, because so much has been learned about what makes an appraisal system effective, a clear set of must-dos can be established to provide a road map for creating effective individual performance appraisals. If appraisals are done correctly, there is every reason to believe they can be used as a basis for an individual pay-for-performance system and a knowledge-and-skill-based pay system that motivates individuals to perform well and to develop the proper skill mix. Appraisals can also be the basis for determining a total compensation level that correctly places individuals in the market, ensuring that high performers are highly paid.

Traditional Appraisals Without Pay

A second alternative is not to have individual pay for performance or pay for knowledge and skills but still have supervisors do traditional performance appraisals. This makes performance appraisal easier to do and places fewer demands on supervisors. It needs to follow most of the same individual performance appraisal guidelines that are discussed later in this chapter. The problem is that when pay is not involved, supervisors often do not spend enough time doing performance appraisals because performance management is not seen as a serious activity. In essence, it is seen as firing blank bullets. Still, it is appropriate to do appraisals if an organization is willing to commit substantial resources to helping the supervisor do it well and to take steps to ensure that it is a serious activity aimed at skill development, job definition, and performance coaching.

From an organizational point of view, doing appraisals without individual pay for performance is most appropriate when motivation through individual pay for performance is either not possible, such as in certain union and government jobs, or when pay for performance is focused at the group or organizationwide level. This may be true, for example, when profit sharing, gainsharing, or small-group incentives are in place that provide extrinsic motivation.

Team Appraisal

A third alternative is to turn the performance management of individuals into a team activity. This approach makes particular sense in an organization that relies on self-managing work teams and expects work teams to handle issues of skill development, selection, discipline, and pay administration. Creating an effective team appraisal process is a significant challenge and requires a considerable investment in team training. It also requires relatively mature teams. The manager who is responsible for the team's performance has a particularly important role to play. She or he needs to be sure that the appraisal process gets done by the team and that it is done fairly and reasonably. In essence, the manager becomes a facilitator of the appraisal process and a check on its effectiveness and fairness. The appraisal may well include individual pay for performance and skills, but only if the team decides it is appropriate. The work on self-managing teams shows that it can be an effective approach if it incorporates the principles of good appraisals.[3]

Appraisal of the Team

A fourth alternative is appropriate when the work of a team is highly interdependent and, as a result, it is difficult to assign responsibility to individuals for particular performance results. In this alternative, the manager appraises the team as a whole and rewards the team as a whole. Just as with individual performance appraisal, goals are set, performance measured, and rewards distributed. In this case, however, they are distributed to a team as a whole or perhaps to several teams.

The manager does not intervene in internal team processes but encourages the team to deal with its own performance problems. The team pays attention to its competencies and capabilities and to how they can be built internally through individual skill development. In this alternative, there is no individual pay for performance, although there may be social and recognition rewards because the better performance of some individuals is informally recognized by the members of the team. Rewarding everyone with the same pay is specifically intended to create internal inequity in the team with respect to rewards for performance. The expectation is that the members of the team will create social and recognition rewards to offset the inequity that is caused by all individuals receiving the same financial rewards.

Choosing an Approach to Appraisal

Organizational design is perhaps the most important factor in choosing which of the four approaches to performance management should be used. As the Star Model indicates, it needs to fit the organization's structure and key processes. Traditionally managed organizations that are built around functional silos, individual work designs, and hierarchical relationships fit well with individual performance appraisal systems. In most cases it is advisable to use an approach to individual appraisal that ties pay increases and bonuses to the results of the appraisal. If the work design is such that it is difficult to do individual appraisals, the best approach may be to focus appraisals on individual development and possibly tie pay increases to the development of skills and knowledge.

The situation is quite different in organizations that follow the new logic in order to create high-performance organizations. In these organizations team-based appraisals are usually the appraisal approach of choice. Team-based appraisals fit well because individuals have a good knowledge of each other's work, and the work is done by teams. Often team-based appraisals are a necessity in these environments because, with very flat organization structures, managers often do not have the knowledge or the time to conduct effective one-on-one appraisals.

Appraising teams and appraising individuals in the context of a team requires a significant change in how most organizations operate their performance appraisal system and more basically how they think about organizational effectiveness. Despite all of the literature on teams and the increased adoption of teams, most organizations still have individual performance appraisal systems and individual merit-pay systems. These practices conflict directly with the development of highly effective teams but fit the values and experiences of most managers. Simply measuring an individual's contribution to the team in a traditional performance appraisal system is not the answer. As I will discuss further in the next chapter, an entire redesign of the performance management system is needed—a redesign that supports team structures and builds on what is known about the determinants of appraisal effectiveness.

Keys to Performance Appraisal Success

No magic list of activities can guarantee that an organization will have a successful performance management system. However, the research on performance management does establish the key features of a system that make it more likely that appraisals of individuals will produce positive results. It is important to emphasize that the performance appraisal process must be considered as a system. The implication of this is that the practices that make up the system cannot be looked at as separate items or activities. They need to be adopted as an entire package so the system has all the elements required for successful operation.

Performance management should be a continuous process that takes place over an extended period of time. Thus, the activities that are part of the process need to be designed and explained in a meaningful way so that individuals have a sense of being appraised regularly, fairly, and comprehensively. Bearing in mind that individual practices are not sufficient to make for a successful appraisal process, let us turn to a consideration of specific features that, when combined into a system, can make individual performance appraisals successful.

Work Design

I said this earlier, but it is worth saying again: individual appraisals require individual work assignments. In some work situations, such as direct sales, jobs largely involve individual work; in others, such as oil refineries and chemical plants, the work is highly interdependent, team-based work. Such work does not lend itself to the use of an individual performance appraisal system. However, work in which individuals can carry out activities autonomously and accomplish objectives lends itself to individual appraisals because it is possible to come up with quantitative measures of performance and to attribute to one individual most of the responsibility for the outcomes. An example helps to highlight this point.

In sports such as hockey and soccer, an individual often scores a goal only as a result of the coordinated activity of a large number of players. In this case it is hard and often undesirable to focus on assessing the performance of individuals; it is better to focus on assessing the team's performance. But in sports such as track and field and golf, individuals are largely responsible for how fast they run or how low their score is. Thus, it is important to focus on the performance of each person, not the team's performance.

Hierarchical Process

Performance appraisals need to be driven by a hierarchical process in which supervisors evaluate their direct reports at all levels in the organization. All too often, however, the senior executives in an organization are not appraised and do not appraise their subordinates. The result is that performance appraisal becomes something the people at the top tell middle management to do to lower-level employees.[4] Needless to say, this sets up a negative dynamic with respect to the way appraisals are thought of and done. Among other things no senior role modeling is visible, and senior managers are not held accountable for their performance. The recommendation here is clear: performance appraisals need to be done and done well at the top of an organization. The CEO needs to be evaluated by the board of directors and so on down the organizational hierarchy. This sends a clear message that performance accountability exists at all levels and gives senior management a chance to model the right kinds of performance appraisal behavior. The impact is especially great when the organization releases the results of the CEO's appraisal to all employees, which does in fact happen in a few organizations.

There can be a second important outcome when boards of directors actively appraise the performance of the CEO and others in senior management. Particularly if the goal-setting part of the appraisal process is done well, it can help establish the strategic direction of the organization and provide a set of goals and measures that form a basis for the performance objectives and goals of individuals throughout the organization. In the absence of an effective performance management system at the top, these are often missing as key drivers of performance appraisals at lower levels.

Jack Welch of GE is the poster boy for how a CEO can model good performance appraisal behavior. Welch sets precise performance targets for all his direct reports in GE and monitors them throughout the year. At the end of the year every one of Welch's direct reports is given a handwritten, two-page performance evaluation. Attached to the detailed evaluations are Welch's jottings from a year earlier specifying particular goals and objectives. Written in the margins are comments on how well the individual performed against each objective. The notes include congratulations as well as criticisms.

When Welch deals with his direct reports, every salary increase, every bonus, and every stock option grant comes with a talk about expectations and performance. He often sends personal letters and comments that reinforce his focus on rewarding performance. Bonus awards and stock option plans are usually quickly followed with clear statements as to what is expected for the next year. Welch requires that his behavior be replicated by each of his direct reports. They are expected to use their goals and objectives to drive the goals and objectives that are set for their subordinates. The result is a cascading down of objective performance measures and performance-appraisal-based rewards for performance.

Quality of Appraisals

Measuring the effectiveness of appraisals is a key way to indicate their importance and to motivate managers to do a good job of appraising performance. It is also a way to give managers feedback about how well they do appraisals and how well the appraisal process is unfolding. Thus, it is critical that systematic measurement of the effectiveness of the appraisal process take place. This measurement should include an audit of the quality of the written documents produced in the appraisal process, the gathering of survey data on how individuals feel about the appraisal events, and measures of the timeliness of the appraisal meetings and reports.

In the absence of effectiveness measures, it is hard to judge how well managers do appraisals and to reward them accordingly. Thus, there is a real danger that the appraisal will be seen as an optional activity. Recognizing this, PECO Energy Corporation ties its managers' raises and bonuses to their successfully completing the appraisals of their direct reports.

The Goal-Setting Process

The appraisal process is greatly facilitated when specific, quantifiable goals are set for job performance and acceptable levels of performance identified in advance. In order to do this, managers and subordinates need to sit down before the performance period begins and establish what measures will be used and what performance levels need to be achieved. The research on goal setting suggests that the more mutual the setting and establishing of goals, the more likely individuals are to accept the goals, be motivated by them, and see the performance appraisal process as a fair and reasonable one.[5]

The most frequently raised issue about goal setting concerns goal difficulty. Particularly since Jack Welch began emphasizing "stretch goals" in GE, the question of how difficult goals should be has been debated. The research evidence on motivation that I mentioned in Chapter Three has a clear answer to this. Setting performance goals that are too easy can result in suboptimal performance because individuals feel that once they have achieved the goal, they need to do no more. Stretch goals can be powerful motivators if they are not so difficult that the individual feels they are unachievable. This leads to the suggestion that when only one performance goal is set for each measure, it should have at least a 20 to 30 percent probability of being achieved. Better yet, for each performance measure, multiple goal levels should be set, with reward size increasing as goal difficulty increases.

In order for goals to be motivating, individuals need to believe they are worth accomplishing. Sometimes individuals will be motivated to accomplish a goal simply because they have agreed that it is reasonable and one they can achieve. When this occurs, the goal-setting process itself can be a powerful motivator because it ties feelings of success and self-esteem to goal accomplishment. When goals and results are public, esteem in the eyes of others can also be tied to being able to successfully accomplish a goal. Of course, financial rewards can also help lead individuals to believe that goals are worth achieving and can supplement motivation that is based on self-esteem and the esteem received from others.

Input to Appraisal

Individuals should have an input opportunity at the end of the performance appraisal period. They need a chance to present their version of how well they have performed their work assignments against their preset goals. My research suggests that it is important for individuals to have this opportunity before a performance judgment is reached by their appraiser.[6] In the study we did for GE, we found that in many parts of the company individuals were first judged and then given a chance to comment on the overall appraisal judgment that had been reached. In this scenario, employees told us that they felt they had been tried and convicted before they had a chance to present their case. They also reported that supervisors were unwilling to change appraisal ratings. This was true, even when there was significant evidence that the supervisor had made a wrong decision because he or she did not have all the needed information or had erroneous information. The solution to this is simple: gather data from subordinates about their performance before appraisal judgments are made.

Rewarding Performance

As I mentioned earlier, one of the most complex and persistently debated issues in individual performance appraisal is when and how the appraisal results should be tied to changes in pay. It has been consistently found that discussing development needs and the amount of a performance-based pay action at the same time is very difficult. When money and development are discussed together, most people who are being appraised tend to remember only the discussion about money and some of the discussion about how well they performed. The development part of the discussion either never takes place or the individual being appraised doesn't remember it. This is hardly surprising. Money is important to most people and in many cases they are given at least some feedback that reflects negatively on their performance.

One solution to the conflict between the discussion of pay and the discussion of development is to separate the pay discussion from the performance review discussion. In some companies, it is separated by as much as six months. This may have the desirable outcome of creating a better discussion of performance and development needs, provided both parties' interest level remains high. But it eliminates one of the major positives of the whole appraisal activity, motivating individuals by tying pay changes to individual performance. This raises the interesting question of whether it is possible to have a good development discussion and tie pay closely to performance.

I believe the answer is yes. The key is separation, but not the kind that is often used. The discussion of pay for performance and past performance needs to be separated from the discussion of development needs and activities. This inevitably means two separate discussions between the appraiser and the person being appraised—one in which past performance and the resulting pay increase is discussed and a second, separated by a significant time period, in which the development and career situation of the individual is discussed. When a knowledge-and-skill-based pay system is in place, pay changes related to skill development need to be discussed at this time or perhaps at a third meeting that focuses on just skill certification and pay.

The development discussion often is best done on the basis of an individualized schedule. In the case of highly ambitious new hires, once a year may not be enough; for R&D scientists, once a year may be too often. I have interviewed many researchers and other professionals who consider an annual development plan irritating and insulting because it does not fit their career trajectory.

It often is best to involve people other than an employee's direct supervisor in the development discussion. One way to structure this process is to have the discussion at the request of the person who wants career development advice and to let the employee and his or her supervisor decide who will conduct it. This can help ensure that those who do the assessment and career development work are knowledgeable about the earning and career opportunities available in the organization and about the individual's performance and competencies.

Under the skill-based pay systems in many plants, often skill development appraisals are done by people other than an employee's direct supervisor. In many of these plans, individuals indicate when they have mastered a particular skill or piece of knowledge and ask to be appraised. Depending on who is in the best position to judge their skill and knowledge, some combination of peers, technical experts, and the individual's supervisor do the appraisal. In most of the skill-based plans that I have studied, this process works well, at least in part because the expertise of the appraiser is well established and the individual initiates the appraisal process. But it can be initiated in other ways. I have seen it work successfully as a regular annual event in which individuals get feedback about their development and make plans for future development activities.

The growing trend toward putting human resource management systems on company intranets has created an interesting option for how and when development discussions are held. Sonoco has a development feedback process that is intranet-based. It is initiated by the employee and allows the employee to determine who does the assessing. It uses a standard form and provides feedback directly to the individual. Sprint Corporation has developed a similar system that is tied to the competencies it wants all its employees to have.

Hewlett-Packard, among other companies, has developed an "expert system" approach to development and career planning that can be accessed by all employees. It provides individuals with an opportunity to assess their interests and gives them career advice based on how their interest patterns fit with different types of careers. It also makes available a complete list of all the job openings in the corporation and makes it easy to apply for the jobs. The advantages of this system are many and include the fact that individuals can operate on their own career planning schedules and do not need to involve anyone higher up in the organization. In essence it is a self-scheduled, self-administered approach to development and career management, so there is no conflict with the pay and appraisal processes. It also makes information about the opportunities that exist more open and available so that individuals can use it to find career opportunities. Finally it reduces the paperwork load and advice-giving demands on both managers and the HR department.

One downside of appraising and rewarding skill development is that it may divert employees' attention away from performance and focus it too much on development. If the decision is made to have skills assessed as part of the individual performance appraisal, it is particularly important that there be some pay-for-performance system in the organization to offset the focus on skills. Possible alternatives are team pay-for-performance plans and any of the organizational pay-for-performance plans that I discuss in Chapter Ten.

Frequency

One of the most frequently asked questions about performance appraisal is, How often should it be done? There is no definitive, universally correct answer; the answer depends on the situation. One concept that I find useful is *time span of discretion;* it was developed by Elliot Jacques and refers to the time it takes to judge the impact of a person's performance once the person has performed a task.[7] At the lower levels of many organizations, the time span of discretion is extremely short, sometimes just minutes or even seconds, whereas at the top it is often years or even decades long. For example, poor performance on the part of an assembly line operator is often immediately obvious, whereas strategy decision making by CEOs and boards can take years to evaluate. At the top it may be getting shorter because of the rapid changes that are occurring in the business environment and in technology, but it still is usually longer than one year.

Although theoretically correct, it is foolish to argue that appraisals should be done every few seconds at the lower end of an organization and only every decade or so at the very top. Realistically, some kind of appraisal probably needs to be done for everyone in an organization at least annually. Clearly, in research labs and in top management jobs, an annual appraisal needs to be balanced by a consideration of indicators of long-term performance and the trend of performance, not just one year's performance.

In some jobs it may make sense to have appraisals more frequently than every year. For example, in sales and in many production situations, appraisals often should be done weekly, monthly, or quarterly. A key issue here is the availability of good quantitative performance data on which to base the appraisal. When the data are available and appropriate, it makes sense to have relatively frequent appraisals and to tie rewards to them. This is an important part of establishing a clear line of sight for a pay-for-performance system. Rewards need to follow the behavior quickly in order to establish a motivating reward system. This is essentially the same point I made earlier when I discussed separating the appraisal event from the pay change: rewards for performance that are given long after the behavior has been completed are poor motivators.

Timing

Closely related to the issue of how frequently appraisals should be done is the choice between an anniversary date and a focal point appraisal schedule. In anniversary date systems the clock for the performance appraisal usually starts when an individual is hired into the organization or takes a new job. Once a certain amount of time has elapsed (usually a year) from this date, the individual is appraised. In focal point appraisals everyone is reviewed at the same time; in most cases it is at the end of the calendar or fiscal year. I know of no definitive research data that suggest whether the focal point or anniversary approach is most popular. My guess is that the focal point approach is the more popular and becoming even more so.

Although there are arguments for both schedules, I believe that the better choice is the focal point review. I prefer it because it is most likely to lead to valid measures of performance. Because all evaluations are done at the same time, it is easier to make comparisons among the performances of different individuals and groups. It also allows appraisals to be done when most of the typical measures of performance are collected for the purpose of reporting on the financial performance of the organization. When individuals are appraised before the year end, financial performance results may not be available. Further, comparisons among individuals are difficult to make because the time period of performance that is being evaluated is different for each individual. It is quite possible that because of different business conditions it may have been more difficult for one person to perform well than for another. Finally, it is hard to use meetings and other devices to adjust ratings for leniency and other biases when they are not all done at one time.

The major disadvantage of the focal point review schedule is that when performance-based pay is used, it leads to a large, once-a-year increase in the operating costs of the company (particularly if bonuses are paid). It also creates a heavy workload on managers when appraisals need to be done. The latter problem is often somewhat moderated by the fact that managers get in the "habit" of doing appraisals. In fact, sometimes they prefer doing a number of appraisals at the same time because they do not have to relearn and restart the appraisal process a number of times throughout the year.

One of the worst timing errors that I have seen with performance appraisals involves delaying individuals' appraisals when they have a poor performance period. The logic seems to be that after a poor performance period, eligibility for a pay raise should be delayed and, therefore, so should the next appraisal. It uses timing as a way of reducing an individual's pay, thereby punishing them for their poor performance. A much better alternative is to give no pay increase to someone who has performed poorly but to relatively quickly make them eligible for a new appraisal and, if warranted, a pay increase. This makes it possible to say to an employee, "If you perform well in the next period of time you can immediately get a pay increase." This is a much better approach to motivation than to say, "You are not eligible for a performance review and a pay increase for a longer time because of your past performance."

Project work presents a particular challenge with respect to the timing of performance appraisals. Typically, the best time to assess somebody's performance on a project is when the project ends. An exception is when the success or failure of a project is not known until considerably after it is completed. In the case of new-product development teams, for example, it may not be known until the product has either moved into production or into the market. In any case the assessment of an individual's contribution to a project should be made based on the timing of the project, not on a traditional calendar basis. Similarly, if a reward is to be tied to performance on the project, it too should be based on the life cycle of the project, not on an arbitrary company calendar.

Contingent workers present an interesting situation with respect to performance management. Appraising them on the typical annual cycle often does not make sense because they are unlikely to be in an organization for a full year. Not appraising them makes no sense because often the only incentive that exists to encourage them to work effectively is a performance appraisal system that ties rewards to performance. A logical approach with contingent workers, therefore, is to specifically review and reward them based on a performance cycle that is developed with an eye toward how long they are expected to work for the organization.

Individuals who are new to the job, either because they have been promoted or hired from the outside, often need special performance management treatment in focal point review systems. In their case it often makes sense to give them a performance review after they have done their job for a fixed amount of time. How long that period of time should be, of course, depends on the nature of the job and how quickly it is possible to get a sense of their performance.

In many cases it makes sense to give new employees an early pay adjustment based on how quickly and well they have mastered their work. This is consistent with paying people for their skills and knowledge, and it can be an incentive that encourages them to quickly master the skills necessary to do their work. It can also be a powerful retention device for employees who are in high demand because it can position them more quickly than a normal system would at a relatively high pay position in the external market.

Promising a quick performance review can also be an advantage in attracting employees. It is a way of saying to new recruits that the organization is not a rigid bureaucracy that has to wait for a particular date in order to give feedback and raise people's pay. It can be a particularly effective recruiting tool if one result of the performance review can be a significant pay increase. It is also a relatively low-risk way to attract individuals because it only commits an organization to a higher pay rate once individuals have shown that they can do the work.

Measures

Performance measures are critical to the success of any appraisal process. Many appraisals fail because the performance measures consist of ratings that are made on vaguely or poorly defined traits such as reliability, communication skills, customer focus, and leadership. These traits are difficult to judge and almost always lead to communication breakdowns and misunderstandings between appraisers and subordinates.

The alternative to measures that focus on general traits and personality dimensions are behavior- and outcome-based measures that quantify or at least clearly identify the behaviors that are needed. For example, if the term *reliability* refers to completing work on time, the appraisal should focus on whether work is completed on time and or how late the work is, not on whether the employee is reliable. This is a simple example, but it makes the point that in order to have agreement among raters and between those doing the ratings and those being rated, it is important to focus on and measure observable behaviors and the business outcomes they produce.

It is particularly important to focus on business outcomes in order to establish a relationship between the business strategy of an organization and the appraisal process. If growth is an important business objective, the behaviors that lead to growth need to be identified and each person assessed against those behaviors. For example, a salesperson might be appraised on the proportion of sales that come from new products, on the number of suggestions made for product innovation or changes, and on the opening of new sales territories and customer accounts.

In addition to leading to poor communication between supervisors and those being appraised, vague trait measures also are particularly subject to stereotypes and unfair discrimination. Court case after court case has affirmed that in order for an appraisal to be valid, it must measure behavior and the business outcomes the behavior produces.[8] If the appraiser simply measures a global, vaguely defined characteristic such as communication skills, dependability, or innovativeness, there is likely to be an adverse impact on minorities.

Measurement Scales

For a number of purposes it is useful to have an overall rating of performance that goes beyond a straightforward description of behavior. Overall or summary ratings of performance are often used for the allocation of pay increases as well as in determining promotion and work assignments.

Organizations typically ask supervisors to make appraisal judgments on one of two types of rating scales. The first type has from two to an infinite number of categories that range from high performance to low performance. Each individual is then placed along the scale in one of the performance categories.

The second type of rating scale requires supervisors to put their subordinates in order from best to worst, depending on how well they have performed. The latter, ranking ordering approach leads to each individual being ranked in a sequence that is equal to the number of employees. In some companies these rankings are integrated on a companywide basis so that employees are ranked from 1 to a number equal to the total number of employees. In one company I studied, this resulted in one employee being ranked number 1 and another as number 3,038.

Rank ordering has no place in most organization for the simple reason that the detailed data that are needed in order for individuals to be judged so precisely are not available. When many people are being ranked and poor performance data exist, error and randomness come into play, with the result that individuals are always unfairly ranked.

What about rating scales? How many points should there be on the scale? After years of studying performance rating systems, I believe that in most situations the correct answer is three levels of performance. If there is a significant learning time required for the job, it may be important to have a fourth category of employees who are new to the job and just learning how to perform it. A three-category rating system typically provides all the information that is needed to handle pay increases and identify who is appropriate for promotion.

There is no magical right number of categories to place people in, but it is reasonable to say that in most situations fewer is better. For example, PECO Energy Corporation uses only three categories: "great," "OK," and "needs improvement." This simple system provides all the information the company feels it needs to manage its employees. It replaced a five-point scale that had produced much more complicated, but not more useful, ratings.

Managers can almost always accurately identify a small group of truly outstanding performers who separate themselves from the rest. They also can identify a small (sometimes nonexistent) group that performs badly and probably should be dismissed. Once they have identified these two groups, what's left is a large group of employees who perform well and should be encouraged to stay with the organization. Splitting them into more groups is usually an error-filled, unnecessary, counterproductive activity.

One group that may not get treated fairly in a three-category system includes the above-average but not outstanding performers. They often feel that there is little opportunity for them to get the top rating and that they are being unfairly grouped with the average and below-average performers. In some instances, this is a compelling argument, but it should only lead to adding an additional performance category if good measures exist that allow a supervisor to clearly identify these employees. A similar argument can be made for identifying employees who are somewhat below average. From a pay-for-performance perspective it makes sense that they should get smaller increases and be told that they can get an average or mid-sized increase only if they perform better. Again, the key determinant of whether to identify this group of employees is whether sufficiently precise performance measurement is possible.

Although it may make sense to use a five-category rating system when good performance metrics are used, supervisors are well trained, and the information is needed for pay or promotion purposes, going beyond five categories is another matter. This is rarely advisable because it is not needed for making reward decisions, and it calls on managers to discriminate among levels of performance at a level of precision that is difficult to attain. Thus, placing employees in more than five categories makes little sense unless good quantitative performance data are available.

One final comment needs to be made on the use of different rating scales: it is almost always wrong to have an even number of categories, with no middle or average category, so that everyone has to be put in either an above-average or below-average category. This is an almost impossible task when people are being rated because the middle of the performance distribution is where the least precise data and the most people are. It is better to leave the average performers together as a single, coherent group than to try to separate people who are very similar into performance categories such as slightly above and slightly below average.

Appropriate Distribution

Colleges, high schools, and grade schools have grade inflation. Companies have performance rating inflation. Over time in many organizations, more and more employees are rated highly, even though the organization's performance fails to show the same type of upward movement. What is going on is a major breakdown in the performance appraisal system. All too often the solution organizations try is the "forced distribution" approach.

Organizations tell their raters that they can only have a certain percentage of their employees in each of the rating categories. This has a number of negative effects. It almost always produces false data because the distribution of actual performance rarely meets the distribution called for by the appraisal system.

Forced distribution advocates correctly argue that in any group, someone has to be the best and someone the worst. But it does not necessarily follow that the difference between the best and the worst is very large or significant or that the individual rated worst in a particular group is a poor performer. Someone who is rated low in one group may nevertheless be a good performer when compared to the total population of employees. When small groups are being rated, there is no guarantee that the average performance level will be the same from one group to another. Thus, it is dangerous to force distributions of any kind on relatively small groups of employees.

Most companies use the normal distribution or bell-shaped curve as their guide to how many people should fall in each category. The reality is that the true performance of most groups of employees does not match a normal distribution. In fact, organizations spend years training and developing employees so that the distribution will not be normal, yet appraisers are told they have to match a normal distribution. They respond by disowning the results of the appraisal process. For example, they tell low-rated employees that someone has to be in the low category and it is their turn this year. They also rotate individuals into lower categories in order to meet their annual quotas.

Having fewer categories can help the problem of appraisal inflation to some degree. With just three, it is possible to have a very careful definition of what is required to be in the very top category. Particularly if a well-defined, three-category system is combined with clearly developed anti-inflation norms, inflation can be controlled. It often helps to provide a "suggested guide" that indicates what percentage of employees are expected to fall into each category.

Bringing supervisors together and forcing them to defend their appraisals is another potentially effective way to reduce inflation.

It helps make apparent to managers that their ratings have an effect on others and that in order to have fairness and integrity there has to be some consistency about how individuals are rated across different work groups. Left on their own, supervisors are inclined to be lenient, partly because it is a way of capturing pay increases for their employees and has no obvious cost to them. Creating a situation in which they must defend their ratings to their peers creates a pressure that can help avoid inflation.

PECO Energy has two sets of meetings to support its performance management system. One set at the beginning of the year brings appraisers together to develop and calibrate goals and objectives. The second set, at the end of the year, are used to allow managers to discuss and justify their ratings.

The results of an effective series of performance review meetings can be tied into a human resource review process that is focused on the development of employees throughout the organization. Particularly when this process is led by senior managers, it can be an important part of a company's overall human resource management process because it can make the organization aware of employee development needs and facilitate development moves. It can also identify individuals whose retention is key to the success of the organization.

Correct Appraiser

Supervisors are the most obvious source of appraisal data but clearly not the only ones. In all too many appraisal systems, however, supervisors are the only appraisers used, and as a result potentially valid and useful appraisal data are lost. There is an increasing recognition of this problem. A number of companies, including General Electric, Honeywell, Hallmark, and General Mills, use a 360-degree appraisal process.[9] This rather catchy term simply refers to asking peers, customers, subordinates, and perhaps others—in addition to the supervisor—to do performance ratings.

It is hard to argue against the wisdom of using multiple raters. For example, in the case of a manager, often that person's subordinates see the manager's behavior more clearly and frequently than the person's boss does. In a team environment, team members who are peers often see more of an individual's behavior than a manager does. The challenge in developing valid performance measurements is to determine what behaviors are needed for success and then to identify which appraisers are best positioned to judge those behaviors. The final step is to develop an appraisal system that has good measures and captures valid data from appropriate appraisers.

Despite the obvious advantages of multiple appraisers, it is important to point out that the dynamics of appraisal get increasingly complicated as more and more appraisers are added to the mix. Each one is likely to have unique biases and issues when making appraisal judgments. For example, peers may be in competition with each other for a pay increase, and this may influence what they have to say. Subordinates may have a particular vendetta and as a result conspire to undermine tough but effective managers. I could cite other examples, but it is hardly necessary. At some point the appraisal judgments of individuals need to be evaluated from the perspective of their likely validity and objectivity.

Often the best use of ratings from customers, peers, and subordinates is for coaching and development purposes. They can provide valuable data about how a person needs to develop in order to be seen as effective in dealing with others. Many of the 360-degree appraisal processes that exist in organizations today, including the ones at Sprint and Sonoco, are used for developmental purposes only. This has two advantages: (1) it often makes it easier for the individual to hear the feedback because it is not quite as threatening, and (2) it reduces the possibility that individuals will be biased in their ratings because of competitiveness with the individual.

Training Appraisers and Appraisees

Appraisal is in many respects an unnatural act. It is a little more natural in Western than in Eastern cultures, but most individuals are not prepared to do it well. If there is an appraisal effectiveness gene, it is a recessive one—which leads me to a simple recommendation: appraisers need to be trained in how to conduct a productive appraisal process. They need to know more than just the theory of appraisal. They need a chance to practice appraisals in a simulated appraisal situation.

Being appraised is not a comfortable or frequent event for most people. Thus, those who are appraised need training as well. They need to understand what the process is like and what their rights and expected behaviors are in an appraisal situation. Again, this type of training is best delivered by simulations that provide different types of appraisal feedback and give individuals a chance to respond.

Although it is rarely done, it makes a lot of sense to train supervisors and subordinates together. This creates a shared understanding of what the appraisal process is like, how it should be run, and what its expected outcomes are. It ensures that the appraiser and the person being appraised have a common understanding and are simultaneously exposed to the same description of the appraisal process. This can help them hold each other accountable for how well the appraisal goes. It also can take much of the mystery and some of the anxiety out of the appraisal process.

Information Management

Current, accurate, easily accessible records of each individual's performance management history are an important part of every effective performance management system. They help establish a clear understanding of all decisions that are made about measures, goals, and rewards, and they build a documented performance history for each employee.

Organizations that have intranet-based human resource management systems should post performance information, along with person descriptions, on the system. This creates a single database that contains specifications of the knowledge and skills each individual should have, an assessment of what attributes they have, and the work assignment and performance history of every employee. To be useful, this database must be updated on a regular basis, as knowledge and skills change and performance goals are met and reset.

There are numerous advantages to having an easily accessible, centralized database of the knowledge, skills, and performance history of an organization's workforce. It can be a crucial tool in knowledge management in that it can provide easily accessible information on the knowledge and skills currently at the organization's disposal. It can be used to monitor how effectively important organizational strategic goals are being translated into operational measures and goals for specific individuals and to assess how well goals are being met. It can also provide information to all employees on what is happening elsewhere in the organization and what sorts of resources are available in-house. As a result, it can allow them to coordinate their work more effectively with that of others.

Developing Effective Appraisal Systems

It should be apparent that developing and operating an appraisal system is not a simple task. They truly are systems, and, as with all systems, many features must be right if they are to work. The list of issues that need to be considered is long, and relationships among the issues are complex. This raises an important question: Who should design performance appraisal systems?

It is possible for a consulting firm or the human resource department to design an appraisal system and then install it and train individuals in its use. This approach has at least two important weaknesses, however. First, it often fails to capture important information about special issues that need to be considered in the design. Often, employees throughout an organization, rather than somebody from HR or a consulting firm, have the best idea of what needs to be measured, what supervisors are capable of, and what problems should be addressed. Second, when employees don't design their own system they have to be sold on its advantages. When they or their representatives are actively involved in the design of the system, it helps not only to educate them about the system but to convince them of its advantages.

Often the best answer to the question of who should design an appraisal system is the individuals who will be affected by the system (or their representatives). It is particularly important that they be involved in the design when the organization uses teams and other new-logic approaches to management in which everyone is required to take part in the appraisal activities, and there is a commitment to employee involvement in decisions that affect the workforce. In new-logic organizations, widespread commitment to and understanding of the appraisal system is critical to its success.

Because performance appraisal systems are complicated, employees should not be turned loose to do design work on their own. Good design requires technical knowledge as well as system design thinking. Thus, it is important to provide design help and resources to any group that is designing a performance appraisal system; designers need to know the possible options as well as the pluses and minuses of those options. Perhaps most important, they need to understand the best way of sequencing the activities that are involved in doing a performance appraisal and to understand all the elements that need to be built into a performance appraisal system in order for it to be successful. They must, for example, understand that it needs to involve goals, employee participation, correct rating scales, and all the other features we have just reviewed. Although it is difficult to design effective systems, my experience is that when employees understand the features that contribute to performance appraisal effectiveness, they can design an effective system.

Conclusion

The best way of summarizing this discussion of performance appraisal effectiveness is to say that performance appraisal should not be abandoned in most organizations; instead, it should be reinvented on a selective basis. The challenge is to move from the traditional, dysfunctional approach to one that incorporates the recommendations made in this chapter. Completely eliminating performance appraisal is not an answer; elimination does not deal with the reasons appraisals were created in the first place. Individuals need to be guided and encouraged to develop particular skills and to direct their performance toward critical organizational outcomes. The challenge is to develop approaches to do this that fit the new logic of organizing and the need to reward excellence. How to do this in teams will be considered in the next chapter.

| **Rewarding Team Excellence**

Teams have emerged as a widely used design approach in large organizations for a number of reasons, including the changing nature of work, their fit with employee involvement and total quality management programs, and the development of more and more knowledge about how to design and operate teams. National survey data indicate that virtually all U.S. corporations currently use teams.[1] The types of teams they use differ, however. Four types can be identified: (1) parallel teams, (2) work teams, (3) project teams, and (4) management teams.[2]

Types of Teams

The four types of teams differ from each other in three major ways. First, teams either perform the basic work of the enterprise or supplement the regular work flow. Second, teams vary in the degree to which they move power, knowledge, and information to team members. Third, teams can be temporary or permanent structures. Because the four approaches differ significantly, they tend to fit specific situations, produce different results, and require different reward practices. I will describe each of the four types of teams and then discuss the type of reward practices that fit each type.

Parallel Teams

Parallel teams supplement the regular organization structure and perform problem-solving and work-improvement tasks. Examples of parallel teams include problem-solving teams, quality circles, quality improvement teams, survey feedback teams, and employee participation teams. Parallel teams are used more widely than any other team design; over 85 percent of Fortune 1000 companies have them.[3]

Improvement-oriented teams are called parallel teams because participating employees are taken out of their regular organizations and placed in separate team structures with different operating procedures. Parallel teams usually meet regularly (each week or two) and follow a defined problem-solving or quality improvement process. Employees are trained in the use of these processes. Parallel teams make recommendations that are considered by the management hierarchy. Typically, no change results unless the recommendations are approved by management.

Parallel teams often contribute useful ideas about how to improve quality and productivity. The literature on teams reports many cases in which quality improvement teams have saved companies thousands and even hundreds of thousands of dollars with their suggestions. However, parallel teams have several limitations. They have difficulty achieving organizational legitimacy, and they are not very powerful when it comes to competing for time, money, information, and other resources. They are difficult to sustain and may introduce conflict between those who are involved and those who are not. Middle managers and staff professionals who are required to respond to and implement many of the recommendations often have competing objectives and perceive the teams as creating extra work for them and treading on their turf. As a result of their weak position and the resistance they meet, even the good ideas that teams develop often are not used. Thus, over time the costs of operating parallel team programs may outweigh their benefits.

Work Teams

Work teams are responsible for producing a product or providing a service and are self-contained, identifiable work units that control the processes involved in transforming inputs into measurable outputs. Work teams are performing units in which members report through the team and are responsible for the group's performance.

Work teams are found most frequently in manufacturing settings, but they are applicable to any situation in which people are interdependent and can be made collectively responsible for part or all of a product or service. Examples include production teams, assembly teams, administrative support teams, insurance claims processing teams, and customer sales and service teams. The use of work teams has significantly increased over the past few years, with 78 percent of Fortune 1000 companies reporting that they used work teams in 1996, compared to 28 percent in 1987.[4]

In order for work team members to take responsibility for their team's performance, they must feel in control of the work processes and make key decisions about how the work is done. In actuality, the degree of management responsibility given to teams varies significantly. Typically, work teams control how a task is performed but not what tasks they do. They have discretion over work methods, the scheduling of activities, and the assignment of individuals to tasks; performance and quality standards usually are set by management. Sometimes teams are responsible for personnel functions such as performance appraisal and the hiring and firing of team members. The names used to describe work teams reflect the variability in their authority. Frequently used names are *self-managing teams, self-directed teams, autonomous teams, semiautonomous teams,* and *shared management teams.*

All or most of the knowledge and skills needed to do the work of a team usually are located in it. Typically, members are cross-trained so that they can do most or all of the tasks that fall within their team's area of responsibility. Team members tend to rotate their tasks on a regular basis.

The research on work teams suggests that installing work teams has a positive impact on performance and improves the job satisfaction of team members.[5] Most studies have documented quality improvements as well. The results with respect to safety, absenteeism, and turnover have been more equivocal. The most reliable cost savings come from the need for fewer supervisory and staff personnel. Dramatic cost savings, quality improvements, and productivity improvements are often described in the popular business literature.

Project Teams

Project teams typically involve a diverse group of knowledge workers such as design engineers, process engineers, programmers, and marketing managers who are brought together to conduct projects for a defined but typically extended period of time. These knowledge workers apply their disparate specialties to developing innovations and fulfilling customer requirements. Examples of project teams include new-product development teams, information system design teams, and new-factory design teams.

Project teams usually are assigned unique, uncertain tasks and are expected to innovate and produce; they cannot rely on standardized procedures because they are creating something new. Their products are identifiable and measurable, but measurement may be difficult because the value of their output may not be known for a long time after the work is completed. For example, the degree to which a new product meets the requirements of customers and achieves significant market share may not be known for several years.

Project teams usually have broad mandates and considerable authority. They are assigned the responsibility for making key decisions within broad strategic parameters. Within these parameters, they typically have discretion over the definition of project outcomes and work methods; members usually have the technical and business knowledge required to make project-related decisions. Project teams need to respond to the requirements of their sponsors and customers, so they must balance the need for independent thinking with responsiveness to key stakeholders and make sure that appropriate external communication occurs. Without an alignment between project team decisions and strategic objectives, projects are unlikely to be successful.

Finally, project teams are temporary structures that disband once projects are completed. In a project-based organization, members often get assigned to new projects when their current project is finished. Frequently, the membership of project teams changes over the life cycle of a project. A core team may be involved from the beginning to the end, with other contributors added as needed. Further, the composition of a project team may include contributors dedicated to it full-time and others who are part-time.

Management Teams

Without question, the least frequently used and the most poorly understood type of team is the management team. It has only recently begun to attract research and discussion. The success of work teams has raised the issue of whether the same kinds of advantages that occur when employees are organized into work teams can be obtained by creating management teams.

There are some obvious potential advantages to having a group of well-trained managers operating as a team. Often management work is unpredictable and difficult to schedule, so having an interchangeable group of individuals who can be used where and how they are needed is an advantage. Further, a cohesive management team can be a powerful integrating device that may make one or more levels of management unnecessary because the team takes on the coordinating work that is normally done by higher levels of management. Finally, management teams have the potential advantage of selectively capitalizing on the skills that are present in different managers. For example, if a manager is particularly good at doing performance management or team building, he or she can be used in this role across a number of the teams or individuals who report to the management team.

Unlike the other kinds of teams I have discussed, it is difficult to specify the characteristics of management teams. One reason for this is their relative newness; another is that they may operate at multiple levels in the organization and thus do quite different things. Increasingly, organizations are saying their top management group is a team, just as they are talking about first-level managers being in teams.[6] Clearly, the characteristics of a top-level team and those of a first-level supervisory team are likely to differ, particularly with respect to their authority and skill mix. Critics of the management team idea frequently point out that many management teams are teams in name alone. In reality they are simply groups of individuals who come together occasionally to discuss common issues.

Despite the diversity of management teams, some elements are common to all of them. Management teams typically have a stable membership, and the members are full-time, with the possible exception that some members may do some specialized functional work along with being part of the management team. The teams are permanent and are expected to provide integration, leadership, and direction for the parts of the organization that report to them. In order to be effective they also need a number of different skills.

Rewarding Team Members

A key requirement for the effective operation of any kind of team is learning on the part of team members. They need to learn how to operate as team members, and they need to learn about the organization and its work processes and methods. This is particularly true when the team is self-managing and when the individual team members need to work in a highly interdependent mode. A key issue in many types of teams is the management of lateral processes. This is often best facilitated by individuals on teams learning multiple steps in production and service processes so they can communicate with those who come before and after them in the work flow.

Person-based pay that rewards skill and knowledge development can be a powerful tool for encouraging individuals to learn the lateral skills that are necessary in order to make teams effective. Knowledge-and-skill-based pay that focuses on technical skills is particularly important if the team is doing complex knowledge work, and it is impossible for any one individual to learn everything necessary to address the kind of issues that come up in the work process. This is often true in management, project, and work teams. A typical approach that is taken when depth knowledge is needed is to identify a few individuals as depth experts and reward them with extra pay for their expertise. In the absence of a knowledge-and-skill-based pay system, there is often no way to reward this kind of depth.

Overall, because of its impact on skill development and retention, some form of knowledge-and-skill-based pay is the pay system of choice for most if not all types of teams. However, there is variation in the skill needs of the different types of teams. Thus, the importance of using knowledge-and-skill-based pay, as well as the kind that is needed, varies from one type of team to another.

Parallel Teams

Parallel problem-solving teams (for example, quality circles and suggestion teams) are often the ones that have the least need for knowledge-and-skill-based pay. They rely on individuals to contribute their ideas to various problem-solving activities. Because the team activity is not a full-time commitment for members, investing heavily in learning additional skills is often not worthwhile. A few additional skills may be needed to aid in problem solving and in developing effective group processes, but people often learn these skills without needing to be paid for doing so.

Knowledge-and-skill-based pay that encourages cross-training, like the pay-per-skill approach, can sometimes be a significant aid because it gives individuals a better overall understanding of the work process. It can also improve people's ability to problem solve, diagnose, and innovate in work system design. There remains a question, however, as to whether it is worth investing in cross-training simply so that individuals can be more effective for the short time they are active in a parallel team.

Work Teams

Self-managing production and service work teams typically have a great need for learning and development. Depending on the kind of production or service process the teams perform, this learning may involve simply cross-training so that individuals can understand the entire work process and better coordinate their work. Alternatively, it may involve developing particular kinds of management and technical expertise so that supervisors and staff support are not needed.

Because of the learning and development required in work teams, knowledge-and-skill-based pay is particularly appropriate. One of the first skill-based pay plans in the United States was installed in the team-based General Foods plant in Topeka, Kansas, over three decades ago; the plant had skill-based pay from its inception. Its approach to pay encouraged individuals to learn all of the tasks their team was asked to perform, following the pay-per-skill approach I discussed in Chapter Six. As individuals were certified as having learned a skill, they got anywhere from 25 to 50 cents added to their hourly pay rate. Over time, most reached the top pay rate; in effect, they almost doubled their pay from their entry wage rate. Skill certification was handled by a peer appraisal process, except in a few cases when technical experts were brought in to certify the more complex specialized skills.

The approach used in this plant is very similar to the ones used in many manufacturing locations today. It is used most commonly in process technology operations such as chemical plants, oil refineries, and other situations in which highly interdependent team behavior is needed. The pay-per-skill approach is typically not used in union situations. Union-organized plants tend to establish two, three, or four pay rates; over time, individuals progress from an entry wage to a fully skilled wage, and some continue progressing to an expert level. This progression is based on the learning of certain packages of skills. In that respect it is similar to the pay-per-skill approach, but instead of pricing individual skills it bundles them together, sometimes giving individuals choices about which sets of skills they learn in order to complete a package that will allow them to move to the next higher pay rate. This approach is slightly simpler to administer than the pay-per-skill approach because it involves fewer pay rates.

An alternative to skill-based pay is to establish a small number of flexible, generic job descriptions. This approach reduces some of the dysfunctional features of a traditional job-based system, but unlike skill-based pay, it does not motivate individuals to learn a specific mix of the skills that contribute to work team effectiveness.

Project Teams

A common success factor in project teams is the presence of some individuals who have knowledge of multiple functions.[7] Thus, a knowledge-and-skill-based pay system that rewards breadth learning is a particularly good fit.

When complex project work is involved, it is often impossible to have one person with a good knowledge base in all of the functions that are required to make a project successful. This doesn't mean that there can't be a number of individuals who have mastery outside a single function, however. Indeed, members' knowing several functions is critical to enabling the project team to integrate its work and to make good trade-offs among the demands of the different disciplines in developing a new product or service.

In job-based pay systems, it is hard to get individuals to learn multiple functions because there is usually no reward for doing so; indeed, there may be punishment for learning a second function. For example, an individual who learns a new function in connection with a lateral move may not achieve a higher pay grade and is further likely to lose out on merit-pay increases or bonuses because others in the new area have more expertise. Thus, in order to encourage lateral career moves, an organization may have to do more than simply use a pay-per-skill approach. Often lateral career tracks need to be developed so that individuals will be significantly rewarded for making cross-functional moves.

If a project team's work involves complex knowledge work, depth expertise in one or more areas is often critical to its success. Knowledge-based pay, which rewards people for developing deeper and deeper levels of expertise as in a technical ladder, can be a very helpful tool here. Not only does it reward people for developing important knowledge that supports the organization's core competencies, but as I mentioned in Chapter Six, it helps retain technical experts by paying them more than they would be paid in many traditional job-based structures. The typical approach here involves defining multiple levels of technical expertise in disciplines such as engineering, accounting, finance, and human resources. Each level has a set of knowledge and skill descriptors attached to it, and when individuals demonstrate that they have mastered the knowledge and skill set at a new level, they are given a promotion and a pay increase.

Management Teams

In many situations a strong case can be made for the use of knowledge-and-skill-based pay when management teams are used. Creating successful management teams often requires considerable skill on the part of managers, who must learn how to operate as a team and to become more cross-functionally knowledgeable. Traditional job-based pay is unlikely to reward this type of learning, whereas a knowledge-and-skill-based pay plan can reward the development of teamwork and team leadership skills. Similarly, cross-functional skills can be identified and rewarded. Knowledge-and-skill-based pay can also be used to encourage individuals to develop depth of expertise. This can be particularly helpful in management teams that are working in high-technology areas or functional specialty areas.

Teams and Person-Based Pay

Given the positive fit between knowledge-and-skill-based pay and teams, it is not surprising that the research evidence on the use of this approach to pay shows that it is most frequently used in team-based organizations.[8] This is particularly true with respect to work teams that carry out production and service tasks. There is less information available on how much it is used in conjunction with project and other kinds of teams. A good guess, however, is that the use of project teams tends to increase the adoption of person-based pay.

As more and more organizations move toward being team-based overall, the pressure to adopt knowledge-and-skill-based pay is likely to grow. This relates to the point I made earlier that in team-based organizations, individuals do not so much have jobs as they have roles and temporary task assignments. Given this, it is neither practical nor logical to base a person's pay on his or her job. It makes more sense to base pay on the person's value to the organization, that is, on the skills and knowledge the person has that are relevant to the organization's competencies and capabilities. This can also encourage people to learn skills and develop knowledge that can help them become more effective team members.

Table 9.1 summarizes what I have said about the applicability of person-based pay to teams. As can be seen, slightly different uses of pay for skills and knowledge fit each of these types of teams. Thus, the challenge is to design skill-and-knowledge-based pay systems that fit the type of team that is the focal point of the design process.

Performance-Based Rewards for Teams

Because teams differ in their characteristics, objectives, and structure, no single pay-for-performance approach fits all of them. Thus, in the remainder of this chapter I will discuss separately how each type of team should be rewarded for performance.

Parallel Teams

Parallel teams do not represent a fundamental change in the structure of organizations, thus they have the fewest implications for

Table 9.1. Teams and Person-Based Pay.

Type of Team	Person-Based Pay
Parallel	If necessary, use to encourage cross-training and development of team skills.
Work teams	Use to motivate cross-training, development of self-management skills, and some depth skills. Retain most skilled team members.
Project	Use to motivate development of depth expertise and cross-functional knowledge. Retain critical knowledge assets.
Management	Use to motivate development of depth and team expertise, as well as cross-functional knowledge and lateral career tracks.

performance-based rewards. Indeed, it is possible to argue that no pay-for-performance system is needed to support the activities of parallel teams. However, there is evidence that rewards can and should be used to motivate effective problem-solving team performance.

Advocates of participative management have suggested for a long time that the Scanlon plan and other gainsharing plans that will be discussed in Chapter Ten fit extremely well with the use of problem-solving teams.[9] There is a history of more than sixty years of combining suggestion groups with the type of cost-saving bonuses that are part of gainsharing plans. Virtually every review of the research on these plans argues that they improve the economic performance of an organization.[10] They work particularly well when gainsharing is combined with open financial-information systems and participative decision making. The major motivational weakness of gainsharing plans is that the line of sight between a suggestion and the size of the bonus is weak. A group can make a major improvement breakthrough and receive only a small bonus in return because the savings are shared among all employees in an organization and because many other factors influence the size of the bonus.

Profit-sharing, stock option, and stock ownership plans that cover all employees can also be supportive of problem-solving groups. They distribute financial rewards that may be slightly related to the effectiveness of the problem-solving groups and to the implementation of their ideas. Their major weakness, of course, is line of sight, and consequently they do not have a significant impact on the effectiveness of problem-solving groups.

Donnelly Corporation, a successful auto parts manufacturer, is a good example of a company that for decades has worked hard to relate its problem-solving team activity to the size of team members' bonuses. Through extensive education and communication programs, Donnelly has done a good job of informing the workforce both about the economics of the business and about the financial impact of the suggestions that the workforce develops through its problem-solving meetings.

Donnelly is not an isolated example. A number of other Scanlon companies, including Dana Corporation and Herman Miller, have used the same approach. It is hard to determine exactly how good a line of sight they have developed, but there is little doubt that the logic of bonuses for everyone based on improvement suggestions is well accepted and generally seems to be meaningful.

The alternative to gainsharing and profit sharing is to give bonuses, stock, recognition rewards, or other valued rewards to teams for their suggestions. A number of organizations have used this approach, which, in most respects, is simply a group version of the suggestion award programs that reward individuals for submitting suggestions. An estimated savings amount is calculated, and the team that contributes the idea is given a percentage of the estimated savings.

Group suggestion reward programs can have a strong line of sight but can lead to a number of problems. One problem is that often the estimated savings are not realized, so individuals are rewarded even though the company does not gain. Further, individuals may feel they are not rewarded fairly when they get only a small percentage of the savings. There are usually issues of who should be included among the recipients of the bonus. Finally, to be useful most suggestions have to be accepted and implemented by many people. The typical suggestion program does not reward people for accepting and further developing suggestions, so they may not be motivated to implement the suggestion. Quite the opposite, of course, is true with gainsharing and profit-sharing plans in which no one gains unless an idea is successfully implemented and gains are created.

Clearly incompatible with parallel suggestion teams is the use of approaches that reward individuals for their suggestions. These approaches are in direct conflict with the idea of teams developing ideas. They reward the wrong kind of behavior and compete directly with group suggestion and problem-solving approaches. When rewards for individuals have been used along with rewards for problem-solving teams, individuals have been known to claim ownership of ideas that were developed as part of the group problem-solving process, sometimes submitting them through individual suggestion reward programs in hopes of getting a bonus. Not surprisingly, with individual reward programs in place, people are much less willing to share their ideas and thoughts in a group setting than they are when only collective rewards for groups developing a suggestion are offered.

A number of organizations use a recognition approach to rewarding parallel teams for their successes. Unfortunately, there is virtually no research evidence to indicate how effective recognition rewards are in this application. The variety of recognition vehicles used is enormous. Some companies emphasize appearances before senior executives, while others give symbols that, in some cases, involve significant outlays of money (for example, clocks, TVs). Although little research has been done on recognition programs, my guess is that they can be powerful if they are used astutely. The key is to give rewards only when groups accomplish something significant and to deliver rewards that are valued by the group.

Determining what is valued by a group can be a challenge in recognition programs. Obviously, there are cultural differences in how much various types of recognition rewards are valued. For example, there may be differences within a group as to the value of a trip to a ball game or a chance to present an idea to the CEO. With the exception of the issue of how much recognition rewards are valued, most of the other considerations with recognition programs are the same as those involved in giving financial rewards for producing an idea.

Xerox Corporation provides a good example of a company that has extensively used recognition to reward quality improvement teams. They run a high-quality, companywide TV broadcast that features the improvement ideas of carefully selected teams. There is no question that this is a powerful reward and that teams compete hard for the honor of being on the telecast and receiving the attention and recognition that it provides. It helps that the CEO of Xerox hosts the program and is knowledgeable about the suggestions.

Work Teams

There are a number of distinctly different ways to reward performance when work teams are used. One is to reward the individual team members for their performance. A second is to reward the teams for their performance. A third is to reward team performance indirectly by rewarding organizational performance. Additional alternatives can be created by using a combination of the first three.

Perhaps the most common way to reward the members of work teams today is to appraise their individual performance. Instead of rewarding the team as a whole, organizations simply add a dimension to the performance appraisal of individuals that focuses on how good a team member they are. This usually counts toward their overall appraisal score and determines the amount of pay increase or bonus they get. In essence, it continues the individual pay-for-performance practices of most organizations but adapts them slightly to a team environment.

In several ways, rewarding individuals for being good team members creates conflicting motivations that can be self-canceling with respect to effective team behavior. It asks individuals to compete for a given amount of money but changes the basis of the competition from individual performance to performance as a team member. In other words, individuals end up competing with other team members for who is the most helpful, cooperative, and best contributor. This keeps the performance focus on the individual rather than the team and does little to get individuals to focus on how effectively the team is performing. Thus, it makes sense to reward individuals on the basis of their performance as individual team members only when work teams do not need highly interdependent behavior in order to be effective.

When a reward system formally appraises and rewards individual performance, the pressure is reduced on the team to appraise and deal with poor performers. Indeed, when the performance appraisal used is a forced-distribution rating system, it becomes in the best interests of individuals to have some poor performers on their teams. Thus, they are much less likely to encourage and support performance improvement on the part of poor performers and to create a team of "all-stars" than when there is a collective pay situation in which poor performers hurt everyone's opportunity to earn a bonus. When teams are rewarded collectively, they often handle the problems associated with someone who is not contributing their fair share to the team's performance. They also, in many cases, will recognize and reward the best performers because it is in everyone's best interest to have good performers on the team.

It is unlikely that everyone in a typical group or team will accept the idea of having only team or collective pay for performance and no individual pay for performance. This brings us back to the point I made in Chapter Four that in a team-based environment, people who are focused on getting rewarded for individual performance should not be put on teams. They belong in individual jobs with individual incentive-pay plans.

There are three ways of directly rewarding the performance of an entire work team. First, rewards can be tied to team performance through the use of a merit-pay or incentive-pay system that bases salary increases or bonuses on team performance. Second, special awards can be provided to teams in order to recognize outstanding team performance. Third, a gainsharing or profit-sharing plan can be used that pays all teams the same bonus amount or pays bonuses that are funded by the overall plan but adjusted to reflect the performance of particular teams.

Team Performance Pay

The most powerful way to motivate team performance is to establish objectives and metrics for successful team performance and link rewards to team success. Performance pay in the form of salary increases or bonuses is then distributed equally to team members based on the results of a team performance appraisal. In order for team performance pay to work, there must be clear and explicit objectives, accepted measures, and good feedback—the same conditions I reviewed in Chapter Eight concerning individual performance appraisal. Team performance appraisals can also provide opportunities for teams to conduct self-appraisals that are based on customer evaluations and other performance measures that are used in the determination of team ratings.

If the work of team members is not highly interdependent, it may make sense to combine team and individual pay for performance. A bonus pool can be created, based on team performance, and divided among the team members using the kind of measures of individual performance that I discussed in the previous chapter. If this is done, it is essential that managers solicit input from team members about the relative contributions of individual members to ensure the validity and completeness of the data.

A mature work team may be able to use a team evaluation meeting to reward individuals for their contributions to the team's performance. The decision process is more likely to be effective if team members assess team performance before they assess individual performance so that team performance sets the framework for individual performance. By having teams do appraisals of individuals in which they divide up a pool of money that originally was generated by the effectiveness of the team, individuals are rewarded for being cooperative in producing the bonus pool but still recognized as individuals.

Team bonus plans can also be created that are driven by formulas and objective measures. Selectron Corporation provides an interesting example of an organization that decided to use formula-driven team bonuses in order to support the creation of self-directed production work teams. Selectron is a very successful Silicon Valley high-tech corporation that is a contract manufacturer of circuit boards and electronic products. It also packages software and is well known for its high-quality products and rapid growth. Not only is Selectron one of the few high-technology firms to win the U.S. National Quality Award (1991), but in 1997 it became the first company to win the award twice.

Despite its success, the company decided in the early 1990s that it needed to improve its performance because of growing competition and a shrinking competitive advantage. It set up self-directed production teams that were charged with the responsibility for an entire part of the production process. In its California manufacturing operations Selectron created 240 teams.

When Selectron began its movement to teams, a companywide variable pay plan was already in place. It had begun in 1985 and involved discretionary bonuses that focused more on effort than on performance. The plan had no ability to focus on team performance and did not support the right team behaviors. So a participative design process was begun to create a new pay plan. The team-based plan that resulted was installed in 1995.[11]

The new team-based bonus system is funded by measures of location profit and return on assets. It provides a quarterly bonus payment to the members of all teams. The company set the maximum bonus that individuals can earn at a conservative 5 percent of base pay. The amount the members of teams receive is based on the quality of the team's output and productivity, as measured against a team goal; the members share equally in the payout. Temporary employees participate in the plan, as do nonexempt employees who are not on teams. Members not on teams are expected to set individual goals so that they can receive bonuses.

The goals of individual teams are based on a negotiation process with the team manager that leads to the setting of different goals for each team. This is required because of the different products that are produced by the teams.

One of the most unusual features of the Selectron variable pay plan is that it was participatively developed in order to ensure commitment to the plan on the part of team members as well as managers. There was also an effort to be sure that the development process fit the overall management style of the organization. An extensive communications and training program was used to introduce the plan. After the plan's introduction an extensive meeting and communications program was used to develop a more in-depth understanding of the plan.

The results of the pay plan implementation have been positive. The quality and productivity performance of the teams has improved. In addition, overall satisfaction with the pay system has improved significantly because individuals feel that they have more control over how much they are paid. The pay plan has also encouraged individuals to learn more about the organization's financial—and overall—performance. A key element of the plan is the public posting of team goals, which has stimulated teams to reach their goals and has led to peer and manager recognition for performance.

Interestingly, the group providing the biggest obstacle to the successful installation of the variable pay plan was the managers. They saw it as causing them to lose power and raised a number of concerns that slowed the implementation process. The organization repeatedly stressed to the managers that the changes were needed to meet competition and that it was critical to the long-term success of the organization that this plan be installed and be successful. The financial results seem to justify the installation of the plan. Among other things, the defect rate went down substantially, saving the organization $18 million in the first nine months the plan was in place.

Overall, the movement to a team-based pay plan at Selectron seems to have improved the fit between the pay system and the organization design and management style. This occurred because the company shifted what was measured and how teams were rewarded. The success of the plan is also likely due to the involvement that occurred in the design of the plan and to the extensive communication and training process associated with its implementation.

The experiences of Motorola highlight a major problem with team-based bonuses. For years Motorola had team-based incentive plans in many of its manufacturing facilities. The bonuses were often quite large and were targeted to meeting specific performance objectives. In many cases, the bonuses did motivate the teams to perform well as teams but did a poor job of recognizing the interdependencies that existed among the teams. Because Motorola tends to have large manufacturing facilities that do relatively complex work, its teams often need to cooperate with each other in order to produce products. They also need to share a number of key services such as maintenance and technical support. Because of the team incentive plans, a considerable amount of conflict developed among the teams over who got first access to help and support; in addition, there was tremendous focus on the inequities that were perceived to exist when some teams got large bonuses (30 percent or larger bonuses were possible), and others did not.

Ultimately, Motorola decided to abandon team-based incentive plans because they failed to produce a cooperative environment in the workplace and caused too many parts of the organization to optimize their performance at the cost of the performance of the overall organization. The lesson from Motorola is clear. Strong team incentive plans should be used only where teams operate relatively autonomously with respect to their production and service needs.

The experience of Levi Strauss with work-team-based bonuses is a graphic illustration of both their strengths and their limitations. Until 1992 virtually all Levi Strauss employees in the garment manufacturing process were on individual incentive plans. They were paid on a piecework basis and did just one task, over and over, for an entire day. This created a highly repetitive but in some ways efficient work process. Employees who spent day after day sewing pockets on jeans became quite skilled at it. The variations in performance usually resulted simply as a result of how motivated they were. Because of the incentive plan, by and large they were quite motivated; as a result production was relatively high in the company's piecework plants.

In 1992 Levi Strauss began to change to work teams and team-based bonuses. There were a number of reasons for this, including the management philosophy and values of Robert Haas, the CEO and owner of the company. He believed strongly in having good working conditions and in employee involvement. He heard about self-managing work teams and thought they were more in line with his values than the traditional individual jobs approach to manufacturing. He was also concerned about a particular problem with the jobs in Levi's plants that teams potentially could solve. The repetitive motion used in assembly tasks in the garment industry often leads to employee injuries and to high worker compensation costs. He hoped that by rotating production tasks within teams of employees, the amount of repetition and hence the number of employee injuries could be reduced.

The conversion to teams proved to be a mixed blessing. On the positive side, as might be expected from the fact that there were team-based bonuses, strong peer pressure developed on all employees to be good performers. The pay of some previously outstanding performers actually dropped with the movement to a team bonus. They in turn put pressure on the poor performers to hold up their end of the team's performance so that everyone could get a good bonus. Workers did switch jobs, and this provided relief from the repetitiveness of the individual piecework approach. The teams were also able to reduce some work-in-process inventory and to respond more quickly to the market's need for particular styles and colors of clothes. Overall speed and the lateral management processes in the organization improved.

The downside of the movement to team-based pay was also significant. The pressure on poor performers often reached an unacceptable level, and they became overstressed by the system. This resulted in problems with worker disability claims. An overall decrease in productivity was another result. Despite the peer pressure, the strong line of sight that existed with the individual incentive plan simply provided more incentive than did the group bonus plan. In addition, of course, employees had to learn multiple tasks, and because of the learning curve and start-up time on new tasks they often were not as productive as employees who simply did one task hour after hour, day after day. Interestingly, this fit well with my research on employees who manufacture surgical sutures. Like garment assembly, it is a very simple, repetitive, individual task.

The movement to teams at Levi Strauss clearly illustrates the problems with using team incentives in situations where independent, repetitive tasks exist. When all is said and done, it usually doesn't make sense to use teams and collective incentives when the work consists of independent, repetitive tasks; teams simply do not add value. Indeed, they may actually reduce production and increase the number of management problems because they create interdependencies and complexities that were not there before and that do not help get work done any better.

Special Awards

The second way of linking pay to team performance is through the use of special reward and recognition programs. In contrast to appraisals with goals and formula-driven approaches, they usually reward exceptional performance after it has occurred on an unscheduled basis. They can be motivating and enhance team cohesiveness. A certain pride comes from being associated with a successful team, and public recognition can solidify it.

In order to be effective, special awards should be used only to recognize truly special team achievements. Extraordinary performance is likely to be rare; therefore, special rewards are often best used to supplement and not to substitute for other team pay-for-performance systems.

Organization-Based Pay for Performance

The use of gainsharing, goalsharing, profit-sharing, and stock plans constitutes the third major approach that can be used to provide rewards to teams for performance. As I will discuss in the next chapter, they focus on the combined performance of teams. These plans typically give the same amount of reward to all teams in a particular work unit or location. They suffer from a poor line of sight but can be effective in motivating team performance and may be the best choice if the work of teams is highly interdependent. The greater the interdependence between work teams, the more pay-for-performance systems should operate at the organizational level.

Choosing an Approach

In choosing among the different approaches to rewarding work teams, it is important to remember that, as the Motorola example highlights, rewarding a work team for its separate performance is not always appropriate. The critical issue here is the degree of integration and differentiation. If the team is not highly autonomous (differentiated), providing rewards at the team level may be counterproductive. When there are critical interdependencies between a team and other parts of the organization that need to be accounted for, rewarding a team for its own performance may push differentiation too far.

There are many types of interdependency among teams. For example, work teams in manufacturing plants often work separate shifts, but what happens during one shift affects other shifts. In addition, interdependencies with staff groups may be important. When a work team develops its way of doing things and members become close, members may become myopic in their understanding of the needs of the broader organization; suboptimization and an unwillingness to share learnings can be the result. The use of a gainsharing or profit-sharing plan that rewards team members based on the performance of the larger organizational unit can serve to integrate the team into the rest of the organization and act as an offset to the strong cohesiveness that tends to develop in work teams.

In general, an organization composed of work teams needs to make sure its pay-for-performance systems motivate the right kinds of team performance. As I will discuss further in Chapter Eleven, this often is best done through a mix of team-level and organization-level pay-for-performance systems.

Project Teams

Project teams present a particularly interesting challenge for reward systems, often requiring a reward system that is specifically designed to support them. Pay-for-performance systems that focus on individuals and measure and reward performance on an annual schedule are a poor fit with project teams. The obvious first choice for motivating a project team is a reward system that establishes measures for successful group performance and sets rewards that are tied to the accomplishments of the group. It also is desirable to have the rewards distributed at the time the team completes its project. Thus, one popular and effective approach to rewarding project teams is to give spot bonus awards when they complete their projects.

Rewarding a project team's performance may be particularly difficult if, as is often true, the membership of the team changes during projects. It may not make sense to reward everyone equally when some people are there for 10 percent of the team's activities, whereas others may be there for 100 percent of the time. Unequal rewards are a possibility, but it can be difficult to determine how large they should be because the amount of time spent on the team may not be a good measure of someone's contribution to a project.

One example of a kind of pay bonus plan that can be created for project teams is provided by a high-technology firm. They do new-product design by creating cross-functional, dedicated teams that are charged with developing a new product. At the beginning of the design process, teams are given a number of milestone targets to meet, and the members are told to dedicate their efforts to the development process until the new product is ready for manufacturing. In the case of this technology company, specific bonus amounts are tied to reaching the key milestones in the product development process. Equal dollar amounts are given to all members of the product development teams when the goals are met. The bonuses can add an additional 20 to 30 percent to the employees' annual pay, so the incentive is more than just a symbolic one. The incentive plan, however, ends before the product is actually in the marketplace, so the employees are not rewarded based on the ultimate success of the product.

One alternative or complement to rewarding project group performance at the end of each project is to rely on a gainsharing profit-sharing plan or stock ownership system that covers a total organizational unit. This may be the preferred alternative to rewarding individual teams when, in fact, the teams' activities have a major impact on the effectiveness of the unit. It also may be the preferred alternative if measuring the performance of individual teams is difficult. It clearly makes the most sense when organizations want their project team employees to have a long-term, organizationwide focus.

When individuals operate relatively independently, it may be desirable to focus on individual performance in a project team environment. The best approach to doing this is to measure the contributions of individuals to the success of the overall project. In many cases peer ratings, as well as customer satisfaction ratings, need to be used. Peer ratings are particularly critical because, in most project teams, peers are in the best position to assess the contribution of team members.

In organizations where individuals work on multiple project teams over the course of a year, individuals may accumulate a number of ratings that reflect their contributions to each project on which they worked. Their performance-pay treatment then becomes a "simple" derivative of how effectively they performed on each of the projects in which they participated. Alternatively, spot bonuses can be paid at the end of each project.

Management Teams

Many of the same issues that arise when project teams are paid for performance also arise when management teams are paid that way. A major difference exists, however, because management teams are usually permanent teams, so spot bonuses and one-time awards are less relevant. They also may not be as highly interdependent as project teams, which means that a greater possibility exists for rewarding individual performance. Like project teams and work teams, they can either be rewarded as stand-alone entities based on performance appraisals or measures of team performance, or they can be rewarded based on a larger, organizationwide gainsharing, profit-sharing, or stock-based plan. The choice among these is essentially one of the degree to which line of sight and motivation are important versus the degree to which integration of the total work unit is important.

Pay-for-performance plans that focus on an individual team's performance tend to separate that team from the rest of the organization. In the case of management teams, this can be a critical problem because it gives the management team a different reward orientation than the teams and individuals who report to it. Of course, if the management team is supervising relatively unrelated operations or business units, it may make sense to measure and reward the management team separately. However, if the success of a unit they are supervising depends on a high level of integration among the members of the management team and the people who report to them, rewarding them separately does not make sense. Instead, they should be included in either a corporationwide or business unit–wide plan that treats them the same as it treats the teams and individuals who report to them.

Unfortunately, there is no "right" approach to rewarding management teams for performance. What clearly is right is considering the degree to which the team itself needs to be integrated and how integrated the team needs to be with other parts of the organization. Once this is established, it should be used to determine the degree to which the team is rewarded separately or as part of an integrated unit that may include the part of the organization that reports to the team or, in fact, the total organization.

Summary: Rewarding Teams

As is illustrated by the Selectron, Motorola, and Levi Strauss examples, in order for teams to be optimally effective a reward system is needed that recognizes the kinds of behavior and skills that are needed for teams to be successful. Because teams differ, no reward system design is likely to be universally effective. The key is to design a reward system that fits the characteristics of the team and the organizational context in which it operates. This is not a simple task. It requires choosing among the major pay system design options based on the outcomes they will produce when they are applied to a particular type of team in a specific environment.

Table 9.2 summarizes our conclusions so far about the fit between approaches to rewarding performance and four different types of teams. It clearly makes the point that one size does not fit all types of teams. Key to choosing the correct approach is the measurement of performance and interdependence. Valid measures of performance need to be available, and the reward system needs to reinforce the key interdependencies among individuals and among teams; otherwise, the reward system may reward the wrong kind of performance and do more harm than good.

Figure 9.1 shows where different pay-for-performance approaches fit, taking into account the characteristics of individuals. The figure shows four quadrants based on two dimensions: the degree to which the work is independent or interdependent and the orientation of individuals in that work area. One orientation includes highly individualistic people who value individual rewards and who like to work independently. The other includes collectivists who enjoy working with others and value collective and social rewards.

Table 9.2. Teams and Pay for Performance.

Type of Team	Pay for Performance
Parallel	Use gainsharing or other business unit plan to reward savings. Use recognition reward plan for teams, as appropriate.
Production and service	Use team bonuses or business unit bonuses if teams are interdependent. Use individual bonuses that are based on peer evaluations.
Project	Use bonuses based on project success. Also use profit-sharing and stock plans.
Management	Use team or business unit bonuses. Also use profit-sharing and stock-based plans.

Figure 9.1. Approaches to Team Rewards.

	Work	
	Independent	Interdependence
Individualists	Individual bonuses	Misfit
Individuals		
Collectivists	Misfit	Team pay for performance

The figure indicates that the individual work situation and individualists should have an individual pay-for-performance, bonus-type plan. Collectivists, with interdependent work, need to have the kind of team and organizational rewards that treat everyone the same. When there is misalignment between the nature of the individuals and the nature of work, my recommendation is to pay according to the nature of the work. The work is the major determinant of what kind of behavior is needed in a situation; the reward system must therefore fit it. If an incentive is large enough, it may overcome the inclination to be either collectivists or individualists. It can also eventually lead to a self-selection situation in which collectivists leave the individual reward system and individualists leave the collectivist reward system so that everyone is in one of the "fit" boxes.

Conclusion

It is hardly surprising that the traditional approaches to pay do not fit a team-based environment. They were designed to support and reward individual behavior. As long as they remain in this mode, they are at best neutral and in most cases counterproductive to creating effective teams.

Two general approaches to pay do seem to potentially fit best with teams. The first is an emphasis on paying the individual instead of the job, and the second is pay for performance that focuses on collective performance more than individual performance. Taken together, these two approaches can encourage individuals to learn the right skills to make teams effective and can motivate the right type of performance focus on the part of teams and organizations.

Chapter Ten

Rewarding Organizational Excellence

Reward systems that tie pay to organizational performance take a variety of forms, each of which has advantages and disadvantages. This chapter will review the impact on organizational performance of four different approaches to rewarding organizational performance. The first two, gainsharing and goalsharing, usually focus on business units or plants within large organizations. The other two, profit sharing and stock-based programs, typically focus on the performance of the total organization. Before looking in detail at each of the four, I would like to make a few general observations about the advantages and disadvantages of the approaches.

Impact of Organizational Rewards

The major advantage of pay plans that reward organizational performance is the ability to align individual rewards with the strategic performance of the business. This alignment is often better and more easily created at the organization level than at the team or individual level because there are fewer measurement problems at the organization level. An organization's key strategic objectives can usually be stated in terms of regularly collected corporate, financial, and operational measures. This creates the possibility of relating reward amounts directly to the degree to which organizational objectives are accomplished. With team and individual pay-for-performance plans, the organizational objectives often must be converted into appropriate behaviors at the individual and group levels and measures developed for them. Not only does this represent extra work it often is difficult to do because the organization's agenda does not always translate easily into measures that can be used at the individual or team level.

In many respects the major advantage associated with paying for organizational performance is also the major problem with it. It is often difficult for individuals to see how their behavior relates to measures of organizational performance, especially in large organizations and when complex financial measures are used. This is the other side of the coin with respect to paying individuals based on organizational goals and performance. Just as it is hard for managers to translate strategic goals into individual measures of performance, it is often difficult for individuals to see how their behavior directly affects whether or not the organization accomplishes its strategic objectives.

Because the connection between behavior and organizational performance is difficult to establish, individuals and teams often do not develop a clear line of sight between their behavior and the rewards they can receive as a result of organizational performance. Hence the motivational potential of the pay system is small or nonexistent. The research on motivation I reviewed in Chapter Three does suggest one way to offset a poor line of sight. It argues that with very large rewards, individuals will be motivated even if the line of sight is relatively weak. As I mentioned there, this is demonstrated every day as people buy lottery tickets and gamble. Large rewards seem to offset the low probability of winning. There is of course a serious problem with offering very large rewards: they are very expensive.

Because they reward a large number of people in a common manner, organizational pay-for-performance systems can have the effect of integrating an organization. They end up creating a common fate for the entire workforce of an organization, and this can have a positive effect on the degree to which people cooperate across a wide variety of functions and units. In this respect they are like team-based incentives but on a much larger scale. They are able to integrate teams, plants, and total organizations, not just small groups of individuals.

Because of their common impact across an organization, rewards for organizational performance can also have a positive impact on an organization's culture. They can help focus the organization on a common set of goals and create a sense of the importance of individuals supporting each other and working together. Again, there is some similarity here to the impact of team-based reward systems, but organizational reward systems have an impact on the total organization's culture.

Depending on how they are paid out and how large the rewards are, organizational reward systems can affect attraction and retention. On the attraction side companies like Lincoln Electric and Hewlett-Packard, which have long histories of paying large bonuses, are extremely popular places to work, in part because their bonus payments take their total pay package well above market. Another example is Microsoft. It is a very popular place to work, at least in part because of its generous stock option plan, which gives employees the potential to become wealthy. From 1990 to 1998 it issued 807 million stock options to employees and created a number of millionaires.

Organizational pay-for-performance plans can also have a positive effect on retention if individuals believe the plans will continue to pay off. They can be particularly effective in retention if they are paid out in ways that require continued organizational membership.

One potential weakness of organizational pay-for-performance systems is that they typically do not differentially attract and retain individuals. Because they are usually paid out on an equal basis to all employees or as a percentage of base salary, they retain the best as well as the poor performers. Of course this weakness can be eliminated by doing individual performance assessments and using them as the basis for determining how much of an organization-wide reward pool each person will receive.

Gainsharing Plans

The best-known gainsharing plan is the Scanlon plan, which was championed by Joe Scanlon, a union official of the steelworkers union. Much of its initial implementation occurred in the steel industry during the 1940s and 1950s. In the 1960s and 1970s it spread to a number of different types of manufacturing establishments and to some nonmanufacturing locations. Other gainsharing plans include the Improshare plan and the Rucker plan, as well as an infinite variety of custom-designed plans that have been developed for particular work situations. Approximately 40 percent of the largest U.S. corporations have at least one gainsharing plan.[1] It is beyond the scope of this discussion to go into the details of how the various gainsharing plans are structured; a number of books outline these in considerable detail.[2] It is worthwhile, however, to review the general principles on which gainsharing plans are based and to consider where and when they should be used.

Design of Gainsharing Plans

The Scanlon plan and its many derivatives emphasize a win-win philosophy with respect to bonus plans. At the core of this philosophy is the belief that if the employees of an organization work together to improve organizational performance, they can make the organization more successful. The gainsharing philosophy goes on to argue that employees are entitled to a share of the improvements that result from their efforts. Gainsharing plans usually accept the current performance of the organization as the starting point for the plan; they then split the financial gains that come from any performance improvement between the workforce and the organization. The amount of the gain that is shared with the employees varies from as little as 20 percent to as much as 70 or 80 percent of the dollar value of the gains. In most plans the savings in these areas are split 50–50 between the employees and the organization.

In order to create a meaningful line of sight, gainsharing plans tend to focus on organizational units of less than a thousand employees and to measure performance outcomes that are controllable by the workforce. For example, in manufacturing plants they usually focus on such controllable manufacturing costs as labor, scrap, and the use of materials and supplies. The message to the employees is clear: if, through your collective effort, you can reduce the costs that are under your control, it is a win for the organization and a win for you. All employees in the unit are rewarded the same; there is no attention to individual or team performance in determining the amount of the gainsharing payout. Payments to employees are usually made as a percentage of base pay, but sometimes equal dollar amounts are paid out.

Gainsharing has been used in many large organizations where it has been installed in one or more plants or locations. Monsanto,

Dana, Eaton, Weyerhaeuser, and 3M are typical large-company users of gainsharing. They have designed unique gainsharing plans for some or most of their manufacturing locations. This means that each plant or location has its unique measures, and bonus payments are based on the plant's performance. The expectation is that this will produce a line of sight that is sufficient to create a meaningful and motivating plan.

In many respects the Scanlon plan and some of its early derivatives were among the first change efforts to recognize the importance of moving power, information, knowledge, and rewards down in an organization in order to create a viable, motivational situation for all employees. Joe Scanlon emphasized that employees will be motivated only if they are given an opportunity to influence and understand an organization's financial performance. Thus, he called for open communication of financial information and for giving employees input with respect to how the organization operates. His model of employee involvement was essentially a problem-solving suggestion model rather than a self-managing work teams model. He suggested using teams to screen and implement suggestions. Recent installations of gainsharing plans have emphasized their fit with more advanced levels of employee involvement such as self-managing work teams, flat organizations, and "open book" management.

The most difficult issue with gainsharing plans involves maintaining their impact over time. Just as is true with other pay-for-performance plans, particularly critical is the management of the standard against which current performance is compared in order to calculate the bonus. The early plans emphasized the importance of keeping the standard the same unless there are major changes in products, technology, or capital investment. The rationale for this is simple and sensible: if the standard is raised every time employees improve performance, they will quickly lose their incentive to improve performance. They will realize that they are in fact working themselves out of an incentive every time they improve. In short, no good deed goes unpunished. Gainsharing argues that as long as performance is above standard, both sides win; therefore it is reasonable to continue to pay employees bonuses when their performance exceeds its historic level.

It is hard to disagree with the rationale underlying the idea of a fixed historic standard—with one exception. How the organization's performance compares with that of competitors is important. There usually is no problem with paying bonuses as long as the performance of a gainsharing organization exceeds that of its competitors. But problems may arise when performance exceeds the plan's historic standard but falls below or at the performance level of competing organizations. In essence the organization can end up paying a bonus for a performance level that is not competitive and, as a result, end up with low performance and high costs—not exactly a winning business formula. Thus, in the case of long-running gainsharing plans it may be necessary to adjust the standard so that it recognizes the improvements that are being made by competitors and puts the bonus at an affordable level.

When the standard is raised, it must be done in such a way that employees don't feel they are always working their way out of a bonus. Accomplishing this is not easy, but it can be done if organizations have good competitive benchmarking data and have employees who are aware of the overall success of the business versus its competitors. This is another argument for giving employees information that enables them to understand the economics of the business and its competitive environment.

Impact of Gainsharing

A number of studies have looked at the success of gainsharing plans. All report positive results. Typical of the findings is the conclusion that approximately 80 percent of the gainsharing plans in the United States have produced positive financial performance results and have lasted at least three to five years.[3] Some of the most successful examples, such as the plans in Herman Miller, Donnelly Corporation, and the Dana Corporation, have lasted for decades. The plans appear to have provided a significant competitive advantage and have helped these organizations achieve good financial results. There are many fewer examples of successful gainsharing plans in the service sector; the plans' focus on operating cost and historic standards seems to fit better in the manufacturing world than in the service sector.

Gainsharing plans are not necessarily universal attractors of employees. However, as I pointed out earlier, like other variable payment plans they may be good attractors of the right kinds of employees to work in a variable pay environment. Because there is no guaranteed payout with a gainsharing plan, employees who are looking for security and stable wages are not likely to be particularly interested in organizations that offer them, particularly if base pay is low. However, employees who are inclined to believe that companies are fair, like pay for performance, and are willing to take some risk may very well be attracted to companies with gainsharing plans, particularly if they are shown the history of the plan and it has a positive track record.

Clearly, gainsharing is not for every organization. It seems to fit best in relatively stable operations where medium- to small-sized organizational units can be identified that have good performance measures. Stability is important because it makes setting a historic standard easier and makes it worthwhile to develop the sometimes complex and extensive measures that are part of the payout formula. Organizations also need to be willing to engage in at least some form of employee involvement that shares business information, educates employees in the economics of business, and encourages suggestions. Without moving information, knowledge, and power downward, it is unlikely that a significant line of sight will develop and that the plan will be successful. It also helps to create a joint labor-management steering committee to operate the gainsharing plan because it builds trust.

Goalsharing

Goalsharing plans are becoming increasingly popular. Even though goalsharing plans did not start becoming popular until the early 1990s, they may now be more common than gainsharing plans. In some ways they are similar to gainsharing plans; indeed, sometimes they are actually called gainsharing plans. However, they are significantly different in important ways and thus warrant a different name and separate consideration.

Design of Plans

Like gainsharing plans, goalsharing plans pay bonuses when performance is above a standard. They also usually cover most or all employees in a particular company or business unit. They are most frequently installed in part of a company rather than throughout.

They are particularly popular when the business environment is rapidly changing and the company wants to target a particular kind of performance improvement for a limited period of time.

The key differences between goalsharing plans and gainsharing plans are in their stability and approach to establishing measures and standards. Gainsharing plans thrive on stability. They tend to use the same measures and the same standards year after year. They argue that this builds trust, understanding, and behavioral routines.

The logic of goalsharing plans is quite different from gainsharing. Goalsharing plans seek to leverage an organization's business strategy by measuring performance on key strategic objectives. Standards and measures are set on an annual basis and are not necessarily based on historic performance or what was measured and rewarded in past years. They are more likely to be based on measures of what it takes to implement a strategic plan and to be successful in the current business environment. Typically, goalsharing plans establish three, four, or more goals in areas such as quality, customer satisfaction, delivery time, cost, and sometimes profitability. They then tie specific bonus amounts to achieving one or more levels of performance on each of these measures. The plans typically last for a year; at the end of the year a different set of measures and standards may be established as part of a "new" plan, or the old plan may continue.

Goalsharing plans are a particularly nimble reward system. They can quickly change focus as an organization's business strategy changes, and they are usually easy to explain, so they can be used effectively by an organization that is undergoing change and by organizations that have not had a history of employee involvement. Because of their flexibility, they can react to turbulence in the external environment and strategy changes better than gainsharing plans can.

Goalsharing plans can and often do reward things that do not have an immediate or direct dollar payoff for an organization. Whereas gainsharing plans are based on measures of dollar amounts saved, goalsharing plans simply tie measures to bonus amounts. Thus, goalsharing plans can pay bonuses for things that typically are not measured in dollars (for example, quality, customer satisfaction, and accident rates). There is, of course, a risk that bonus payments will be made for performance improvements or results that do not actually affect the financial performance of the company. Examples of this are customer satisfaction and on-time delivery. It is common wisdom that they have a financial payoff, but it is often hard to quantify their impact on a company's financial performance.

Continental Airlines provides an interesting example of using a goalsharing bonus to target the development of a strategically important behavior. In 1994 Continental was providing very poor service to its customers. Its planes were late, baggage was mishandled, and complaints were at an industry high. When new CEO Gordan Bethune took over, he decided to focus on improving customer service. In January 1995 he announced a new plan. Each month that Continental's on-time performance was good enough to place Continental in the top five of all airlines, each employee would receive $65. In February 80 percent of Continental's planes arrived on time—good enough to rank it fourth and slightly ahead of the industry average of 79 percent. Every employee got a check. It was one of the first promises that the airline had kept to its employees in a long time and began a pattern of Continental's improving its on-time service. Management making good on one of its promises not only improved on-time performance, it helped turn the culture in a more positive direction.

Like most goalsharing plans that focus on a single outcome, Continental's plan produced some negative consequences in the areas of performance that were not measured. The planes were landing on time, but the number of lost and delayed bags went up and so did the number of customer complaints. This should hardly be surprising. Employees were emphasizing what they were getting paid for—on-time arrivals. Given the choice between delaying a plane to load a few more bags or meals and having it leave on time, the employees chose to have the plane leave on time. Continental responded to this problem by changing its goalsharing plan to include baggage handling and improved its performance in this area. Continental then decided to give all employees profit-sharing checks equal to 15 percent of the carrier's before-tax earnings.

Balanced Score Card

A considerable amount of writing has been done in the last few years about the importance of using a balanced score card.[4] In the writings of many accountants, this means measuring performance on more than the typical accounting-type measures. They recommend measures that include such things as customer satisfaction, employee satisfaction, and quality. It is hard to argue with this development in accounting; in fact, it is a welcome one because accountants strongly influence the kind of measures that are gathered by corporations. For a long time accountants have neglected measures that may be important indicators of the future direction and health of organizations. Accounting measures provide a financial record of the company and are good indicators of many areas of its performance. However, they are less than perfect predictors of future performance and are not inclusive measures of present performance.

The development of balanced scorecard measures fits well with the idea of goalsharing incentive plans. They require a type of balanced scorecard in order to operate effectively. The challenge with any balanced scorecard approach, or for that matter any pay-for-performance approach, is to get the right measures and to weight them appropriately so that the incentive effects are supportive of the organization's business strategy.

Conditions for Success

For several reasons goalsharing plans run the high risk of being effective for only a short period of time. When companies misuse them by setting unrealistically high standards or changing the measures or standards indiscriminately, there is a definite risk that employees will lose confidence, not only in the plan but in management. The challenge in managing goalsharing plans is to create measures that fit the business plan and to establish goals employees see as fair, reasonable, and achievable. This must be done not just once but year after year if the goalsharing plan is to continue to drive organizational performance.

It is hard to overemphasize the difficulty of establishing and maintaining a line of sight between behavior and rewards when organization pay-for-performance plans are involved. It takes a significant leap of faith for employees to believe that their organization will reward their current performance at a later date, particularly when the organization is measuring not individual but collective performance. Anything that undermines the trust of employees and the fairness and reasonableness of pay plans stands to reduce or totally eliminate a line of sight. Raising the standard, reducing bonus payouts, and unreasonably changing measures are all things that can challenge the credibility of a plan and destroy trust.

Many of the points I made earlier about the challenge of doing individual performance management well are appropriate here. In essence goalsharing plans are nothing more than performance-appraisal-driven bonus plans at the organizational level. Just as with individual and group plans, the process used to explain goals, set goals, and communicate results is critical. When the contracting, communication, and payment process is done well, goalsharing plans can be positive influences on business performance. When they are not done well, goalsharing plans waste time and money.

In many cases where I have seen goalsharing installed, the cash payout is so small that it is unlikely to be motivating, particularly in the long term. Payouts of $500 a year or 1 percent of base pay clearly do not get over the threshold of a financially attractive incentive, particularly when the line of sight is weak. That said, on occasions even a small bonus may be motivating if it is tied to a goal that the workforce is committed to. In these cases it is not the money that's the incentive but the achievement of a goal that employees have committed to reaching. Just as with individual and team goals, commitment to organizational goals is aided by a participative process in which employees establish what they think are achievable performance goals.

Impact of Goalsharing

There is little systematic evidence on the success of goalsharing plans. This is because they are new and also because they often get grouped erroneously with gainsharing plans. A good guess is that in the short term, goalsharing plans often are quite successful. It is less clear that most organizations manage them in ways that cause them to be powerful long-term drivers of strategic performance. Many organizations probably have successful goalsharing plans but over time don't do a good job of managing the goal-setting process and payouts. As a result the plans fail and are abandoned.

I have seen a number of instances where, after some initial excitement and positive results, organizations have tried to save money by raising the standards or reducing the bonus amounts, and the result has been a loss of motivation and the ultimate abandonment of the plan. This is similar to what often happens with individual incentive plans. All too often organizations think they can get more or the same for less by raising the standard, with the result that they get less, and the plan is abandoned.

One way to think about the use of goalsharing plans is exemplified by the Continental Airline example. At Continental there was a progression from goalsharing to profit sharing. In some respects goalsharing can be looked upon as incentive pay for beginners, that is, it can introduce an organization to variable pay with a plan that is relatively straightforward, easy to understand, and not very risky. As everyone in the organization becomes more knowledgeable and sophisticated in understanding the business and reward systems, a logical progression is to go to a more complicated pay-for-performance system that better captures the overall performance of the organization and potentially can produce larger rewards. Thus, the next step may be the installation of profit sharing or perhaps a gainsharing plan that relies on a formula.

In the turbulent business environment that corporations face today, it is highly likely that more and more goalsharing plans will be created. Even with their limitations they are just the kind of reward system that can help companies change by implementing new strategic focuses and processes. However, their nimbleness, agility, and ability to support change is both their greatest strength and greatest weakness. When goalsharing plan changes are managed well, they can make organizations more agile, but when they are managed poorly, they can create mistrust and resistance to change.

Profit Sharing

Profit sharing is the oldest and most commonly used bonus-based approach to rewarding organizational performance. In 1996, fully 69 percent of the Fortune 1000 companies operated profit-sharing plans. This represents virtually no change from the percentage that had profit-sharing plans in 1987.[5]

Design of Profit-Sharing Plans

Most profit-sharing plans use the publicly reported earnings of a company as the measure of performance that determines the amount of the bonus payment that is made to organization members. Usually some minimum level of earnings has to be achieved in order to have a payout; earnings above this level fund a bonus pool that is divided among the eligible employees. The payouts to employees may come in the form of a cash bonus, or they may be used to fund a retirement account.

In order to create a clear line of sight for employees, sometimes certain costs are excluded from the profit measure that is used. For example, interest and taxes are sometimes not considered; similarly, one-time extraordinary costs and write-offs are sometimes ignored. Profit-sharing plan payout amounts are usually based on a percentage of an employee's wages. The amount the individual receives may be modified by an evaluation of his or her individual performance. This, of course, represents an effort to increase the line of sight for employees by adding an individual pay-for-performance component to the profit-sharing plan.

Existing profit-sharing plans differ dramatically in terms of the percentage of the workforce they cover. In 1996, some 33 percent of the companies in the Fortune 1000 covered almost all their employees with profit sharing, whereas 18 percent covered fewer than 20 percent.[6] A few well-known companies such as Hewlett-Packard and Hallmark have plans that cover everyone and have had them since the early days of the company. Other well-known profit-sharing plans include the ones at the Saturn division of General Motors and Ford. These plans were negotiated by the United Auto Workers Union, and the payouts go to all union members. In many other large corporations, however, only the top executives are covered by profit-sharing plans.

Profit-sharing plans differ enormously in how much they pay out. At Hewlett-Packard, the profit-sharing plan has no limit and has paid bonuses of more than 15 percent. Clearly, this is enough of a payout to attract most people's attention.

Many non-U.S. companies have long histories of making profit-sharing payments. This is particularly true in Japan, where large companies make two profit-related payments a year to all employees. The norm in Japan has been that these payments are equal to 30 percent or more of employees' annual pay. Although they are not based on U.S.-type accounting profits, the amount of the payments reflects the corporation's overall financial performance.

Impact of Profit Sharing

Profit-sharing plans have a number of significant strengths and weaknesses. Perhaps their greatest weakness involves their ability to affect the motivation of employees. In large and medium-sized companies it is extremely difficult to establish a line of sight between employee behavior and corporate profitability. As a result profit-sharing plans typically do not have a significant impact on organizational performance. Simplifying and taking out uncontrollable factors when measuring earnings can help a little bit, but in a company as large as Ford, or for that matter Hewlett-Packard, this is not likely to make a significant difference in employees' line of sight. The one exception to this point concerns the very senior managers. They have more control over the reported earnings of the company, and their incentive opportunity is often much greater than it is for lower-level employees. Therefore, the incentive effect of profit sharing is more significant for them.

Profit-sharing plans can be significant motivators in companies with fewer than five hundred employees, where they can act much like gainsharing plans. Indeed, in many small companies, they probably make more sense than gainsharing plans because they can be based on existing measures of performance and can unite owners as well as employees around a common goal for the organization.

Profit sharing, like any other variable pay plan, is not universally attractive to all employees. It does introduce risk in an individual's compensation package and therefore is unlikely to be attractive to someone who cannot tolerate risk and who is suspicious of how large organizations operate and deal with employees. Again, the fact that it is differentially attractive to individuals may not be a major problem. That may be an advantage if it helps attract the kind of employees who will fit an organization's culture.

As I mentioned earlier, profit-sharing plans can have a long-term retention effect when the payouts are delayed. Many companies make payments from their profit-sharing plans to employee retirement plans. This means that employees get no cash payments from the plan unless they stay long enough to qualify for retirement payments. On the downside this probably eliminates any potential that the plan might operate as a significant motivator of performance. However, it can help lock employees into the company because they often have to stay five or more years to become eligible to get a payout when they leave. Placing the payouts in retirement plans, as well as paying out the bonuses earned over a number of years, can retain employees, but as I emphasized in Chapter Six, it often retains the wrong employees. Because profit-sharing payouts are usually made to everyone, even poor employees are motivated to stay.

Perhaps the major advantage associated with profit-sharing plans is their impact on an organization's culture and the way people think about their organization. When a profit-sharing plan covers most members of an organization, there is the potential for it to stimulate interest in the financial results of the organization and to create a culture in which attention is focused on performance. Although profit sharing may not be terribly motivating in the sense of driving people to work harder, it may motivate them to pay attention to financial results and to try to understand the business. This effect occurs because employees want to understand what their bonus is likely to be, where it comes from, and how it is computed. The effect on employees can be a better understanding of the organization and thus more knowledgeable and profit-focused decision-making behavior. Unfortunately, there is very little evidence showing the extent to which profit sharing has this effect. What evidence there is shows that companies with profit-sharing plans tend to perform only slightly better than companies without them (only 1 percent better in one study).[7]

Stock Plans

Stock-based pay plans have become increasingly popular, and that trend is likely to continue. Today most organizations have some form of stock plan for their employees. In 1996, for example, 87 percent of the Fortune 1000 companies had stock option plans.[8] A number of factors have led to the popularity of stock-based compensation, not the least of which is the extremely favorable performance of the U.S. stock market during most of the 1990s. But the changes that are taking place are probably more profound and long-lasting than simply the transitory desire to participate in a rising stock market. Stock ownership can be a way to retain individuals, to motivate them, and to create a culture of ownership. The advantages of stock ownership have a much greater appeal today than they did decades ago because of the greater importance of human capital, the creation of more high-performance organizations, and the increased desire of the workforce to participate in the success of their company.

Design of Stock Plans

There are a variety of ways to reward employees with stock in their corporation. One option is simply to give it to them. A second is to allow employees to buy stock at a substantially reduced price, either directly or in one or more retirement vehicles. Last but not least, employees can be granted stock options that give them the right to buy stock at a certain price. The surest way to create employee ownership is to make stock grants to them directly.

One type of stock plan used in the United States, known as an Employee Stock Ownership Plan (ESOP), allows employees to own part of a company through the creation of a trust vehicle, which actually holds the employee-owned stock. The trust votes the stock and handles the payouts to individuals when they leave the company or retire. ESOP plans continue to grow in popularity, at least in part because of the tax and borrowing advantages they offer companies.[9] In some cases they have been put in place as part of an effort to involve employees more in the company and to change the company's management style. In other cases stock is given in return for wage reductions and work rule improvements. For example, both United Airlines and Northwest Airlines created employee stock ownership plans during the 1990s in return for wage and work rule concessions.

Stock option plans give individuals the right to buy stock at some future date at a predetermined price. If the price of the stock at the time the option can be exercised is higher than the current exercise price, an employee has an incentive to buy the stock but little incentive to hold onto it once the purchase is completed. In fact there is good reason to believe that employees typically exercise their options as soon as they can (assuming the stock price is the above-option price) and immediately sell most or all of the stock they purchase.

Broad-based stock option plans are becoming much more popular, particularly in high-technology companies. Studies suggest that between 10 and 15 percent of all large corporations have broad-based stock option plans.[10] In the mid-1990s a number of U.S. companies started issuing stock options to all or most of their employees. PepsiCo, Monsanto, Merck, Procter and Gamble, Bank of America, Tricon, and a host of other companies have made either one-time or repeated stock option grants to all of their employees. Virtually every Silicon Valley company has made liberal use of them for years.

One Silicon Valley company has given stock options to the significant others of its employees. It has also invited the significant others to a seminar to discuss the company's business model and to explain how stock options work. When I asked the CEO why he did this, he said that it was part of being a family-friendly organization and rewarding family members for their support of the company. He added that he hoped it would make it easier for employees to put in the extra hours it took to be successful because their significant others would back their efforts for the company. In fact, he hoped the significant others would urge the employees to work even harder because now they too could profit from the company's success.

Companywide stock option plans are not limited to high-tech companies like Microsoft. Three successful retail chains—Starbucks, Home Depot, and Lowe's—have had them for years. Over one thousand employees of Home Depot have become millionaires doing what is generally regarded as low-wage work. Starbucks first issued options to its "partners" (employees) in 1991. They got options worth 12 percent of their annual base pay. Each year since then more options have been issued.

A few companies are moving to performance-based stock option plans. For example, Boeing's stock option plan pays off only if Boeing's stock price grows at a five-year average annual compounded rate of at least 10 percent. It also has a sliding scale for vesting the stock options (making them useable): if the company's stock price increases at an annual rate of 14 percent, all options vest; if the rate climbs to 15 percent or higher, executives also receive a 25 percent bonus; if the price increases less than 14 percent, only some of the options vest.

The Boeing plan takes into account the common criticism of management stock option plans that they tend to pay off simply as a result of the general upward movement of the stock market.

However, the plan assumes a stock price increase rate that may not reflect the reality of what happens in the stock market. The market might easily outperform the increase rate in the plan, in which case Boeing does not need to outperform the market in order to have handsome payouts to executives. In fact, it may make payouts even though it underperforms the market. If the market performs poorly, it could make the Boeing options worthless even though Boeing performs well compared to the market. So the plan is potentially risky for Boeing from a motivation and retention point of view. If the stock market performs poorly and this holds down the performance of Boeing stock, no line of sight will exist and no payouts will be made to any executives. This may very well encourage some of the better ones to depart.

A superior approach would be to relate either the vesting of the stock options or the price of the options to how Boeing's stock performs relative to the overall market or to its aerospace competitors. By doing this, a plan can be created in which, if the company performs at or above the market, the stock options will be valuable; if it underperforms, they will not be.

It is possible to reward individuals with stock, even though the company is not part of a publicly traded corporation. By using a device called phantom stock, it is possible to create a reward system that may even be superior to giving employees options in publicly traded companies. Essentially, phantom stock consists of fictional shares of stock to which companies assign a price that reflects the companies' financial performance. Usually the price is determined by an outside analyst, who bases it on how similar companies are priced by public markets.

Phantom stock is particularly appropriate for closely held companies that do not have publicly traded stock and for highly autonomous divisions or parts of large corporations. In the latter case companies and individuals can be given stock or stock options in their business units, in addition to or instead of giving them stock in the total corporation. This makes sense if the company wants employees to focus primarily on their particular division or business unit.

A key advantage of phantom stock is that it can filter out or dampen some of the noise, distraction, and changes in the market price of publicly traded stock that are caused by irrational exuberance and irrational pessimism. In short, it can represent a truer reflection of how the company has actually performed and therefore create a better line of sight for those who are given the stock.

Because phantom stock is usually valued on an annual basis, it can create a longer-term perspective on the part of employees. They do not have to manage Wall Street reactions to quarterly earning statements, for example. Just as with publicly traded stock, companies can give options or they can actually give shares to employees as part of a phantom stock plan.

Companies that are adroit users of phantom stock include Mary Kay and Kinko's. Mary Kay introduced its phantom program in 1985 and focused it on top executives; the program makes cash payments based on the increase in the value of the stock from the date of the initial grant of phantom shares. Mary Kay has launched a phantom stock program every five years since 1985 in order to provide a continuing incentive for senior managers. Among the divisions of major companies that use phantom stock is Putnam Investors, a subsidiary of the insurance giant Marsh & McLennan.

A second alternative to traditional stock is tracking stock. Hughes Electronics, which is owned by General Motors, has tracking stock in its name that is publicly traded. Hughes reports its financial results separately from those of GM. Tracking stock, of course, suffers some of the same problems as regular stock with respect to changes in market valuation. However, it does allow large corporations to provide separate stock incentive plans to their business units. This is an important advantage for corporations that need targeted stock plans to attract, retain, and motivate employees in some of their businesses. The advantages of tracking stock are likely to increase its use in corporations that operate multiple businesses.

Corporations differ dramatically in how much of the workforce they typically cover with stock ownership plans. For example, stock option plans often cover only very senior employees. In one study over half the companies that had stock option plans covered only senior executives.[11] In the case of some of companies (for example, Disney) the size of the stock option grants to senior executives has been truly astounding. Millions of options have been granted to senior executives, whereas none have been given to most of the employees.

ESOP plans typically cover virtually all employees in an organization, so they do not create two classes of citizens—haves and have-nots. Stock purchase plans are typically available to all employees, as is ownership of the company stock through retirement vehicles. Stock grants, however, are often used only for senior management, corporate board members, and some outstanding employees. It is rare to see a company grant stock to most or all of its employees.

Impact of Stock Plans

The effect of stock plans on motivation is likely to be slightly less than the effect of profit sharing because the line-of-sight problem is even more severe than it is for profit-sharing plans. Stock price depends on more than just the somewhat controllable financial performance of the company. It depends on how the stock market evaluates the earnings and the future of the company as well as the economy. These factors are less controllable by the company than the company's earnings are. Thus, even for senior managers, the line of sight for the value of their company's stock may be weak.

The strength of stock as a motivator comes from the amount of reward that can be earned. The amount that can be gained from stock programs as a result of improvement in an organization's stock price is virtually unlimited. The amount of money earned by a number of CEOs during the 1990s puts the payouts from the major U.S. lotteries to shame. Literally hundreds of millions of dollars have been made by some CEOs as a result of their stock options. As I noted earlier, if this amount of reward is available, even a weak line of sight can have a definite effect on motivation. Thus, there is a real possibility that at the very senior levels of management in large companies, stock options are an effective motivator. The same is unlikely to be true for the rest of the employees because they often have fewer shares of stock and a much weaker line of sight.

There are some significant negatives that can occur as a result of stock-based pay plans. A dramatic example of what can happen to the value of a company's stock price when large stock grants are made is provided by Computer Associates. In 1995 Computer Associates instituted a particularly rich stock grant plan for its three most senior executives. At the time the plan was created, some shareholders voiced opposition to it, but the majority voted for it. The plan called for the awarding of a large number of shares to senior managers when the stock price of Computer Associates reached a particular level. That happened in 1998, and the stock was issued. The executives got stock that was valued at $1.1 billion. In order to account for this, the company had to take a write-off of $675 million. It wiped out the company's entire profit for the quarter, and Computer Associates ended up reporting a large loss. The stock price immediately dropped by more than 30 percent.

The experience of Computer Associates is an extreme example of the damage that can occur by giving large amounts of stock to executives, but it is not an isolated example. Many companies have significantly decreased their earnings by issuing large amounts of stock or stock options to their senior executives. Given this, it is hardly surprising that large shareholders and investors are increasingly questioning the practice.

Perhaps the greatest negative impact that is created by stock plans that make only senior executives incredibly wealthy concerns their impact on the rest of the organization. Surprisingly, there is little or no research on the impact of executives making hundreds of millions of dollars as a result of their stock option grants while the rest of the organization does not participate in the plans. An educated guess, however, is that this creates an enormous division between people at the top and everybody else in the workforce.[12] This gap can make it difficult for top-level managers to talk credibly about a shared mission and the importance of everyone working together to create a more effective organization. In short, it can make it difficult for them to be effective leaders because employees view them as the only ones who will profit from improving organizational performance.

It is surprising that there haven't been more visible signs of resentment on the part of employees as a result of the high levels of executive compensation in the United States. Occasionally, it is brought up by unions in organizing drives, and there have been protests when executives have visited their plants and facilities. Executives have also been challenged at their corporate annual meetings, but this is more the exception than the rule. Most likely, the main reason there has not been more outrage directed at the high pay of CEOs is that it has occurred during a period of prosperity in the United States. When everyone is doing better, there is usually less concern that a few are doing very, very well.

Finally, some studies suggest that it is difficult for executives to work together in teams when they have dramatically different compensation amounts and pay structures. This makes good sense because it argues that the executives will not all be motivated to accomplish the same goals and objectives, and indeed, there may be a considerable amount of resentment due to the different compensation levels.

Because stock options don't have to be exercised if the stock price of the company drops, they have a potentially different effect on their holders than direct stock ownership has. When employees and executives own stock in their company there is both an upside potential and a downside potential; with stock options there is only an upside. If the stock goes up, the employees can be big winners; if it goes down, they simply have lost the opportunity to make additional money. With stock ownership individuals can suffer significant losses on an ongoing basis, thus the problem of individuals not caring once their stock options are well under water (have no value) does not occur. Given this reality it is reasonable to assume that most employees and executives would rather receive stock options than stock, particularly if, as is often true, the stock that they receive has to be held for a period of time. Of course if the stock does not have to be held, in many cases it is comparable to giving cash; indeed, the organization might be better off giving cash.

Once options get seriously under water, they may lose their motivational power entirely because employees feel that there is no chance for the stock options to pay off. The same is not true of direct stock ownership. As long as the stock has some value, the holder continues to be concerned about and potentially motivated by changes in the stock price.

The evidence on broad-based stock ownership as a motivator is relatively clear. There is no reason to believe that in most large organizations the ownership of a relatively small number of shares is likely to be a driver of employee behavior. Thus, although granting small numbers of shares to employees can be a rewarding event for employees and appreciated by them, it is unlikely to operate as an effective motivator of performance. The same is true for employees owning stock in the company through their retirement plan or some other vehicle. Stock tends to be a motivator only when the organization is relatively small and significant employee involvement in the operations of the enterprise exists. Relatively small size helps because it creates a sense that collective effort by employees can influence the performance of the company and, ultimately, the price of the stock. Involvement is crucial because it provides the understanding of and ability to influence organizational performance that must be in place for a line of site to exist. This is consistent with the line-of-sight argument with respect to profit sharing and gainsharing.

Stock plans can have a decided impact on employee retention. The general principle is the same one I have focused on throughout the book: the opportunity to achieve substantial rewards in the future can act as a powerful retention device. Thus, stock option plans, ESOP plans, and direct stock ownership plans that offer employees the opportunity to profit substantially from stock ownership can be powerful retention devices for at least as long as employees are required to stay with the organization in order for stock options to be exercised or stock ownership to occur. Once these dates are reached, the retention power of the stock plan disappears, often necessitating the creation of a new stock plan that will provide a continuing retention incentive. This is recognized by the many company stock plans that refresh employees' options every year or every several years.

Sometimes stock plans can actually work against retention. This has happened in the case of Microsoft, where the employee stock option program has been so lucrative that individuals can afford to retire from the company at a relatively young age. Not many employees have taken advantage of this option yet, but it clearly has happened. Individuals in their thirties and forties have left the company to do charity work or to run small businesses because the stock option plan made them millionaires and they can afford to.

Option plans can be a disaster for retention and the culture of an organization if they go significantly under water. In this case they are a constant reminder of the company's problems and can feed a kind of "death march" spirit in which the best individuals—

the very ones needed to turn the company around—leave if they can. The solution to this problem is to give new options to replace the old ones. This can work for retention but may not be supported by investors who see employees being rewarded despite the organization's poor performance.

The use of stock options and stock ownership is a particularly interesting issue with respect to attraction. Particularly in high-tech companies, it has become common to offer stock options when firms try to attract knowledge workers. In many ways this can create a win-win situation. When the stock market is performing well, there is good reason to believe that employees may value stock options at a level that is greater than their cost. Thus, it is very much in the interest of companies to offer stock options because it is a cheap way to attract employees. It is particularly cheap for companies in the United States to offer options because the accounting principles do not require companies to reduce their earnings as a result of making option grants. Options are very attractive to employees because they can receive them and not pay taxes on them until they are exercised. Thus, options can be a win for the company and possibly a win for employees.

Over time, both parties do have to pay for options. Employees have to pay taxes, and companies either have to buy stock and give it to employees or issue new stock and suffer a dilution of their equity capital because there are more shares outstanding. The latter issue is becoming a sticky one with investors. As companies have granted more and more options (some have issued options equal to over 25 percent of the stock that is held by investors), investors have become more and more concerned about the impact of options on their share of the equity in companies. Increasingly, investors are questioning and in some cases voting against the issuance of additional options and shares because they see too large a dilution of their ownership position.

Overall, the impact of stock plans that give real or phantom stock to most or all employees on the relationship between employees and companies is most likely similar to the impact of profit-sharing plans. It does put employees who are on the plans in the same situation as investors and thus can create a positive alignment of interests among these two stakeholder groups. It also can encourage employees to learn more about the business and how the investment community looks at their company. Thus, there is reason to believe that stock ownership on the part of employees can help reinforce a business involvement culture and encourage communication practices that focus on business effectiveness. However, because the impact of stock on the motivation of most members is relatively weak to nonexistent, the effect of stock ownership on an organization's performance is bound to be more indirect than direct.

Impact of Rewarding Organizational Performance

Now that I have reviewed four different approaches to paying for organizational performance, I can state some general conclusions about their impact. Table 10.1 provides a general overview of the strengths of the four plans. The evaluations of their impact assume that the plans are well designed and managed. The table distinguishes between stock and profit-sharing plans that cover only senior managers and those that cover all organizational members.

It is clear that goalsharing and gainsharing potentially are the most effective at motivating strategically appropriate behavior. With respect to attraction, stock plans as a general rule are likely to be

Table 10.1. Impact of Pay Systems.

	Motivation	Attraction	Retention	Culture
Gainsharing	Positive	Weak positive	Positive	Positive
Goalsharing	Positive	Weak positive	Positive	Positive
Profit sharing for top only	Positive for top	Positive for top	Positive for top	Negative below top
Profit sharing, broad-based	Little impact except for top	Weak positive	Positive	Positive
Ownership for top only	Positive for top	Positive for top	Positive for top	Negative below top
Ownership, broad-based	Little impact except for top	Positive	Positive	Positive

the most powerful. Of course, if any of the plans have a history of substantial payouts, that can make them quite attractive to job applicants. All the plans are reasonably good at differentially attracting individuals, because they send a strong message about the culture of the company that can aid the self-selection process.

With respect to retention, stock plans are likely to have the most impact. They are the most effective at generating large rewards in the future for individuals who stay with the organization. Their effectiveness is, of course, somewhat problematic because it depends on the company's stock market performance. All stock plans can lose their power to retain if the stock price falls either below the option price or to a very low value in the case of stock ownership.

Finally, all the plans can have an impact on organizational culture and on the relationship that individuals have to the organization. Gainsharing and goalsharing can perhaps do the most to focus attention on particular strategic objectives. Profit sharing and stock ownership have more impact on causing individuals to focus on the business and the financial results of the company. Stock plans are particularly good at building a culture of ownership; in small companies this can lead to peer pressure for performance. In the case of profit sharing and stock ownership, plans that cover most of the workforce and those that cover just top management produce different results. As is shown in the table, the latter are likely to have a negative impact on the culture because they create a division in the organization.

Conclusion

No one pay-for-performance plan fits all organizations. However, one or more such plans can be used effectively by most organizations. As I will discuss in the next chapter, the key to building an effective pay system for a high-performance organization is in installing the right mix of pay systems that reward organizational performance and fit the business strategy and structure of the organization.

Part Four

Strategic Design

Chapter Eleven

Strategic Reward System Design

Developing a business strategy is a critical step in creating an effective organization. But it is only the first step. Many organizations have good strategies, but only a few implement them effectively. Indeed, often the size of the gap between a business's strategy and the implementation of that strategy is the major determinant of how effective an organization is. The reward system is an important determinant of how effectively a business strategy is implemented. The reward system can play an important role in motivating the development of a winning strategy, but its greatest contribution to organizational effectiveness occurs when it enables and motivates an organization to implement its strategy.

Two aspects of reward systems and their effect on organizational performance are particularly important in strategy implementation: (1) developing an organization with the capabilities and competencies needed to execute the strategy and (2) creating the motivation within an organization to use the competencies and capabilities in a way that supports the strategy. The challenge in creating reward system architectures is to create systems that both help the organization develop the right competencies and capabilities and motivate the appropriate strategic behavior. In this chapter I will focus on our earlier discussions of the impact of rewards on attraction, retention, development, and motivation and how they apply to strategy implementation and the development of a high-performance organization. I will first focus on the elements of a reward system that are needed to develop the right capabilities and competencies and then consider the motivational issues associated with strategy implementation.

Organizational Capabilities and Competencies

Organizational capabilities and core competencies are built on individuals' skills; thus, the reward system must first and foremost support an organization employing individuals with the right skills. This can be accomplished only if an organization attracts and retains the right individuals and motivates them to develop their knowledge and skills.

The details of how the reward system needs to be designed in order to attract individuals with the right knowledge and skills and motivate them to learn depend on the core competencies and capabilities an organization needs. They will be different in an organization that has a chemical process as its core competency and in one with package distribution and tracking as its core competency. Similarly, an organization that wants to develop a capability in product innovation needs individuals with different skills than one developing a capability in lean manufacturing. However, the case can be made that, regardless of the capabilities and competencies an organization wants to develop, some reward system designs are more effective than others. I would like to review the key features that enable a reward system to support competency and capability excellence in an organization.

Person-Based Rewards

A person-based approach rather than a job-based approach is the logical choice for any organization that wants to target the development of individuals and the attraction and retention of those who are highly skilled. This is because person-based rewards that focus on what individuals can do allow organizations to reward skill and knowledge development and to pay individuals according to what their human capital is worth in the labor market. This practice can also motivate people to develop the skills and knowledge an organization needs them to have and position them favorably in the external market so they will be motivated to stay with the organization.

The major challenge in developing person-based pay is to identify and measure the personal characteristics to be rewarded. In virtually every case, the reward system should not reward characteristics that have to do with seniority or loyalty to the organization but should focus on the skills, knowledge, and competencies that individuals have and on how these fit the organization's knowledge management strategy. The characteristics it focuses on must, first and foremost, be determined by the organization's business strategy. Secondarily, they should be determined by the kind of work an individual will be asked to do, as well as the management approach an organization uses.

In my earlier discussion of skills, knowledge, and competencies, I pointed out that skill-based pay is popular in work-team-based organizations and at lower levels in organizations because it fits the work design there. There is little doubt that the best approach for most lower-level and technical jobs is a focus on skills, which can be more objectively and easily measured than competencies and can form a good foundation for determining pay levels and for motivating individuals to learn new skills. When the work is changing rapidly and new skills are needed frequently, a strong case can be made for rewarding individuals with bonuses for learning new skills. Bonuses are superior to pay increases because they do not become an annuity.

The situation is more complex when the work involved is managerial. What seems to make the most sense is to combine what is often measured in competency-based pay plans that focus on behavior and knowledge with what is done in skill-based pay to create a knowledge-and-skill-based pay plan that focuses on three areas of knowledge and skill.

The first is determined by the organization's management approach. For example, the ability to lead work teams and to communicate are often key competencies that individuals need in high-involvement, high-performance organizations.

The second is the set of technical skills and knowledge that managers need. These are specific to the functional or technical area in which they work, so managers' rewards should be based on the mastery of the skills and knowledge in their work area. For example, someone managing a software development group needs considerably different technical knowledge than someone managing a retail store.

The third is also related to the type of position and involves business knowledge and skills. The financial, strategic, and business models that a manager needs to understand are different across business sectors and organizations. Thus, role-specific skills should be developed and rewarded.

Person-based pay systems should put proper weight on the three general kinds of skills and knowledge that individuals must master to perform well. The specific skills that individuals should develop need to be specified in person descriptions like those discussed in Chapter Six. These person descriptions should then serve as a basis for determining pay.

Market Position

I have stressed throughout this book that labor market position is crucial to retaining people. Those who are rewarded at less than their market value tend to leave; those rewarded at or above their market value tend to stay. This leads to a straightforward statement of what an organization should strive for: rewarding individuals who should be retained at or above the market; rewarding everyone else below the market. Successfully accomplishing this, of course, is more easily said than done.

One of the major reasons for installing a person-based system is to enable the pricing of individuals relative to the market. Job-based systems price jobs relative to the market and typically lead to most employees being paid at about the same rate. Often this means the most valued individuals are paid too little and the least valued too much. Person-based pay provides the opportunity to price individuals more strategically in the market.

A major challenge in pricing people is the lack of good market data; most data focus on jobs, not on individuals. One kind of market data, however, is quite observable and readily available: hiring data. Every time a person is hired, an important piece of market data is generated. That is why I argued in Chapter Six that organizations need to pay particular attention to the salary offers individuals get and the hiring rates in their labor markets.

Once market data are obtained, an organization needs to translate those data into appropriate pay rates. One strategy is to consistently be an above-market payer. Most major organizations have chosen to do this by paying their jobs—not individuals—above the market. This strategy has a number of advantages, including establishing that the organization is a good place to work, but it also carries risks. It is a high-cost strategy and can lead to the retention of all employees, not just the very best. It may also not pay the best technical and knowledge workers enough because their pay is determined by the pay range for the position they hold.

An alternative to paying above the market for jobs is to pay above the market for the most valuable employees of the organization and at or below the market for the rest. From a retention point of view, it is hard to argue with this strategy, but it can be difficult to implement because it requires extremely good market data, as well as accurate assessments of employees' skills, knowledge, and performance. It also involves some risk because the misplacing of individuals in the market can lead to the departure of valued employees. In essence, it leaves little margin for error and must be carefully monitored and managed. Finally, paying the best employees above the market may raise internal equity issues. The best way to deal with them is to explain how the pay practices are driven by the strategic needs of the business.

One final issue needs to be considered once a market position is established: How much of the cash compensation paid to get individuals at or above the market is at risk? As I stressed in earlier chapters, variable pay is a critical element in creating a motivating pay approach, and the more that can be put at risk, the more motivating a pay-for-performance approach can be. However, creating large bonuses or stock awards often requires that organizations reduce employees' base pay to a point that is significantly below the market for them. In a bad performance year for an individual or the organization, this can put key individuals below the market in terms of their total compensation. If competing organizations are doing well, they may seize this opportunity to hire people whose compensation has dropped below the market.

There is no easy solution to the retention problems that are caused by having large amounts of variable pay. However, the risk can be somewhat reduced by making stock or bonus payments contingent on staying with the organization for several years. That way, one bad period will not automatically mean that an employee is poorly paid. This is exactly what Amazon.com has done. It combines very low levels of cash compensation with large stock option grants that cannot be exercised for several years.

Another effective approach is to be sure there is always at least enough variable pay available so that particularly high performers can be paid at or above market. As I will discuss later in the chapter, this can be accomplished by creating the right combination of individual, group, and organizationwide pay-for-performance plans.

Equity Focus

As I have repeatedly stressed, developing and maintaining organizational competencies and capabilities requires attracting and retaining individuals with the right talents and skills. In turn, this means aligning an organization's reward levels with the external market. Typically, individuals leave organizations because they can do better elsewhere, not because they are unhappy about what some else inside their organization is making. Similarly, individuals are attracted to an organization because of what they are offered relative to other offers, not because of what somebody doing a different job in the organization offering them a job is paid.

The implication here is obvious: the focus of pay systems needs to be on the external market, not on internal pay comparisons. This straightforward conclusion is contrary to the way many organizations operate. They do not ignore the external market but neither do they ignore the internal market. They compare internal jobs to each other in order to determine how much to pay them and argue that an important core principle in their pay system is internal equity. This leads to many debates about how to compare apples and oranges—in other words how to compare radically different kinds of jobs and determine what a fair internal comparison process looks like.

It is easy to understand why companies might want to offer fair pay according to both the internal and external markets. The promise of receiving fair pay is attractive to everyone. The problem is that focusing on the internal market denies the reality of how the market for human capital operates. The market does not price individuals on the basis of jobs but on market demand for identifiable skills and knowledge. It sometimes acts in surprising and distressing ways because of rapid changes in the demand for certain skills and the resultant shortages of those who have them. It is also influenced by historical patterns of bias and discrimination. As distressing as the realities of the market may be, it is still the market—not internal equity—that matters when the issue is the attraction and retention of human capital.

Organizations that focus on internal comparisons often miss important changes in the market; as a result, they have great difficulty attracting and retaining individuals in high-demand, "hot talent" areas. They also end up paying many people more than they need to when they bring all of their pay rates up to those for the highest-paid jobs. In short, although having an internal focus is common, it ignores the laws of supply and demand and from a human capital point of view is doomed to be ineffective.

Moving to an external equity focus means moving away from traditional job evaluation processes and internal job-to-job comparisons and stating clearly that external equity is the focus. It means pricing individuals and sometimes jobs directly in the external labor market and paying them according to what the market says they are worth. In many respects this an important part of moving from an organizational culture that is focused internally on equality, entitlement, and loyalty to one that is focused on the external market and that defines fairness in terms of an external reality rather than a set of internal comparisons. It means adopting a core principle that says pay equity doesn't mean equality but rather pay that is market-driven.

Degree of Hierarchy

The development of the core competencies and organizational capabilities needed to create high-performance organizations requires that organizations not have a strictly hierarchical approach to reward allocation. The development of technical skills and knowledge is not optimized in organizations that tie pay to hierarchy because when they do it, organizations cannot effectively reward people for becoming technology experts. In hierarchical systems even the most important technical contributors usually end up being paid less than most managers because their jobs are less highly evaluated.

In the case of organizational capabilities, a very hierarchical organization often stands in the way of developing good lateral processes and effective self-managing teams. Hierarchical reward systems create status differences and reinforce power hierarchies that actively work against decision making at lower levels and individuals communicating with each other across hierarchical levels.[1] Finally, hierarchical reward systems often encourage individuals to develop the wrong skills, that is, those associated with higher-level positions and upward mobility. They often do this at the cost of individuals developing the skills and knowledge to operate effectively in the roles they have.

In considering the movement to a less hierarchical reward system, it is important to distinguish between what is required in order to meet the external market and what are optional indicators of hierarchy. With cash compensation, it is impossible and unwise to ignore hierarchy. The reality is that to pay the market rates for higher-level managers, these employees have to be paid more—sometimes quite a bit more—than most other employees because the market pays more. A few organizations have tried to deny this reality and have suffered as a result. For example, Ben & Jerry's Ice Cream systematically underpaid senior managers in order to create a more egalitarian internal environment. As a result they had problems attracting competent senior managers and ultimately had to abandon the policy.

The situation is somewhat different with respect to the many nonfinancial rewards that are attached to hierarchy—special parking places, large offices, and other status symbols. Like many reward system practices, the degree of hierarchy with respect to nonfinancial rewards may be important in selectively attracting and retaining the right employees. Managers who want very hierarchical status and perquisite systems are not usually the kind of managers who operate effectively in a high-performance organization that values involvement. Those who are right for the new-logic organizations do not find them attractive, so such rewards should be minimized or completely eliminated.

Employment Contract

The traditional *employment* contract or deal clearly does not focus on an organization's competencies and capabilities; the *employability* contract represents a better fit. It calls for individuals to continue to learn and develop and for the organization to help them do so. My research shows that organizations are more successful at developing new capabilities and changing when they have an employability contract than when they have a contract focused on job security.[2] Organizations are more agile when people feel that their continued employment depends on accepting change and adding the skills and competencies necessary to function effectively in the new environment. In addition, the research suggests that they need to think their performance is an important determinant of how secure their job is. In several respects these findings are not surprising. They very much fit the expectancy theory approach to motivation, which argues that individuals behave in ways they feel are rewarded. With an approach based on high seniority, job security, and loyalty, rewards are clearly for staying around and surviving rather than for learning and changing.

An example of a company that has developed a well-stated employability contract is Allstate Insurance. The contract, a mutual commitment contract that is skill- and performance-oriented, is given to all employees (see Exhibit 11.1). Allstate used videos, pamphlets, and talks by the CEO to help employees understand the employment relationship expressed in the contract. Clearly, Allstate wants a relatively long-term employment relationship with its employees, and the contract reinforces this.

Good as the Allstate contract is, it does not fit all organizations. For example, it does not take into account the use of temporary or contingent employees. In organizations that are in rapidly changing businesses, the employment contract may well need to take into account short-term employment relationships and the use of temporary employees. Perhaps the best way to do this is to simply have a second or third contract that makes it clear what the basis of the employment relationship is for contingent employees.

In most cases an employment relationship for contingents should involve many fewer commitments to the individual than the

Exhibit 11.1. Allstate Employability Contract.

You should expect Allstate to:

1. Offer work that is meaningful and challenging.

2. Promote an environment that encourages open and constructive dialogue.

3. Recognize you for your accomplishments.

4. Provide competitive pay and rewards based on your performance.

5. Advise you on your performance through regular feedback.

6. Create learning opportunities through education and job assignments.

7. Support you in defining career goals.

8. Provide you with information and resources to perform successfully.

9. Promote an environment that is inclusive and free from bias.

10. Foster dignity and respect in all interactions.

11. Establish an environment that promotes a balance of work and personal life.

Allstate expects you to:

1. Perform at levels that significantly increase our ability to outperform the competition.

2. Take on assignments critical to meeting business objectives.

3. Continually develop needed skills.

4. Willingly listen to and act upon feedback.

5. Demonstrate a high level of commitment to achieving company goals.

6. Exhibit no bias in interactions with colleagues and customers.

7. Behave consistently with Allstate's ethical standards.

8. Take personal responsibility for each transaction with our customers and for fostering their trust.

9. Continually improve processes to address customers' needs.

Allstate contract makes. It should also state that individual performance, not learning, is the key to being successful and to continued employment. Because contingent employees are typically not around long enough to become involved in the business of the organization and to develop skills and competencies that increase their market value, they may need to be given short-term incentives to motivate them to perform well.

Most organizations do not take time to develop a formal employment contract. Instead, an understanding develops between the individual and the organization that constitutes an informal, often unspoken, contract.[3] In the past this may have been good enough. The loyalty contract was the way corporations operated, and everyone knew what the deal was and behaved accordingly. But as organizations try to gain competitive advantage through developing unique organization designs, capabilities, and competencies, a strong argument can be made that they need to develop clearly stated employment contracts. Such contracts can help attract the right employees and differentiate an organization from its competitors. It can also help focus organization members on the right kinds of behavior. Increasingly, organizations are recognizing the importance of having a contract they can use as a tool in attracting, retaining, and developing the right employees and establishing a performance-oriented culture.

Summary

The features of a reward system that are potentially supportive of developing strategically important competencies and capabilities in a high-performance organization are identified in Table 11.1. Also identified are the features of a traditional reward system that fit well with a more bureaucratic approach to organizing. Having the right features, of course, does not guarantee that an organization's reward system will support a specific strategy. This is simply the outline of an architecture that will allow the organization to develop a pay system that supports the development of specific competencies and capabilities. In essence, the architecture needs to be filled out with detailed policies, practices, and behaviors that identify such things as the kind of skills and knowledge individuals

Table 11.1. Traditional and Strategic Reward Structures.

	Traditional	Strategic
Reward basis	Job	Person
Market position	High	Based on person's skills and knowledge
Equity focus	Internal and external	External
Hierarchy	Significant level differences	Minimal level differences
Contract	Loyalty and entitlement	Employability and performance

need, what market comparisons are appropriate, the degree of hierarchy that makes sense, and the details of the employment contract. These factors will differ significantly by industry and by type of firm. For example, the type of employment contract that works for Allstate is unlikely to be appropriate for Microsoft. The skills and competencies the two companies need are different, and the rate of change in their businesses is different.

Table 11.2 provides two examples of the types of reward system practices that might be associated with different capabilities. The first set is for an organization that wants to have the key organizational capabilities associated with lean manufacturing, that is, a focus on quality, low-cost manufacturing and the effective use of capital and people. The second set is for an agile, knowledge-work organization that is project- and customer-focused. As can be seen from the table, they need somewhat different practices in their reward systems in order to develop the appropriate capabilities.

In addition to developing different capabilities, organizations also need to develop different core competencies. How to do this is not shown in the table because it requires specifying which of many core competencies are needed. What the table demonstrates, however, is that a reward system that pays the person according to the external market, sets the correct market position for pay, has the right degree of hierarchy, and has a well-developed employment contract can support the organization's development of the

Table 11.2. Reward Structures for Organizational Capabilities.

	Lean Manufacturing	Agile Knowledge Work
Skills and knowledge	Quality, self-management	Technical knowledge, leadership skills
Market position	At market	High for core knowledge
Equity focus	Business competitors and local markets	External competitors for skills, national and global skill markets
Hierarchy	Moderate	Minimal
Contract	Employability, possible seniority-based rewards	Employability, soft landing for layoffs, multiple contracts, retention rewards for core employees

core competencies it needs. Establishing a reward system that develops the right competencies and capabilities is the first step in aligning the pay system with the organization's business strategy. The second is creating a performance reward system.

Performance Motivation

Rewarding performance is a key to motivation and therefore to successful implementation of a business strategy. It can also have a positive impact on attracting and retaining outstanding performers. In Part Three I analyzed a wide variety of pay-for-performance systems that can be used to motivate excellence. Each and every organization faces the challenge of putting together the right combination of these pay-for-performance approaches to support its business strategy. The emphasis here should be on combining approaches because it is highly unlikely that a single approach to pay for performance will suffice.

The Star Model that I presented in Chapter One suggests that in determining the right pay-for-performance approach it is not sufficient to look only at strategy. The structure of the organization needs to be taken into account, as does its overall management style, its people, and its key measurement processes. These, like the strategy, need to fit with and drive an organization's performance reward architecture. Achieving a good fit is a complex and dynamic process.

The remainder of this chapter will focus on specifying a pay-for-performance architecture that fits the new logic and that can be adapted to fit most strategies. A word of caution is needed here, however. What follows is not the specification of a complete pay-for-performance approach. As is true of developing competencies and capabilities, the approach needs to be filled in and modified to fit each organization. This is particularly true with respect to the performance measures used; these should be guided by the strategic direction that the organization is taking. With the exception of a few general measures like profitability and cost, it is particularly important that specific measures be developed that reflect the kinds of behaviors needed in each organization at different levels and in different business units. Without this type of customization, it is impossible to align a reward system with the business strategy.

I will discuss separately the type of pay-for-performance reward systems that are appropriate for six different types of employees: board members, senior managers, general production management and service employees, technical and professional employees, and contingent employees.

Board Members

Reward systems for boards in U.S. corporations have recently undergone a major change. Traditionally, board members were paid for attendance at meetings and in some cases also received a lucrative benefit package that included retirement pay. Recently, pressure from institutional investors has led to dramatic changes. Board members increasingly are getting no benefits or retirement pay and are rewarded for performance through stock options or stock grants. One recent survey of the boards of U.S. corporations found that 78 percent of companies now use stock-based compensation.[4] Board members may still get cash payments for board membership and for attending specific meetings, but the major form of compensation is becoming company stock.

It is hard to argue with the movement toward the pay of board members being based on company performance. The only unanswered questions concern what form of performance-based compensation should be used and how much board members should be compensated. The answers to them are clearly suggested by the role boards play in corporations. Fundamentally, they are responsible for the company's long-term performance.[5] They are expected to monitor company performance and select and develop future senior executives. Given these duties, one type of pay-for-performance fits board members particularly well: long-term, stock-based compensation. By giving directors stock-based compensation, an alignment is created between the interests of shareholders and the interests of boards. This serves to make them more than just representatives of shareholders; it gives them a common interest with shareholders.

Of the two major forms—stock options and direct ownership—the right choice seems clear. Every director should own significant stock in his or her corporation. The reason for requiring stock ownership is relatively straightforward. It creates a symmetry with shareholders with respect to both the upside and the downside of corporate performance. In most cases board members should also participate in stock option plans. The recommendation here is that the stock options be long-term options, taking at least three years before they can be exercised. Of course, they should also be given to board members at a price that is at or above the current market value of the stock when they are issued.

Sandy Weill, former CEO of the Traveler's Group (now merged with Citicorp to create Citigroup), is a particularly strong advocate of board members and senior executives owning stock. In 1996 his seventeen-member senior executive planning group agreed not to sell any of their Traveler's stock. The only payment for board members at Traveler's was in stock; they got $100,000 worth of stock each year. They received no retirement benefits, no insurance, no come-to-meeting fees, no fees to be head of a committee—every board member got the same reward: stock. In order to accommodate the tax implications of this, members were allowed to sell enough stock to generate the cash they needed to pay their income tax.

Major corporations in the United States have tended not to do any systematic evaluation of either their boards as a whole or their individual board members. For example, a survey by Korn/Ferry in 1997 found that only 18 percent of boards evaluate individual directors.[6] This clearly needs to change if a culture of performance excellence is to be created in corporations.[7] Both kinds of evaluations need to take place. Boards need to systematically assess how effectively they are operating and what can be done to improve their performance. Similarly, board members need to be assessed regularly in order to guide their development as board members and ultimately to determine whether they should be reappointed.

A few leading companies, including Motorola and Compaq Computer, already do individual and collective board evaluations, but they are the exception. The rationale for not doing them is that boards might be uncomfortable doing evaluations and members who are evaluated might be insulted. The rationale goes on to point out that individuals on boards are very successful and do not "need" to be on boards; as a result valuable board members may be driven off if they are subject to evaluation. There clearly is some legitimacy to this point, but the more important and overriding consideration is the mentality of nonaccountability and the acceptance of less-than-excellent performance that can develop when boards, collectively and individually, are not subject to a performance appraisal.

What is not appropriate, given the role of boards, is to tie rewards to either board performance or to the individual performance of board members. Individual pay for performance clearly does not have a place in the boardroom because of the team and interdependent nature of the work that needs to be done. The argument against rewarding boards as a team rests largely on the problems of measuring board performance separate from corporate performance. Further, board performance measurement and individual member performance management often involve a fairly heavy element of self-assessment; this is difficult to do well when it carries a consequence for the rewards individuals receive.

On the surface it might seem desirable to allow the CEO to evaluate individual board members and the board's performance for reward purposes. This could be done, but it leads to a significant risk of tilting the power relationship between the CEO and the board too strongly in favor of the CEO. A major problem in corporate governance is the dominance of CEOs over boards. Putting reward power in the hands of the CEO goes in the wrong direction. It puts too much influence in the hands of the CEO and too little in the hands of the board members and the board as a collective.

If there is an outside or nonexecutive board chair, it may make sense to have the chair do appraisals. This can be an effective way to reinforce the power of the board chair relative to the CEO. However, in the United States, few corporations have outside board chairs.

Having boards do peer appraisals to determine reward levels is an option. Although this may work when boards have done serious team building, in most cases it probably is not appropriate. Thus, instead of rewarding individual board members or boards collectively for their performance, it makes sense to tie the rewards of board members directly to the performance of the corporation. This gives them a close tie to the shareholders they represent and also to the members of the corporation who own stock. Perhaps most important, it gives them a tie to each other because of the common fate it creates.

Senior Managers

The challenge in compensating and rewarding senior management performance is getting the right mix of short- and long-term incentives and the right performance measures. It is clear that performance-based compensation for senior managers should always include stock ownership. Senior managers need to have a significant ownership interest in their corporations so that they have a common alignment with the board and with shareholders.[8] They are the one group in the organization for which stock price has a reasonably strong line of sight.

Stock options also clearly need to play an important role in the compensation of most senior managers. Stock options are a tax and a financially advantageous way to reward senior managers and can be a significant motivator of their performance. Stock options can also play an important role in attracting and retaining senior managers, so they should be part of the reward package when corporations try to recruit from other corporations.

Variable bonus payments also need to be a key element of executive compensation; the bonus structure should be driven by the business strategy. It typically should include a profit-sharing plan, but that may not be enough. Often profit sharing is not based on measures that are specific enough to aid the implementation of a strategic plan. Senior managers need to be on a bonus plan in which significant amounts of cash compensation depend on measures that are directly related to the strategic plan. For example, if improving quality is a key part of the strategic plan, the compensation of the CEO and other senior executives ought to depend on the corporation meeting specific quality targets. Similarly, if growth is a key objective, bonus payments to senior managers should vary, at least in part, based on identifiable growth targets being met.

Probably the most difficult decision to make when it comes to creating a strategic architecture for a senior management team is whether individual, performance-driven, variable bonus amounts should be used. Often, the best answer is no. Evaluating senior executives and rewarding senior executives as individuals tends to put an antiteam pressure into the senior management group. The exception occurs when the senior management team is managing a group of unrelated businesses. For example, United Technologies and General Electric own a variety of unrelated businesses. The senior managers of those businesses need to be evaluated and awarded bonuses based partly or completely on the performance of their businesses.

One more possible exception to the rule of no individual bonuses occurs when a company is in a single business or set of closely related businesses. In that case it may make sense to modify the amount of bonus an executive gets from a corporate bonus pool by how well they execute their particular responsibilities and the degree to which they meet their objectives. This is a tough call, however, because it clearly moves the organization away from a common fate approach to rewards toward one of greater individual accountability. In general this should be done only if specific quantitative goals can be developed for individuals and their performance against these goals objectively assessed. When this can be done, then and only then does it make sense to divide up a bonus pool that is based on corporate performance among individuals based on their individual performance.

In some respects CEO compensation is a special case of senior management compensation. Although in many corporations CEOs simply have not been subject to a formal evaluation procedure, this is changing. In over 70 percent of U.S. corporations, boards now are doing systematic evaluations of CEOs.[9] The consequences of these evaluations vary all the way from determining whether the CEO continues in the job to determining how much bonus he or she receives. It is hard to argue with the idea that CEOs should be systematically evaluated. As I emphasized in Chapter Eight, it sets the tone at the top of the corporation for a performance-driven culture. It also enables the CEO to deal directly with the next several levels of management around the set of objectives for which he or she is responsible. In essence, it creates the opportunity to cascade goals down the organization and thereby support the strategic implementation process.

What is an open question is whether the CEO evaluation results should influence the rewards a CEO gets. I think the answer in most cases should be yes. At the very least, the evaluation should influence the amount of stock and stock options that a CEO gets, and it probably should influence the CEO's cash bonus. In the absence of a relationship between the appraisal and the reward level of the CEO, the evaluation process runs the risk of being an unloaded gun and therefore an activity that is not taken seriously by either the board or the CEO. Research on what makes for an effective CEO evaluation suggests that many of the points I made in Chapter Eight are applicable here.[10] Goals need to be set, appraisers identified, and feedback given. In this respect, CEOs are "just like any other employee" in an organization. They need goals, objectives, measures, and rewards tied to their performance.

In designing senior executive compensation packages, a final key issue is how much compensation should come in the form of stock and how much in cash. It is difficult to provide a general answer to this question because it depends on the business conditions an organization faces. In a start-up or high-tech firm, the answer frequently is that most should come in the form of stock. In more mature, slower-growth firms, the best approach is usually to tilt the compensation package more toward cash.

With cash compensation the critical issue is how much of it should be guaranteed and how much should be at risk. For senior management, a strong argument can be made for at least half of an individual's compensation being at risk. There is little room for guaranteed pay levels and annuities at the very senior level of management. This group, more than any, should have their reward level tied to the success or failure of the company they are managing because they control it and should be held accountable for its performance. This means they should receive large amounts of stock and variable cash compensation and relatively small amounts of salary, perks, and fringe benefits.

Overall, the clear recommendation is that all senior executives should have a number of different forms of performance-based compensation. This is necessary in order to align their interests with the major group they represent—shareholders—and to motivate effective short-term and long-term performance. Stock is a major way to deal with long-term behavior and align senior executives' interests with those of shareholders, whereas cash compensation bonuses are usually the best way to drive the strategic agenda of the business.

General Management

The management levels below the very senior level should be rewarded for performance much like senior management, except of course with a smaller amount and with a somewhat different mix of rewards. The market for middle- and lower-level managers calls for significantly lower compensation levels and less compensation at risk. Nevertheless, it is appropriate to use a mix of stock and cash bonuses in compensating these managers. In most cases, they should have at least some ownership position in the company and should get stock options. In addition, they should be on a bonus plan that rewards them for some combination of individual and collective performance.

The key issue with middle- and lower-level management is how much of their bonus compensation should be based on the results of the total corporation and how much on the performance of their particular business unit or functional group. As I noted in the discussion of executive pay, in corporations that are made up of unrelated businesses, it is important to tie most of the performance-based compensation of managers to the success of their business unit or units. The rest should be tied to overall corporate results and in some cases to individual performance. Corporate results, in the case of a very diverse company, should play a relatively small role in determining the compensation of most managers. Their compensation needs to be driven primarily by the particular business unit they are in and its strategy. This means tying bonuses to accomplishing strategic objectives and perhaps creating phantom or tracking stock so that individuals can participate in the success of their business unit.

It is important to create a strong business unit focus in unrelated business corporations because that is where a line of sight can be established, and that should be the focus of the individuals managing them. In the case of managers who are in manufacturing or service locations, their compensation may also include a local bonus that is tied to a gainsharing or goalsharing plan that covers their particular work location. These managers should have compensation plans that reward them for corporate and business unit performance and for their local unit's business performance.

The situation needs to be different in corporations that consist of a single business or several closely related businesses. There the largest part of a manager's pay for performance should be determined by the results of the overall corporation and should include stock. This is an important way to send the message that the company has a common set of goals and needs an integrated set of behaviors. The remaining pay for performance in a manager's overall reward package may be based on the performance of the unit or area that he or she is responsible for. Again, this can be accomplished by the use of a goalsharing or gainsharing plan.

Depending on their specific role, middle- and lower-level managers may or may not have part of their bonus payment determined by their individual performance. If they are managing a relatively independent unit such as a staff group or a research and development group, it may make sense to have an individual reward component in their total compensation package. In most cases, it should be used to modify the bonus amount that comes as a result of being in a particular business unit. In this way both business unit performance and individual performance are recognized. Thus, the managers should be motivated to achieve as individuals and to cooperate and work with others to see that their business unit is successful.

Overall, the suggestion is that most managers should have multiple forms of pay for performance. Some of their rewards should be tied to corporate performance, some to business unit performance, and, in some cases, yet another amount should be tied to individual performance. A combination of their stock and bonus payments should make up at least 20 percent of their compensation so it is a significant performance driver. For more senior managers the number should be much greater than 20 percent.

Production and Service Employees

Having an effective pay-for-performance structure for nonmanagerial employees is particularly critical. They are most likely to hold jobs that are not greatly challenging and intrinsically rewarding and therefore are most likely to show a performance gain as a result of an effective pay-for-performance plan. They are also often the furthest away from the strategic agenda of the business; thus, it is particularly important to have reward systems that guide their behavior and align their performance with the business strategy. Most individual pay-for-performance systems are unlikely to be effective for first-level employees unless they are doing independent work. The challenge, therefore, is to create for them the right mix of team, business unit, and organizationwide rewards for performance.

Critical to the creation of a high-performance organization is giving everyone in the organization some sense of being part of a larger business or organization. Thus, the first recommendation is that all employees be covered by either a profit-sharing plan or some type of stock plan. The stock plan can be a direct ownership plan or a stock option plan, depending on what makes sense from a financial and administrative point of view.

In the best of all worlds, employees would have a stock plan and some participation in a profit-sharing plan that makes cash payments on a regular basis. Even when combined, however, the stock participation and the profit-sharing participation of first-level employees should not involve a large percentage of their total compensation. It cannot be motivating because the line of sight for these employees is so limited. What it can do, however, is create the sense of common fate and business focus that is needed in order to have a high-performance organization. In the case of smaller organizations it can do more than just create a sense of common fate and alignment from top to bottom. It has the potential to be a significant motivator. Therefore, in small organizations larger amounts of an individual's total compensation package should be based on stock and profit sharing.

In large organizations the most difficult design challenge in compensating first-level employees is paying for performance in a way that will be strongly motivating. Gainsharing and goalsharing represent one possibility, as they can be powerful drivers of performance in smaller, highly interdependent production and service situations. Where they are appropriate, typically no additional pay for performance is needed or desirable. Gainsharing or goalsharing, combined with a corporate profit-sharing or stock program, is all that is needed. When goalsharing and gainsharing are used as the primary motivational programs, it is important that they offer significant bonuses to employees. As I mentioned earlier, 10 to 15 percent is probably enough to motivate most employees. In situations where goalsharing and gainsharing are not particularly good vehicles, team bonuses may be used. As I noted in Chapter Nine, these can be effective motivators if teams perform relatively autonomous operations; having them usually precludes having individual incentive plans.

Technical and Professional Employees

An increasingly large percentage of employees in major corporations work in technical and professional positions. These jobs or roles may be either nested within teams or be individual contributor positions. Often the individuals in these positions are key carriers of corporate competencies and capabilities, and they need to be motivated to support the strategic direction of the business. This suggests that in most cases they need to be compensated like managers. There is one important difference, however, in project teams and in individual contributor roles: individuals may need to be on a team-based bonus plan or on an individual bonus plan. For example, if they are on a product development team, it may make sense to tie a significant amount of pay to the successful performance of the product. If they are doing individual staff support work, it may make sense to reward them with an annual individual bonus payment that is based on their individual accomplishments.

Instead of giving rewards for key individual contributions in cash, it is often advisable to give stock or stock options. This has two positive effects: (1) it ties future rewards to the performance of the corporation, and (2) it can act as a retention device—a critical issue if they are high-value-added employees. They can, for example, be given restricted stock that doesn't vest for several years or stock options that can't be exercised for several years. This can be an effective retention device as well as a motivator while they wait for the stock to be theirs.

Contingent Employees

The increasing use by corporations of noncore or contingent employees raises a number of interesting issues about how they should be rewarded. In many respects they can be the most difficult employees to motivate. Because they have a tenuous connection to the organization, it is difficult to get them to identify with its long-term strategic goals and objectives. Also, they are often hired to do work that is not intrinsically challenging or motivating. As a result of their situation, a number of the traditional reward mechanisms do not fit them particularly well. For example, giving them stock options or stock grants hardly makes sense if their employment tenure with the organization is expected to be relatively short. Similarly, offering them a promotion or a once-a-year merit increase does not make sense. Even gainsharing and goalsharing are often poor fits because the employees are not there long enough to understand them, much less collect a bonus. Of course, if contingent employees work long enough to understand and influence a bonus plan, it makes sense to include them in it.

As a result of their very different status, often noncore or contingent employees end up being paid on an hourly rate with no pay-for-performance provision. It is understandable why this happens, but a strong argument can be made for creating special pay-for-performance packages for contingent employees. Particularly appropriate are bonus plans that will only be paid if the employee satisfactorily completes a certain period of employment. A cash bonus plan of this type has the potential advantage of both retaining individuals until they have completed the project or work they were hired to do and providing them with an important motivator to do it well. In the absence of any form of pay-for-performance plan, there are two big risks with contingent employees: (1) that they will find a permanent position and leave early and (2) that they will not be motivated to perform particularly well while they are working as contingent employees.

It also may make sense to give contingent employees a limited, cafeteria selection of benefits. If they will be on the job more than a month or two, they may want to have the ability to convert some of their cash into vacation days and health insurance, for example. Having benefits available is not likely to be a performance driver, but it may well be a way to attract the best possible employees to contingent positions and to encourage them to stay. In essence, it is a way to make salary dollars go further by allowing them to be converted into a more valued form of reward. This can have the effect of retaining employees in contingent positions who might otherwise leave.

Pay-for-Performance Architectures

The major points I have reviewed so far are summarized in Table 11.3. The table shows that pay plan designs need to take into account the overall organization structure, as well as the position of individuals in that structure. The table recommends pay programs for two organization types: a single business and a multiple, unrelated business. These two types call for different weightings of the elements of a pay-for-performance strategy. The weightings reflect the degree to which individuals are interdependent on a corporationwide basis. In the single-business corporation, there is much more need for an overall alignment among employees. In a multiple-business corporation, the issue for most employees is alignment within a particular business unit. Thus, corporationwide pay-for-performance vehicles warrant little weight at the lower organizational levels in independent business units.

The Eastman Chemical Company, which became an independent company in 1994, provides a good example of putting incentives

Table 11.3. Pay-for-Performance Architecture.

	Single-Business	Multiple-Business
Board	Stock ownership and options (5)	Stock ownership and options (5)
Senior management	Stock (4), profit sharing (4), corporate bonus (4)	Stock (4), profit sharing (4), business unit bonus (3) corporate bonus (3)
Management	Stock (3), profit sharing (3), team or unit bonus (2)	Stock (2), profit sharing (2), business unit bonus (3)
Employees	Stock (1), profit sharing (1), team or unit bonus (2)	Stock or profit sharing (1), team or business unit bonus (2)
Technical and professional staff	Stock (3), profit sharing (2), team or individual bonus (2)	Stock or profit sharing (1), business unit bonus (2), team or individual bonus (2)
Noncore	Individual bonus (3)	Individual bonus (3)

Note: Numbers represent a proportion of total compensation (5 = very large, 4 = large, 3 = medium, 2 = small, 1 = little or none).

from top to bottom in a single business corporation. When the company split from Kodak, all employees were asked to put at least 5 percent of their compensation at risk. Managers were then required to purchase and continue to own stock in Eastman Chemical. The money that employees gave up in base salary to put at risk can be put into an employee stock ownership plan if company performance justifies it. If the company does not meet its annual performance target, the employees get nothing. If they hit or exceed their target, the bonus can be up to 30 percent of their annual pay. The amount of the bonus over the 5 percent that goes into stock is paid out in cash. The measure of performance that is used is return on cost of invested capital. This measure makes sense because of the capital-intensive nature of the chemical business. The objective of the Eastman plan is to provide significant payout opportunities for all employees, based on how the company performs against a key strategic goal: return on invested capital.

Conclusion

The overall direction of my discussion of pay for performance has been toward increasing the number and size of rewards that are based on performance. In high-performance organizations, large rewards for collective performance are appropriate, as is having individuals on more than one pay-for-performance plan. This is a major shift in thinking for many corporations, but it is clearly supported by research evidence suggesting that in order to create high-performance organizations, employees throughout the organization need to have a financial stake in the business. As I will discuss in the next chapter, when this is combined with other reward system features, it can make the reward system a major contributor to organizational effectiveness.

Chapter Twelve

Creating High-Performance Organizations

The design of all systems—not just the reward system—is critical to an organization's performance. Rewards alone won't suffice; other features are needed as well. Employee involvement is one example. Many of the reward system practices I recommended in Chapter Eleven will not be effective unless the organization is managed in a way that supports employee involvement. Significant amounts of information, knowledge, and power need to be present at all levels of an organization in order for the reward system practices to be effective. For example, it does not make sense to reward skill and knowledge growth unless employees throughout the organization are encouraged to grow and develop. Organizations need to provide employees with training and development experiences and grant them decision-making power so they can use what they have learned.

With respect to pay for performance, a critical issue is line of sight. Gainsharing plans, profit-sharing plans, and stock plans all have weak lines of sight and thus require a management style that helps individuals develop a line of sight to organizational performance. There is no mystery as to how to do this: good measures should be used and made public. Employees need to understand the plans and know how the business operates. Finally, employees must have the power, either individually or collectively, to influence the operating effectiveness of the organization. In short, they should have their voices heard and be able to base what they say on good information and knowledge. When this occurs, it is possible to create an effective reward system that rewards something other than individual performance.

Managing Change

Changing an organization's systems and practices so that they align with its business strategy and follow the high-performance approach is clearly called for by the Star Model, but is much more easily said than done. Changing complex organizations is an enormous change-management challenge.[1] It is beyond the scope of this book to discuss in detail all of the change management issues that are involved, but I will address several that are particularly relevant to the reward system in the sections to follow.

Sequence of Change

The first issue involves timing, that is, deciding when the reward system should be changed. I know of no systematic research that looks at large-scale organizational change efforts and establishes when that should happen. Many managers and consultants argue that it should be left until later in a change effort because changing pay systems is difficult and starting with it is risky. If it is not successful, the entire effort can falter. However, pay has been used as a lead element in many successful and comprehensive organizational change efforts, and I believe it can be a good first step.[2]

The first question that any change effort needs to address is, Why is change needed? In the absence of a reward system that bases pay on performance, this may be a difficult question to answer. However, when the pay system promises significant rewards if the change effort is successful, it is easy to answer and employees are much less likely to resist change. They won't say, for example, "I can see how this is good for senior management and the shareholders, but I can't see how it's good for me."

A common problem with change efforts is that they move slowly and methodically when they should move rapidly to keep up with the rate of change that the environment demands. Starting with pay system change can speed up the overall change process precisely because it so obviously demands change in other areas.

Given the potentially positive role of pay in motivating change, its successful use as a lead activity is not surprising. The Scanlon and other gainsharing plans are perhaps the premiere examples of pay plans that are used to begin change; they are frequently used as ice breakers. As I discussed in Chapter Ten, the research on gainsharing plans shows they can be a successful lead change, but an important point needs to be made here: other systems need to change rapidly. If all that changes is the reward system, particularly if the change involves installing a gainsharing or goalsharing plan, individuals will not have the information, knowledge, and power to understand the plan and influence payouts. Thus, there is enormous danger that employees will be told they can earn a bonus, but the news will have no impact because they will not see what they need to do to earn it.

The alternative to beginning with reward system change is to start with some combination of training, information sharing, and power sharing. It is often easy and safe to start with training and information sharing, and many organizations do choose to change them first. Although this is a safe approach, it is almost always a slow one. There is always more information to share and more training and development to do. Often the slowness of change efforts that start with training and development is a result of the reward system's failure to support individuals as they learn new skills. If no rewards are related to the new information employees receive, the information is perceived as of little interest or value, and the change effort is likely to falter.

Leading with major changes in power is in many respects the most problematic way to start a change effort. Without rewards being tied to how successfully the newly shared power is exercised, there is a real risk of power sharing without accountability. Reward systems are a powerful form of accountability and can help ensure that power is used effectively by those who obtain it. The sharing of power, even if it is combined with the information and knowledge needed to use it effectively, can be a dangerous thing in the absence of appropriate reward system changes. In practice, a strongly employee-driven use of power may not result in performance that is aligned with the strategy of the business. Instead of leading to strategically aligned behavior, it can lead to behaviors that are intrinsically rewarding and satisfying. Thus, reward system changes often are needed to create accountability for performance and the motivation to accomplish strategic goals.

There is a significant positive side to beginning a change effort with reward system change: if the change is successful, it can have a powerful and positive effect on the organization's culture. As I illustrated earlier with the example of Continental Airlines installing a goalsharing plan, it can dramatically increase the credibility of management and help to change a failure culture into one that believes it can change and get results. It can also show that management will reward the organization for performance improvements.

If multiple reward system changes are needed, it may be desirable to make them at different times during a large-scale effort. Indeed, it may make sense to strategically position reward system changes along the timeline of a change effort. Creating organizational pay-for-performance systems such as profit sharing and stock option plans can be a powerful driver of change efforts and are often best done early. It does not necessarily follow that changes such as moving to an external equity focus and to knowledge-and-skill-based pay should be put in place at the same time. It may well make sense to delay some reward system changes until changes are made in the structure of the organization and in the measurement systems and processes. These changes may stimulate demand for further reward system changes. Correctly designed and positioned reward system change can then be used to stabilize newly installed changes in how information, knowledge, and power are distributed.

Overall, reward system change resists easy characterization as something that should be done early or late; it is an important potential motivator and institutionalizer of change that can be used anywhere along the timeline of a large-scale change effort. The design challenge is to position specific reward system changes correctly in the process so that they are a positive force for creating high-performance organizations.

Change Process

Critical to the success of any change effort is the process used to manage it. Some theorists have argued that the process should mirror the desired end state.[3] In other words, if the change effort is designed to create employee involvement, the change process itself should involve a high level of involvement. In support of this view is the research on skill-based pay showing that basing pay on skills works best when employees are involved in designing the pay system. Similarly, research evidence suggests that gainsharing plans and other collective bonus plans tend to work best when there is an appropriate amount of employee involvement in their design.

There are two major reasons for having employees involved in designing reward system changes. First, they are the ultimate customers of the new reward system, and, by having them involved, a strong commitment to the change is developed. Not only do employees become committed to the new reward system, they are willing to persuade others that the system makes sense. Often they are much more credible proponents of a new system than are human resource managers or senior managers.

The second reason for having employees involved in the design is that they have relevant information. They may not know the technical details of different reward systems, but they know a lot about the workplace and the people there. Thus, they are a great source of insights as to how people will react to particular plans and what special considerations need to be taken into account.

The challenge in reward system change is to identify the right amount and kind of employee involvement in the design process and in the change process overall. In the case of gainsharing plans, the right amount usually means a task force that does the design and makes a recommendation to senior management, which then approves or disapproves it. This approach seems to work well. In most of the pay system change projects that I work on, task forces are staffed by representatives of the affected employees and are deeply involved in the design process.

One potential danger of employee involvement in reward system design is that employees may end up regarding it as a pseudo-participation exercise. This occurs when their efforts and recommendations are deemed "unreasonable" and rejected by management. All too often, the reasons given for rejection were known before the design activity even began, but senior management didn't communicate them to the employees. This leads to my strong recommendation that senior management make it clear before the participative design exercise starts what boundaries the new pay system has to fit within. They need to specify a design box into which any recommended changes must fit. If a particular kind of reward system design will not be acceptable, the design task force members need to know that at the outset.

I usually handle this by having senior managers make a list of the key elements they are looking for in the new reward system. These can be somewhat general but must be specific enough to rule out most unacceptable designs and practices. The instructions to task forces should place a heavy emphasis on the strategic plan of the organization and highlight how the reward system should be aligned with and support it.

Although employee involvement in designing new pay systems is usually a good idea, in one situation it may not be: when the employees already in an organization are not the kind the organization needs in order to implement and effectively operate its business strategy. It hardly makes sense to ask employees who are a poor fit with the business strategy to design a reward system that is intended to support it. Senior management should design the new reward system in cases like this and use it as a way to selectively retain employees who are a good fit with the strategy.

Involvement in the reward system should not stop with the design process. Employees also need to be involved in the operation of the reward system. This is particularly true with respect to knowledge-and-skill-based pay and pay for performance. These plans tend to maintain their credibility and viability only when individuals throughout the organization are involved in administering and continually improving them.

Like any organizational practice, reward systems need to adapt to changing environments and business strategies. This argues for a continuous improvement process that regularly assesses and updates reward systems. In most instances employees should be included in these assessments. In the absence of participation and understanding, people are unlikely to be committed to a continuous change process that regularly updates the reward system.

The kind of involvement employees have in system administration and change should vary dramatically, depending on the reward system activity and the management approach of the organization. Most or all employees need to be involved in the performance appraisal process, the setting of goals, the design of goalsharing plans, and the determination of bonus amounts. With other issues, involvement may be appropriately limited to focus groups that comment, for example, on a new design. In still other cases, employee task forces may need to regularly assess pay plans and revise them. This approach is frequently used with gainsharing plans and works quite well.

Leadership and Reward Systems

No matter how well designed reward systems are, they cannot operate effectively without competent leadership. Leaders need to provide a sense of direction, mission, and credibility for reward systems. When all is said and done, reward systems in general and pay-for-performance systems in particular require trust in order to be effective. Trust can be nurtured by having individuals involved in the design of the system and in its ongoing operation, but it cannot survive without the support of credible and effective leaders.

With respect to reward systems, it is crucial that leaders do what they say and say what they do. That is, they should be very clear about how the reward system works, and there should be a strong correspondence between what leaders say and how the reward system actually operates. They should also make the reward system highly transparent and visible to all employees; people trust systems when they are run by people they trust and when they can see how the systems operate. Leaders who are not public about the administration of rewards and who are unclear in stating how the system operates doom reward systems to failure.

The most effective leaders with respect to reward systems are able to state a clear set of goals for the organization and align the reward system with those goals. They continually talk about the goals of the organization and about the rewards associated with achieving the goals. They involve individuals in the work of the organization in ways that lead them to accept the goals and be motivated to achieve them.

It is impossible to separate the issue of leadership from the way executives and managers themselves are compensated. As I mentioned earlier, in the United States there has been a tremendous growth in executive compensation—a spurt unmatched by the compensation levels of other employees. This growth has raised a number of questions about effective leadership; among these is whether it has undermined the ability of very highly paid executives to lead effectively.[4]

Although there is little research evidence on the effects of reward levels on leadership, I believe that very high rewards for executives decrease their effectiveness as leaders unless certain conditions apply. The most important of these concerns whether the organization has created a common fate in the organization among all its employees, that is, whether or not the executives and the shareholders are the only ones who gain as a result of improvements in organizational performance. If only executives gain higher pay, their ability to provide leadership—not just concerning reward system issues but the overall goals, objectives, and mission of the organization—is seriously undermined. They, in essence, are put in the position of appearing to be self-serving individuals who are simply getting what they can from the organization. This undermines their moral authority to lead and very much limits their ability to talk about a common vision and direction for the organization. This point argues strongly for the reward system structure I discussed in Chapter Eleven, that is, one in which employees throughout the organization participate in its success. When that happens, it adds both moral authority and a belief in a common destiny to the leadership efforts of senior management.

An employee once said to me, "I don't mind if the CEO makes more money as long as I do too." He went on to say he didn't even mind if the CEO made much more money, more rapidly than he did, as long as he was well paid relative to his peers in other companies. This raises an important point. Compensation throughout the organization needs to reflect the relative performance of the company. High executive compensation is certainly troubling in its absolute amount, but it is particularly troubling when CEOs are highly compensated for leading companies that are performing poorly.

A particularly grievous example occurred when a large bonus was paid to the CEO of AT&T, Robert Allen, at a time when AT&T's earnings were doing poorly and a large layoff was announced. This event undermined Allen's credibility and his ability to lead AT&T. What was wrong here, of course, was not that Allen was making a lot of money but that he was getting additional "performance-based" pay at a time when the organization's performance did not justify it.

The situation with Allen is far from unique; there are other examples in the corporate world. One of the most extreme cases occurred at Disney when Michael Ovitz made over $100 million in a year and then was fired. This is clearly neither a good pay practice nor a good leadership practice. It leads to a simple principle that executives in companies should adhere to: compensation levels should be determined by the comparative performance of a company in its industry.

High-performing organizations should have highly paid executives; poorly performing companies should have poorly paid executives. The emphasis here is on relative performance. As I noted in Chapter Ten, all too often the emphasis in executive compensation is on absolute performance and stock price. With this model, individuals can become incredibly wealthy simply because the stock market is performing well. They also can have very poor rewards if the stock market is performing poorly. In most cases a fairer system is to judge them on how their company performs relative to others in their industry. This creates the possibility of individuals profiting handsomely in a down market if their company outperforms its competitors or of being poorly rewarded if their company underperforms others in an up market.

Even with a focus on the market and the relative performance of companies, there still may be an enormous difference between the pay of individuals at the very top of large organizations and those at the bottom. This gap has grown dramatically in some countries in recent years. In large U.S. corporations it grew from a ratio of 60:1 or 70:1 during the 1960s and 1970s to more than 300:1 in the late 1990s.

I do not believe there is one right spread from top to bottom. In a free-agent, knowledge-based economy, wide variations in pay for different skills, as well as for different levels in the hierarchy, are likely to become increasingly prevalent. Because organizations cannot ignore markets, they will end up with wide variations in the amounts that they pay. What organizations can and, I believe, should do is be sure that their differences in compensation are well justified in terms of performance and market pricing and that individuals at the lower compensation levels at least earn a living wage.

What constitutes a living wage varies from situation to situation and country to country, but it should be above the poverty level and include an upside opportunity if the organization does well. The latter point is particularly important. Individuals can tolerate large pay differences in their organization and in their society if everyone has a fair opportunity to increase their compensation. This argues strongly for a common fate orientation toward rewards, even though some may enjoy a relatively better fate than others. It argues strongly against a winner-take-all society in which a few do extremely well but most do poorly.[5]

Overall, the suggestion is that people throughout an organization, particularly executives, should be rewarded based on the comparative performance of their company and that their rewards should be strongly market-based. For leaders to have credibility, a common fate should be created within the organization so that when executives win, everyone wins, and when they lose, everyone loses. This alignment is a critical element in providing a leadership platform for executives to stand on and to providing the kind of direction that is necessary to manage and operate a high-performance organization.

Information Openness

Fundamental to the creation of a high-performance organization is the movement of information about the pay system throughout the organization. This is a critical step in giving employees an understanding of the business and in making pay systems effective. Without it, employees are not likely to have a good understanding of how performance is rewarded or, for that matter, a great deal of trust in the reward system. Keeping pay secret often leads people to make inaccurate judgments about the fairness of the pay system and how well others are paid. They tend to overestimate the pay of individuals like themselves and as a result often feel more dissatisfied than they would be if they had accurate information. This brings front and center an important issue: how open to be with respect to pay information. Historically, the policy in most organizations is best described as secrecy with a need-to-know orientation.

Organizations usually give out general information about their pay systems and sometimes provide information about pay ranges and job evaluation systems. They do not, however, indicate what individuals earn, and in most cases they share neither salary survey data nor information about what is behind the determination of merit payment amounts and bonus amounts. In short, they keep a considerable amount of pay information secret. It is clearly time for a change. Organizations need to be much more open about how they manage and administer pay. People are becoming more sophisticated and knowledgeable consumers of company pay information and practices.

A number of factors have converged to provide people with more information than ever about how companies pay. The amount of press coverage of pay practices has tremendously increased in the United States and other parts of the world. The primary focus has been on executive compensation, but there are also frequent articles and stories about companywide stock option plans, gainsharing plans, and a host of other compensation practices.

The World Wide Web is transforming the whole process of salary comparison and communication in dramatic and important ways. Thanks to the Internet, employees can get a great deal of information about what the job market pays for their skills. A number of Web sites giving pay data are available to people so they can be on a more equal footing with companies concerning the market pricing of jobs and skills. Web sites listing job openings and pay rates are maintained by hiring companies as well as by search firms and employment agencies.

Internet-based services are available to help people assess their skills and career opportunities and determine their market value. Services and books are available that tutor employees on how to bargain for pay when they join a new company, how to get a pay increase, and how to manage their finances, given the increased prevalence of variable pay plans and stock option plans.

As market data become even more readily available, it is inevitable that employees will focus more and more on the external market and on whether they are paid relatively well or poorly. Companies need to respond to this by providing a clear public statement of the value proposition that they offer employees. This is fundamental to their attracting, retaining, and motivating employees who fit their strategy and approach to organizing and managing.

Perhaps the only question left to be resolved concerning pay openness is whether the pay of most individuals should be made public. In the United States it is already public in the case of senior executives because it must be put in proxy statements. Pay is also public in many self-managing work teams and other situations where groups and teams decide what their peers should be paid. Much to the surprise of many traditional thinkers in management, this has not caused a massive uproar or revolution. That is not to say that employees are necessarily happy with what they find out about what others are paid, but when explanations are offered and appropriate changes made, it has not proven to be a highly contentious issue. In many cases it has led to a better understanding and acceptance of the pay system and to positive changes.

As high-performance organizations increasingly operate with teams and share business information through intranets, it logically follows that the pay rates of individuals will be made public. Indeed, making them public promises to make much clearer the kinds of knowledge and skills the organization needs to develop and should allow more and more people to make intelligent decisions about their career tracks. In essence, public pay rates can be a positive reinforcer of the argument that individuals are responsible for their own careers and for their compensation. This is clearly much easier to argue when individuals have information about the compensation consequences of their decision making than when they do not.

Particularly in the case of organizations that have effective pay systems and pay well relative to the market, there is a tremendous advantage to be gained from making pay rates and policies public. Because pay secrecy leads to misunderstandings and perceptions that are more negative than the reality of how pay is actually administered, companies that want to establish a high-performance culture can gain from making pay information public and open to discussion. Openness can increase trust, perception of fairness, understanding of the business, and respect for the organization and its management.

In addition to making pay public, it makes sense for organizations to encourage employees to provide salary data that suggest how their pay compares with the market. It clearly is better for the organization to find this out as a result of its members raising the issue than as a result of members leaving to join another organization.

Overall, open pay fits with high-performance organizations, employability, self-management of careers, the creation of high-trust environments, access to financial information, and the movement of employees to a free-agent mentality. Thus, it is not a question of whether organizations will make pay public; the question is when and on what terms it will occur.

Core Principles

Communicating the major features of reward systems and establishing the credibility of the systems are major challenges. Done poorly, they undermine the effectiveness of not just the reward system but an organization's entire culture-building effort. In order to contribute positively to the culture, the reward system needs to stand for key features of how the organization will be managed, and individuals need to know what the system stands for.

One way to establish what the reward system stands for is to have a short list of core principles that are understood by all and are touchstones for the system. In most situations, these should become relatively permanent parts of the organization and its culture, though from time to time they may need to be changed, adapted, and brought up to date. The principles should be created by the kind of process that I have presented in this chapter, that is, with open discussion and much employee involvement. They should include the major reward system design elements that I have discussed throughout this book: pay for performance, the employment contract, pay for jobs or skills, market position, internal-external equity focus, degree of hierarchy, decision processes, and communication.

No two organizations are likely to have exactly the same core principles. Indeed, the key to success is the participative development of the core principles and their fit with the organization's strategic plan and the business issues it faces. Once the core principles are developed, they should be used to attract new employees and to help them determine whether they represent a good fit for the organization. The principles should also guide the development, as well as the operation of the reward system.

Loyalty and Commitment

Throughout this book I have argued that the traditional loyalty contract between individuals and organizations is obsolete and that such contracts are often not the best deal for either individuals or

organizations. They can prevent people from getting the best return on their skills and human capital and prevent firms from obtaining and developing the best human capital. The so-called
employability contract is a potential substitute because it can benefit both individuals and organizations—but it is not without risks.
Clearly, it will not work unless individuals and organizations accept
the new responsibilities that go along with it.

The key challenges that the employability contract presents for
organizations are familiar: attraction, retention, and motivation.
In some respects these challenges are more difficult to meet with
an employability relationship than with a loyalty relationship. Substitutes for loyalty need to be put in place. Retention rewards that
are used in a targeted way are an effective substitute for the retention effects of loyalty. Pay for performance can be a substitute for
the motivation effects of loyalty.

Perhaps the most difficult changes organizations need to make
concern employment stability. Increasingly, organizations are likely
to include individuals with different degrees of job security and stability. Organizations are likely to continue to have a group of core
employees who are relatively long-term members; in dealing with
them, the traditional retention-type reward system practices may be
used. For example, it makes sense to offer retirement plans to core
employees and to significantly increase their rewards as they gain
more knowledge, skills, and ability. It also makes sense to do some
new things, such as paying them for their skills and knowledge.

Organizations are also likely to employ a group of noncore employees who may be difficult to motivate from a performance point
of view and difficult to retain as long as the organization would like
to retain them. As I noted earlier, organizations need to be clear
in identifying these people and skillful at rewarding them both for
staying with the company as long as they are needed and for performing well. This suggests the use of employment completion
bonuses and awards, as well as significant amounts of variable compensation. It rarely suggests stock ownership or stock option plans.

With respect to core employees, an important principle that
can facilitate retention is the idea of a soft landing if they are laid
off or terminated. In today's environment, individuals take a considerable risk when they stay at a particular organization for a long
time. Thus, they need to be assured that the organization will support their transition to a new situation if they no longer fit where

they are. This does not need to be done for noncore employees. They join with exit in mind and are not expected to make a long-term commitment.

Levi Strauss provides a dramatic example of a company that has made sure its downsized employees enjoy a soft landing. When it closed eleven U.S. factories because of cost pressures, the company spent $200 million on the slightly more than six thousand affected employees. That is an average of over $31,000 for each employee—significantly more than the employees' average annual salary. The severance package included eight months of salary, additional pay based on length of service, and company-paid health benefits for eighteen months. Unlike most severance packages, which require workers to stay to the last day to collect, Levi Strauss workers were eligible for the package even if they found a new job immediately. Indeed, the company rewarded them with a $500 bonus check when they found new work. The message delivered to those remaining was clear: making a commitment to Levi Strauss is low-risk because we will look out for you if and when we have to reduce our staff.

When an organization has employees with employability contracts, managing the workforce is much more complex than when an organization has a loyalty-deal workforce. Organizations need to worry about who will maintain the organization's culture, core competencies, and organizational capabilities. This usually means retaining key individuals, which, in turn, means being very much in touch with the external labor market and being able to change their rewards as the market changes. It may also mean paying some key individuals at above-market rates. This certainly can be accomplished, particularly with the use of a knowledge-and-skill-based pay system, but it is not an easy task. It requires a clear focus on the external market and on the strategic needs of the business. It also means making a continuing effort to identify the organization's key employees and attending to their satisfaction, development, and rewards—financial and otherwise.

In many cases properly motivating key employees requires developing in them an organizational ownership mentality. They are the ones who must make the extra effort to see that the organization is doing well and adapting to key changes in the environment. At times they need to put their own interests temporarily aside in order to improve organizational performance. In the absence of a loyalty contract, this kind of behavior cannot reasonably be expected from individuals who do not share in the organization's long-term financial success. Thus it is particularly important that they own stock and have stock options. It may also make sense to give them formal employment contracts.

Human Capital Self-Management

The growing importance of human capital and the new employment contract is likely to create great opportunities and great risks for employees. Those who are in demand will be well paid and highly rewarded, but the breakdown of traditional job-based pay systems is likely to lead to even more dramatic differences in how well individuals are paid. In the future these differences are less likely to be tied to a hierarchical level and more likely to be tied to technical knowledge and skills.

Successfully navigating the changes in demand for certain kinds of knowledge and the rewards attached to that knowledge requires that people be focused on the market for skills and for the condition of their human capital. Those who ignore the external market and the development of their own capital are at high risk of not being able to maintain their pay level and, ultimately, of becoming unemployable. Given this reality, it is reasonable to expect people to operate with a greater sense of enlightened loyalty to their own careers, and they are likely to change in other ways as well.

The growing focus on human capital, free agency, and the Web has the potential to significantly change the way people find jobs and manage their employment relationships. Historically, some individuals have been represented by unions in their dealings with organizations. They have found that their greatest bargaining power occurs when they join together and speak with a collective voice. This approach may be a good fit for individuals who do work where human capital is not important. However, it is a poor fit for individuals with a high value who are in situations where individuals vary considerably in their value. Because unions tend to negotiate for common pay rates and working conditions, high-value individuals usually lose out.

A more appropriate model for high-value individuals is the agent model that operates currently in sports, entertainment, and other fields. There, it is clear that in order to maximize their market value, individuals need to be represented by agents who know the labor market and are skilled marketers and negotiators. Although we are probably a long way away from seeing most employees deal with companies through agents who negotiate contracts for them, we may not be that far away from many high-talent individuals having agents. In many cases, executive search firms and lawyers already serve this function for senior executives. Given that an outstanding software engineer or chemist may be just as valuable as a senior executive, it is not too great a leap to argue that individuals who bring excellent human capital of many kinds to organizations will have agents who negotiate their employment packages, worry about their job placement, and establish them as a human capital brand.

It is also possible that new unions will develop or old ones will reinvent themselves to serve people of high human capital value. It is interesting to note that the players in the major sports, as well as the entertainers in the movie industry, are unionized and have agents. In their case, the union fulfills one set of needs and the agents fill another. In the entertainment industry, some unions provide benefits such as retirement plans and insurance that are not provided by the relatively temporary employment relationships they have. The agents worry about the contracts the entertainers enter into and the work they do. Together, the agents and the unions provide a relatively individualized package of rewards and support services.

In some sports where individuals are represented by both agents and unions, the combination has not worked well (for example, in American basketball and football). Unions have agreed to limit and in some cases reduce the pay of their members, whereas agents have tried to prevent this from happening.

It is possible that some combination of agents and unions could develop in highly skilled professions like engineering and computer science. However, I think agents are more likely to develop than unions, but both certainly are possible.

Another alternative is the development of more organizations that act as relatively permanent employers of technical knowledge experts and lease their employees to corporations that need a particular technical specialty for a period of time. This model serves the individuals in terms of providing them with continuing benefits and security while dealing with the needs of organizations for high levels of expertise in particular areas. In some areas, organizations that provide technical experts have already developed. So far they have primarily focused on staff services such as accounting, information technology, and human resource management, but they could extend to many core and functional competency areas.

Finally, more and more people are likely to self-manage their human capital—increasingly possible in light of the information that is available today. Job searches already constitute a major use of the World Wide Web, which provides ways for individuals to assess their skills, apply for jobs, and offer their services to employers. Individuals can set up personal Web sites featuring work samples and videos to market themselves and establish their brand. People can auction their work time on a variety of specialized Web sites. There is every reason to believe that as more and more information becomes available on the Web, the trend of employees self-managing their careers will accelerate.

Rewarding Excellence and Public Policy

The impact of the new employment contract and reward strategies that focus on rewarding excellence promises to significantly change the relationship between individuals and society. Thus, it challenges governments to alter the way they think about governing and regulating the way organizations treat employees. Elsewhere I have argued that the adoption of the new logic of organizing and the pay practices associated with it are inevitable and desirable at the societal level.[6] This argument is based on the new reality of global competition and the belief that countries and societies need to develop highly talented, mobile human capital in order to be competitive.

Rewarding excellence promises to create a society of highly mobile human capital, the key element in creating a society that can adapt to a rapidly changing competitive environment. Human capital that is both mobile and knowledge-flexible is crucial to creating start-up organizations that develop new industries and businesses and to creating traditional organizations that are able to change their capabilities and competencies as the business environment changes. Thus, rather than try to protect the old ways of working and organizing, governments should support the movement to the new logic of organizing and to rewarding individuals based on their performance and skills. This movement is in the best interest of societies because it is the best guarantee of continuing economic growth, development, and prosperity. It is also advantageous to those employees who develop the right skills and knowledge and demonstrate high levels of performance.

Governments can do a number of things to support the development of new-logic organizations and to prepare individuals for a world of work that is dominated by organizations that reward excellence. It is beyond the scope of this book to go into them in detail, but it is worth identifying the major actions that need to be taken.

1. *Develop human capital.* Critical to individual, organizational, and societal well-being in a globally competitive world is knowledge development. Unfortunately, it is not always in the best interest of individual organizations to support the knowledge and skill development of their workforce. Therefore, the government has a role to play in human capital development: to support individuals' growth and development. The effort should start with providing an adequate educational system but continue throughout people's lives. As technologies become obsolete, so do skills and knowledge. Thus, people need to learn new skills and start new careers. In the best of all worlds, of course, they would be able to afford to pay for this themselves or be supported by a company, but sometimes individuals need support because they are not being supported by a company or they have not planned well.

2. *Create retirement and health benefits that are available and portable.* Because individuals are likely to have multiple careers with multiple organizations, it is critical that they have access to retirement and health care benefits as they move from organization to organization, are self-employed, or are in contingent employment positions. Unfortunately, it is often not in the best interest of organizations to provide benefits to temporary or short-term employees; as a result, many who need them are not covered.

Health care is a particular problem in countries that do not have a government health service. For example, in the United States many workers do not get health insurance coverage when they are self-employed or in contingent employment positions. Retirement is a particular problem in high-tech organizations because in many cases organizations do not want individuals to stay a long time and therefore do not make retirement benefits available. Government is the logical entity to either support private retirement plans that are portable and vest quickly or to provide retirement plans.

3. *Protect low-skilled employees.* Low-skilled employees in developed countries are likely to have a great deal of difficulty earning a living wage. In an economy based on excellence, there is little opportunity for individuals whose skills are readily available virtually anywhere in the world.

The Internet has increased the divide between the skilled and the unskilled in the United States. In 1999 households with incomes of $75,000 or higher were twenty times more likely to access the Internet than those with the lowest incomes.[7] They were also more than nine times as likely to have a computer at home. The implications of this for the future employability of members of these households is clear: low-income family members are likely to lack one of the most important skills that well-paying jobs require, the ability to use information technology. In addition, they are unlikely to develop the kind of worldview and valuable technical knowledge that can be gleaned from the Internet. In short, they will have lower human capital values and, consequently, lower pay rates. Thus, a major consequence of the Internet may be further division in the developed countries between the haves and the have-nots. This phenomenon has been called the "digital divide."

One way of helping low-skilled people, of course, is to provide training. As I mentioned earlier, it is important that governments do this. But not everyone can profit from training or take advantage of it, so it is important to create a safety net of government policies and practices that prevent employees from being paid less than a living wage and ensure that they will be covered by minimal health care and retirement programs.[8]

4. *Support consistency in reward practices throughout organizations.* At the present time the law in most countries, including the United

States, demands that employees at all levels be treated the same with respect to many pay and benefit practices. But some laws demand different treatment. For example, U.S. law requires that some employees be treated as nonexempt employees and be paid for overtime work; another law prevents nonmanagement employees from participating in certain kinds of pay decision making unless they are members of a union.

The new-logic thinking clearly argues for encouraging organizations to treat everyone the same when it comes to pay and reward systems. This does not necessarily mean that everyone should be paid the same amount but that they should participate in the same pay and reward programs. The implications of this for governments are straightforward: they should not try to regulate the total pay of individuals (except to ensure a living wage), nor should they require pay programs that cause organizations to treat people differently.

5. *Support choice of rewards.* In order to adjust to change, organizations need new human capital, and they often need a diverse workforce. Diversity of many kinds is a precondition to dealing effectively with a complex, diverse environment. The implication of this for reward practice is clear: reward systems need to allow individuals choice because they differ in what they need and value. Government policies should support organizations giving individuals choices when it comes to health care, retirement, time off, and the other rewards that organizations offer.

Conclusion

Throughout this book I have made the point that the reward systems in organizations need to be reinvented. The traditional approaches to rewards have been made obsolete by dramatic changes in the importance of human capital and the growing use of organization and management as a source of competitive advantage. Clearly, no single solution fits all organizations, just as no single approach fits all individuals. However, there are some general reward system practices and structures that organizations can put in place to help them create an effective approach to managing human capital. The overall theme of these approaches is rewarding and focusing on excellence. Employees need to be rewarded for excellent organizational and in some cases individual performance, and excellent employees need to be identified and paid for the skills and knowledge they have.

For individual human capital investors, excellence is also a critical theme. In order to be highly rewarded and valued, individuals need top-flight skills and knowledge. Of course, just having good skills and knowledge and performing well is not enough. The knowledge and skills must be in areas that are in strong demand, and human capital investors need to seek out organizations that value and reward human capital. Traditional bureaucratic organizations are not the place for individuals who have a high level of human capital and performance excellence. They need to find organizations that truly reward performance and knowledge development.

Individuals who have outstanding skills and knowledge and great performance records are likely to have very high pay levels in the future. Human capital investors who have a large amount of capital to invest are likely to see increasing returns over the next decade. They are a scarce resource at this point—a resource that is critical to the success of most corporations. Whether human capital investors will get a better return than financial capital investors in the future is still an open question, but there is good reason to believe they will.

The 1990s was clearly the decade of the financial investor. The twenty-first century, however, is likely to see increasingly high return on human capital, not just for the human capital investors who end up as senior executives but for a wide array of investors who have high levels of knowledge and skill and excellent performance records. The future is unlikely to reward individuals who lack human capital. Nothing is likely to occur that will make the world comfortable for people with poor skills and little knowledge. Thus, it is up to individuals to make themselves safe by developing their human capital so that they can be a part of organizations that reward excellence. There is little doubt who will dominate business in the twenty-first century: organizations that can attract, retain, develop, motivate, organize, and manage excellent individuals.

Notes

Introduction

1. E. E. Lawler III, *From the Ground Up: Six Principles for Building the New Logic Corporation* (San Francisco: Jossey-Bass, 1996).
2. T. Stevens, "Chief Among Us," *Industry Week,* 1998, *247*(31), 24–33.
3. T. H. Davenport and L. Brusak, *Working Knowledge: How Organizations Manage What They Know* (Boston: Harvard Business School Press, 1998).
4. P. Cappelli, *The New Deal at Work* (Boston: Harvard Business School Press, 1999).
5. R. S. Johnson, "The Jordan Effect," *Fortune,* 1998, *137*(12), 124–130.
6. R. L. Brummet, E. G. Flamholtz, and W. C. Pyle, "Human Resource Measurement: A Challenge for Accountants," *Accounting Review,* 1968, *43,* 217–224; E. G. Flamholtz, *Human Resource Accounting* (Encino, Calif.: Dickinson, 1974).
7. T. H. Davenport, *Human Capital* (San Francisco: Jossey-Bass, 1999).
8. E. G. Chambers and others, "The War for Talent," *McKinsey Quarterly,* 1998, *3,* 44–57.
9. J. Pfeffer, "Six Dangerous Myths About Pay," *Harvard Business Review,* 1998, *76*(3), 108–120.
10. Lawler, *From the Ground Up.*
11. G. T. Milkovich and J. M. Newman, *Compensation,* 5th ed. (Burr Ridge, Ill.: Irwin, 1996).

Chapter One

1. B. Gates, *Business @ the Speed of Thought* (New York: Warner Books, 1999).
2. E. E. Lawler III, *The Ultimate Advantage: Creating the High-Involvement Organization* (San Francisco: Jossey-Bass, 1992); A. M. Mohrman Jr., J. R. Galbraith, E. E. Lawler III, and Associates, *Tomorrow's Organization: Crafting Winning Capabilities in a Dynamic World* (San Francisco: Jossey-Bass, 1998).
3. Lawler, *From the Ground Up.*

4. E. E. Lawler III, with S. A. Mohrman and G. E. Ledford Jr., *Strategies for High Performance Organizations: The CEO Report* (San Francisco: Jossey-Bass, 1998).

5. M. A. Huselid, "The Impact of Human Resources Management Practices on Turnover, Productivity, and Corporate Financial Performance," *Academy of Management Journal,* 1995, *38,* 635–672.

6. D. Ulrich and D. Lake, *Organizational Capability* (New York: Wiley, 1990); Lawler, *From the Ground Up.*

7. C. K. Prahalad and G. Hamel, "The Core Competence of the Corporation," *Harvard Business Review,* 1990, *68*(3), 79–91.

8. Lawler, *From the Ground Up;* Mohrman, Galbraith, Lawler, and Associates, *Tomorrow's Organization.*

9. E. E. Lawler III, *High-Involvement Management* (San Francisco: Jossey-Bass, 1986).

10. J. R. Galbraith, *Competing with Flexible Lateral Organizations* (Reading, Mass.: Addison-Wesley, 1994).

11. Mohrman, Galbraith, Lawler, and Associates, *Tomorrow's Organization.*

12. J. R. Galbraith, *Organization Design* (Reading, Mass.: Addison-Wesley, 1977).

Chapter Two

1. Milkovich and Newman, *Compensation.*

2. E. E. Lawler III, *Strategic Pay: Aligning Organizational Strategies and Pay Systems* (San Francisco: Jossey-Bass, 1990); G. D. Jenkins Jr., G. E. Ledford Jr., N. Gupta, and D. H. Doty, *Skill-Based Pay: Practices, Payoffs, Pitfalls and Prospects* (Scottsdale, Ariz.: American Compensation Association, 1992).

3. Lawler, *Strategic Pay.*

4. P. K. Zingheim and J. R. Schuster, *Pay People Right!* (San Francisco: Jossey-Bass, 2000).

5. A. Kohn, *Punished by Rewards* (Boston: Houghton Mifflin, 1993).

6. Lawler, *Strategic Pay;* J. Cameron and W. D. Pierce, "Rewards, Interest, and Performance," *ACA Journal,* 1997, *6*(4), 72–81.

7. C. M. Christensen, *The Innovator's Dilemma* (Boston: Harvard Business School Press, 1997).

8. Lawler, Mohrman, and Ledford, *Strategies for High Performance Organizations;* J. R. Schuster and P. K. Zingheim, *The New Pay* (San Francisco: New Lexington Press, 1992).

9. Lawler, *Strategic Pay.*

10. Lawler, Mohrman, and Ledford, *Strategies for High Performance Organizations.*

11. J. Pfeffer, *The Human Equation* (Boston: Harvard Business School Press, 1998).
12. C. Handy, *The Age of Unreason* (Boston: Harvard Business School Press, 1990); C. Handy, *The Age of Paradox* (Boston: Harvard Business School Press, 1994).
13. Lawler, *Strategic Pay.*
14. Lawler, *High-Involvement Management.*

Chapter Three
1. C. C. Pinder, *Work Motivation in Organizational Behavior* (Upper Saddle River, N.J.: Prentice Hall, 1998); G. D. Jenkins Jr., A. Mitra, N. Gupta, and J. D. Shaw, "Are Financial Incentives Related to Performance? A Meta-Analytic Review of Empirical Research," *Journal of Applied Research,* 1998, *83,* 777–787.
2. W. F. Whyte (ed.), *Money and Motivation: An Analysis of Incentives in Industry* (New York: HarperCollins, 1955); E. E. Lawler III, *Pay and Organizational Effectiveness: A Psychological View* (New York: McGraw-Hill, 1971); R. B. McKenzie and D. R. Lee, *Managing Through Incentives* (New York: Oxford University Press, 1998).
3. R. L. Heneman, *Merit Pay* (Reading, Mass.: Addison-Wesley, 1992).
4. Ibid.
5. W. E. Deming, *Out of the Crisis* (Cambridge, Mass.: MIT Press, 1986).
6. Lawler, Mohrman, and Ledford, *Strategies for High Performance Organizations.*
7. Kohn, *Punished by Rewards;* F. Herzberg, *Work and the Nature of Man* (Orlando, Fla.: Harcourt Brace, 1966).
8. Ibid.; E. L. Deci, *Intrinsic Motivation* (New York: Plenum Press, 1975).
9. A. H. Maslow, *Motivation and Personality* (New York: HarperCollins, 1954).
10. Herzberg, *Work and the Nature of Man.*
11. E. E. Lawler III, *Motivation in Work Organizations* (Pacific Grove, Calif.: Brooks/Cole, 1973).
12. C. G. Worley, D. E. Bowen, and E. E. Lawler III, "On the Relationship Between Objective Increase in Pay and Employees' Subjective Reactions," *Journal of Organizational Behavior,* 1992, *13,* 559–571; A. Mitra, N. Gupta, and G. D. Jenkins Jr., "A Drop in the Bucket: When Is a Pay Raise a Pay Raise?" *Journal of Organizational Behavior,* 1997, *18,* 117–137.
13. V. H. Vroom, *Work and Motivation* (New York: Wiley, 1964); L. W. Porter and E. E. Lawler III, *Managerial Attitudes and Performance* (Homewood, Ill.: Irwin, 1968).

14. Lawler, *Motivation in Work Organizations*.
15. E. Locke and G. P. Latham, *A Theory of Goal Setting and Task Performance* (Upper Saddle River, N.J.: Prentice Hall, 1990).
16. Lawler, *Motivation in Work Organizations;* Pinder, *Work Motivation in Organizational Behavior.*
17. J. S. Adams, "Toward an Understanding of Inequity," *Journal of Abnormal Psychology,* 1963, *67,* 422–436; J. S. Adams, "Injustice in Social Exchange," in L. Berkowitz (ed.), *Advances in Experimental Social Psychology,* Vol. 2 (Orlando, Fla.: Academic Press, 1965).
18. R. Folger and M. Konovsky, "Effects of Procedural and Disruptive Justice on Reactions to Pay Raise Decisions," *Academy of Management Journal,* 1989, *32,* 115–130; J. Greenberg, "Looking Fair vs. Being Fair: Managing Impressions of Organizational Justice," in B. M. Staw and L. L. Cumming (eds.), *Research in Organizational Behavior,* Vol. 12 (Greenwich, Conn.: JAI Press, 1990).
19. Pinder, *Work Motivation in Organizational Behavior.*
20. B. Schneider and D. E. Bowen, *Winning the Service Game* (Boston: Harvard Business School Press, 1995).
21. A. J. Rucci, S. P. Kirn, and R. T. Quinn, "The Employee-Customer-Profit Chain at Sears," *Harvard Business Review,* 1998, *76*(1), 83–97.

Chapter Four

1. N. Schmitt, W. C. Borman, and Associates, *Personnel Selection in Organizations* (San Francisco: Jossey-Bass, 1992).
2. Pinder, *Work Motivation in Organizational Behavior.*
3. J. R. Katzenbach and J. A. Santamaria, "Firing Up the Front Line," *Harvard Business Review,* 1999, *77*(3), 107–121.
4. Lawler, Mohrman, and Ledford, *Strategies for High Performance Organizations.*
5. Lawler, *Motivation in Work Organizations.*
6. J. P. Wanous, *Organizational Entry: Recruitment, Selection, and Socialization of Newcomers* (Reading, Mass.: Addison-Wesley, 1980).
7. Schmitt, Borman, and Associates, *Personnel Selection in Organizations.*
8. M. R. Barrick and M. K. Mount, "The Big Five Personality Dimensions and Job Performance: A Meta-Analysis," *Personnel Psychology,* 1991, *44,* 1–26.

Chapter Five

1. Milkovich and Newman, *Compensation.*
2. E. E. Lawler III, "Paying the Person: A Better Approach to Management?" *Human Resource Management Review,* 1991, *1,* 145–154.

3. R. H. Frank and D. J. Cook, *The Winner-Take-All Society* (New York: Free Press, 1995); A. J. Slywotzk (ed.), *Profit Patterns* (New York: Random House, 1999).
4. Schuster and Zingheim, *The New Pay;* Zingheim and Schuster, *Pay People Right!*
5. E. E. Lawler III, "From Job-Based to Competency-Based Organizations," *Journal of Organizational Behavior,* 1994, *15,* 3–15.
6. W. Bridges, *Job Shift: How to Prosper in a Workplace Without Jobs* (Reading, Mass.: Addison-Wesley, 1994).
7. Lawler, *From the Ground Up;* Mohrman, Galbraith, Lawler, and Associates, *Tomorrow's Organization.*
8. Lawler, *Strategic Pay.*

Chapter Six

1. Lawler, Mohrman, and Ledford, *Strategies for High Performance Organizations.*
2. Ibid.
3. Lawler, *High-Involvement Management.*
4. Jenkins, Ledford, Gupta, and Doty, *Skill-Based Pay.*
5. Ibid.; Lawler, *From the Ground Up.*
6. P. K. Zingheim, G. E. Ledford Jr., and J. R. Schuster, "Competencies and Competency Models: One Size Fits All?" *ACA Journal,* 1996, *5*(1), 56–65.
7. L. M. Spencer and S. M. Spencer, *Competence at Work* (New York: Wiley, 1993).
8. A. M. Mohrman Jr., S. M. Resnick-West, and E. E. Lawler III, *Designing Performance Appraisal Systems: Aligning Appraisals and Organizational Realities* (San Francisco: Jossey-Bass, 1989).

Chapter Seven

1. Deming, *Out of the Crisis.*
2. Whyte, *Money and Motivation.*
3. Heneman, *Merit Pay;* S. Kerr, "On the Folly of Rewarding A While Hoping for B," *Academy of Management Journal,* 1975, *18,* 769–783.
4. J. M. Smithers (ed.), *Performance Appraisal* (San Francisco: Jossey-Bass, 1998).
5. Lawler, Mohrman, and Ledford, *Strategies for High Performance Organizations.*
6. Whyte, *Money and Motivation.*
7. *Wall Street Journal,* July 8, 1998, p. 1.
8. Lawler, *Pay and Organizational Effectiveness.*

Chapter Eight

1. Mohrman, Resnick-West, and Lawler, *Designing Performance Appraisal Systems;* Smithers, *Performance Appraisal;* G. P. Latham and K. N. Wexley, *Increasing Productivity Through Performance Appraisal* (Reading, Mass.: Addison-Wesley, 1994).

2. H. H. Meyer, E. Kay, and J.R.P. French, "Split Roles in Performance Appraisal," *Harvard Business Review,* 1965, *43,* 123–129.

3. S. A. Mohrman, S. G. Cohen, and A. M. Mohrman Jr., *Designing Team-Based Organizations: New Forms for Knowledge Work* (San Francisco: Jossey-Bass, 1995).

4. J. A. Conger, D. Finegold, and E. E. Lawler III, "Appraising Boardroom Performance," *Harvard Business Review,* 1998, *76*(1), 136–148; J. A. Conger, D. Finegold, and E. E. Lawler III, "CEO Appraisals: Holding Corporate Leadership Accountable," *Organizational Dynamics,* 1998, *27*(1), 7–20.

5. Locke and Latham, *Theory of Goal Setting and Task Performance.*

6. Mohrman, Resnick-West, and Lawler, *Designing Performance Appraisal Systems.*

7. E. Jacques, *Equitable Payment* (New York: Wiley, 1961).

8. Smithers, *Performance Appraisal.*

9. R. Lepsinger and A. D. Lucia, *The Art and Science of 360-Degree Feedback* (San Francisco: Jossey-Bass, 1997); W. W. Tornow, M. London, and CCL Associates, *Maximizing the Value of 360-Degree Feedback* (San Francisco: Jossey-Bass, 1998).

Chapter Nine

1. Lawler, Mohrman, and Ledford, *Strategies for High Performance Organizations.*

2. Lawler, *From the Ground Up.*

3. Lawler, Mohrman, and Ledford, *Strategies for High Performance Organizations.*

4. Ibid.

5. Mohrman, Cohen, and Mohrman, *Designing Team-Based Organizations.*

6. D. A. Nadler, J. L. Spencer, and Associates, *Executive Teams* (San Francisco: Jossey-Bass, 1998).

7. Mohrman, Cohen, and Mohrman, *Designing Team-Based Organizations.*

8. Lawler, Mohrman, and Ledford, *Strategies for High Performance Organizations.*

9. C. F. Frost, J. H. Wakely, and R. A. Ruh, *The Scanlon Plan for Organizational Development: Identity, Participation, and Equity* (East Lansing: Michigan State University Press, 1974); R. J. Doyle and D. I. Doyle, *Gain Management* (New York: AMACOM, 1992).

10. Lawler, *Strategic Pay;* Schuster and Zingheim, *The New Pay.*
11. R. Seaman, "Rejuvenating an Organization with Team Pay," *Compensation and Benefits Review,* 1997, *29*(5), 25–30; P. K. Zingheim and J. R. Schuster, "Best Practices for Small-Team Pay," *ACA Journal,* 1997, *6*(1), 40–49.

Chapter Ten

1. Lawler, Mohrman, and Ledford, *Strategies for High Performance Organizations.*
2. Doyle and Doyle, *Gain Management;* J. G. Belcher, *Gain Sharing* (Houston: Gulf, 1991).
3. R. J. Bullock and E. E. Lawler III, "Gainsharing: A Few Questions and Fewer Answers," *Human Resources Management,* 1984, *5,* 197–212.
4. R. S. Kaplan and D. P. Norton, *The Balanced Scorecard: Translating Strategy into Action* (Boston: Harvard Business School Press, 1996).
5. Lawler, Mohrman, and Ledford, *Strategies for High Performance Organizations.*
6. Ibid.
7. A. S. Blinder, *Paying for Productivity* (Washington, D.C.: Brookings Institution, 1990).
8. Lawler, Mohrman, and Ledford, *Strategies for High Performance Organizations.*
9. J. R. Blasi, *Employee Ownership* (New York: Ballinger, 1988).
10. Lawler, Mohrman, and Ledford, *Strategies for High Performance Organizations.*
11. Ibid.
12. E. E. Lawler III, "The Organizational Impact of Executive Compensation," in F. K. Foulkes (ed.), *Executive Compensation* (Boston: Harvard Business School Press, 1991).

Chapter Eleven

1. Lawler, *From the Ground Up;* Mohrman, Galbraith, Lawler, and Associates, *Tomorrow's Organization.*
2. Lawler, Mohrman, and Ledford, *Strategies for High Performance Organizations.*
3. D. M. Rousseau, *Psychological Contracts in Organizations* (Thousand Oaks, Calif.: Sage, 1995).
4. Korn/Ferry International, *Board Meeting in Session: 24th Annual Board of Directors Study* (New York: Korn/Ferry International, 1997).
5. Mohrman, Galbraith, Lawler, and Associates, *Tomorrow's Organization.*
6. Korn/Ferry, *Board Meeting in Session.*
7. Conger, Finegold, and Lawler, "Appraising Boardroom Performance."

8. F. K. Foulkes, *Executive Compensation* (Boston: Harvard Business School Press, 1991).
9. Korn/Ferry, *Board Meeting in Session.*
10. Conger, Finegold, and Lawler, "CEO Appraisals."

Chapter Twelve

1. S. A. Mohrman and T. G. Cummings, *Self-Designing Organizations: Learning How to Create High Performance* (Reading, Mass.: Addison-Wesley, 1989); J. A. Conger, G. M. Spreitzer, E. E. Lawler III, and Associates, *The Leader's Change Handbook* (San Francisco: Jossey-Bass, 1999).
2. Lawler, *Pay and Organizational Development.*
3. N. M. Tichy, *Managing Strategic Change: Technical, Political, and Cultural Dynamics* (New York: Wiley, 1983); A. M. Mohrman Jr. and others, *Large-Scale Organizational Change* (San Francisco: Jossey-Bass, 1989).
4. Lawler, "Organizational Impact of Executive Compensation"; American Compensation Association, *CEO Pay* (Scottsdale, Ariz.: American Compensation Association, 1997).
5. Frank and Cook, *The Winner-Take-All Society.*
6. Lawler, *From the Ground Up.*
7. U.S. Department of Commerce, *Falling Through the Net: Defining the Digital Divide* (Washington, D.C.: U.S. Government Printing Office, 1999).
8. J. R. Galbraith, *Created Unequal: The Crisis in American Pay* (1998).

Index

Other titles by Edward E. Lawler III

From the Ground Up: Six Principles for Building the New Logic Corporation
Edward E. Lawler III
Hardcover ISBN 0–7879–0241–1
Paperback ISBN 0–7879–5197–8

High-Involvement Management: Participative Strategies for Improving Organizational Performance
Edward E. Lawler III
Hardcover ISBN 0–87589–686–3
Paperback ISBN 1–55542–330–2

Designing Performance Appraisal Systems: Aligning Appraisals and Organizational Realities
Allan M. Mohrman Jr., Susan Resnick-West, Edward E. Lawler III
Hardcover ISBN 1–55542–149–0

Large-Scale Organizational Change
Allan M. Mohrman Jr., Susan Albers Mohrman, Gerald E. Ledford Jr., Thomas G. Cummings, Edward E. Lawler III, and Associates
Hardcover ISBN 1–55542–164–4

Strategic Pay: Aligning Organizational Strategies and Pay Systems
Edward E. Lawler III
Hardcover ISBN 1–55542–262–4

The Ultimate Advantage: Creating the High-Involvement Organization
Edward E. Lawler III
Hardcover ISBN 1–55542–414–7

Organizing for the Future: The New Logic for Managing Complex Organizations
Jay R. Galbraith, Edward E. Lawler III, and Associates
Hardcover ISBN 1–55542–528–3

Motivation in Work Organizations
Edward E. Lawler III
Paperback ISBN 1–55542–661–1

Tomorrow's Organization: Crafting Winning Capabilities in a Dynamic World
Susan Albers Mohrman, Jay R. Galbraith, Edward E. Lawler III, and Associates
Hardcover ISBN 0–7879–4004–6

The Leader's Change Handbook: An Essential Guide to Setting Direction and Taking Action
Jay A. Conger, Gretchen M. Spreitzer, Edward E. Lawler III, Editors
Hardcover ISBN 0–7879–4351–7

Strategies for High Performance Organizations—The CEO Report: Employee Involvement, TQM, and Reengineering Programs in Fortune 1000 Corporations
Edward E. Lawler III, Susan Albers Mohrman, Gerald E. Ledford Jr.
Paperback ISBN 0–7879–4397–5